Consumer Reports

Digital
Buying Guide

The Digital Buying Guide covers, in a convenient format, the latest buying tips and product Ratings from CONSUMER REPORTS. Published by the nonprofit Consumers Union, CONSUMER REPORTS is a comprehensive source of unbiased advice about products and services, personal finance, health and nutrition, and other consumer concerns. Since 1936, the mission of Consumers Union has been to test products, inform the public, and protect consumers. Our income is derived solely from the sale of CONSUMER REPORTS magazine and our other publications and services, and from nonrestrictive, noncommercial contributions, grants, and fees. We buy all the products we test. We accept no ads from companies, nor do we let any outside entity use our reports or Ratings for commercial purposes.

OTHER BUYING GUIDES FROM CONSUMER REPORTS

- Best Buys for Your Home
- New Car Buying Guide
- Used Car Buying Guide
- Consumer Reports Buying Guide

OTHER PUBLICATIONS FROM CONSUMER REPORTS

- Shop Smart
- Sport-Utility Special
- Brides Guide
- New Car Preview
- Used Car Yearbook
- Road Tests
- Travel Well for Less
- Consumer Drug Reference
- Guide to Baby Products

Consumer Reports

Digital Buying Guide

The Editors of Consumer Reports

Published by Consumer Reports ◆ A Division of Consumers Union ◆ Yonkers, New York

Consumer Reports Special Publications
    Director & Editor Andrea Scott
    Managing Editor Bette LaGow
    Project Editor David Heim
    Contributing Editors Jeff Fuerst, Kimberly Kleman
    Technology Editor, Consumer Reports Jeff Fox
    Design Manager Kimberly Adis
    Art Director Alison Wilkes
    Contributing Art Director Kim Shake
    Technology Specialist Jennifer Dixon
    Production Charlene Bianculli
    Special Publications Staff Joan Daviet, Merideth Mergel

Consumer Reports Electronics Department
    Vice President and Technical Director Jeffrey A. Asher
    Director of Testing Evon Beckford
    Program Leader Dean Gallea
    Senior Project Leaders Christopher Bucsko, Gerard Catapano, Richard Sulin
    Project Leaders Edward Gleason, Joseph Lazzaro, Robert Lew, Ernst St. Louis
    Assistant Project Leaders Kerry Allen, Susan Daino, Charles Davidman
    Technicians Aaron Fournier, Larry Greene, Maria Grimaldi, Thomas Maung, Artur Pietruch, William South

Consumer Reports
    Vice President and Editorial Director Julia Kagan
    Editor/Senior Director Margot Slade
    Executive Editor/Associate Editorial Director Eileen Denver
    Design Director, Consumers Union George Arthur
    Managing Art Director Tim LaPalme
    Director, Production Operations David Fox
    Director, Survey Research Charles Daviet
    Product Manager, Special Publications Carol Lappin
    Multimedia Product Distribution Manager Tracy Bowen
    Manufacturing/Distribution Ann Urban

Consumers Union
    President James Guest
    Executive Vice President Joel Gurin
    Senior Vice President, Technical Policy R. David Pittle

First printing, September 2002
Copyright © 2002 by Consumers Union of United States, Inc., Yonkers, New York 10703.
Published by Consumers Union of United States, Inc., Yonkers, New York 10703.
All rights reserved, including the right of reproduction in whole or in part in any form.
ISSN: 1530-3713
ISBN: 0-89043-969-9
Manufactured in the United States of America.

TABLE OF CONTENTS

PART 1: UP AND RUNNING

Chapter 1 Plugged in and Turned on
Get the right Internet access 13
Protect your computer system 18
The home network 23
Keep your private data private 27
Do your kids need an online chaperone? 29

Chapter 2 Fitting Images: Photos and Video
In the digital darkroom 34
Lights! Camcorders! Action! 38
Creativity programs 39

Chapter 3 All in the Game
Getting started with video games 42
Outmoded games: They aren't obsolete 43
Gaming online 48

Chapter 4 Rock On: Digital Music
The ABCs of MP3 49
Do-it-yourself CDs 50

Chapter 5 Good Work: Research Tools
Should you bank online? 55
Using the Internet to manage your health 60
Beyond e-mail for good health information 63
Buying travel online 64
Hitting the (virtual) books 68

Chapter 6 Online Shopping: The Virtual Mall
Smart e-tail sites 71
Online auctions: Going, going, dot-gone 77
CONSUMER REPORTS e-Ratings 83

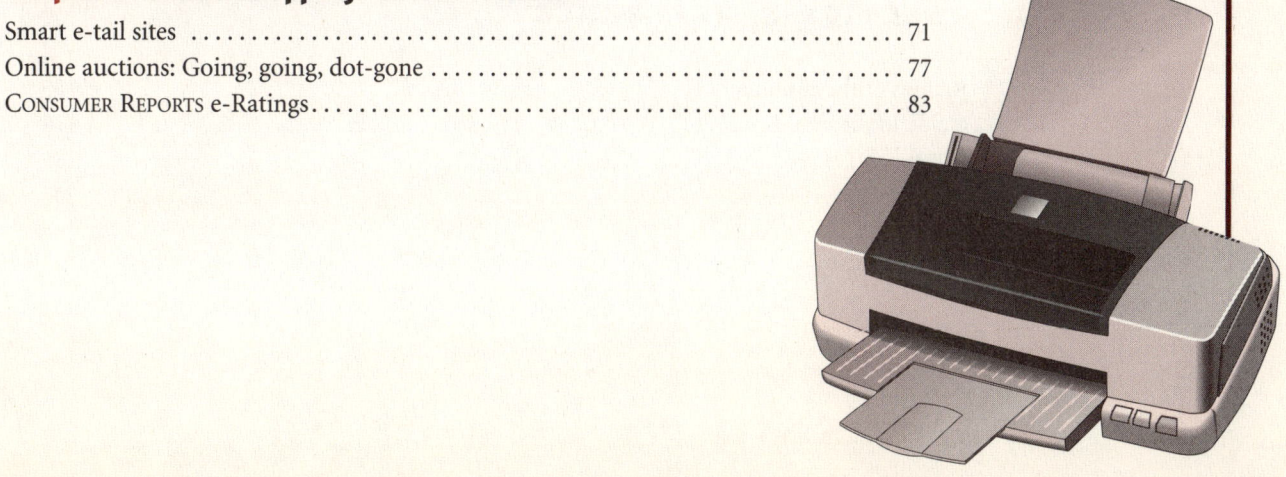

PART 2: SYSTEMS ANALYSIS

Chapter 7 Computing
Desktop computers 99
Laptop computers 104
Monitors 107
PDAs 111

Chapter 8 Picture These
Camcorders 115
Digital cameras 118
Scanners 121

Chapter 9 Sound Investments
CD players/recorders 125
MP3 players 127

Chapter 10 Ink to Paper
Printers 131
Multifunction devices 134

Chapter 11 Telephones
Cell phones 136
Cordless phones 139
Corded phones 142
Cell-phone alternatives 143

Chapter 12 Working in comfort
Ergonomic chairs 145
Workstations 148
Surge suppressors 151

SECTION 3: REFERENCE

Ratings of the equipment 155
Guide to the brands 178
Glossary 185
Index 207

Introduction

Moore's Law, named for one of the founders of Intel Corp., states, in effect, that computer speed will double every 18 months. So far, Moore's Law holds. Computer speeds have been relentlessly accelerating and show little sign of slowing. The computers made in the last two to three years deliver plenty of speed, power, and storage capacity to satisfy all but the most demanding users. That's good news. It means you can concentrate on using your computer for new and, one hopes, enjoyable activities.

To be sure, the computer is still a useful piece of equipment for letter-writing, personal finance and bill-paying, and presentations. It's a supercharged video arcade, with graphics sophisticated enough to please the most easily bored game enthusiast. It's the entrée to the vast and intriguing world of the Internet, with access to e-mail and hundreds of millions of sites where you can speak your mind, consult with a physician, get the latest news, and buy or sell absolutely anything. It's also a dating service, a travel agency, an encyclopedia, a meeting hall, and a shoulder to cry on. And, unfortunately, it can give hackers and other miscreants access to every bit of personal, private information stored inside

The computer is also the linchpin for other digital equipment: cameras, camcorders, scanners, printers, game boxes, and more. The computer is the place where you store, swap, copy, or alter photos, graphics, songs, and games in progress. Hence this edition of the "Digital Buying Guide."

USING THIS BOOK

We can help you make the most of all your digital equipment, and help you decide how to approach new digital activities. This book is divided into three parts. The first, "Up and Running," focuses on how you can use the hardware to best advantage. It includes CONSUMER REPORTS' expert advice on shopping for essential services.

The first chapter, "Plugged in and Turned on," explains options for regular and high-speed Internet access. You'll also find practical advice on how to properly protect your computer from invasion by hackers and viruses, and the best ways to protect children when they surf the web.

The other chapters in the first section cover all the major digital activities that depend on a computer. "Fitting Images: Photos and Video" gives you the essentials to get off to the right start in digital imaging, whether you want to take still photos or home videos. If you're new to computer gaming or want to keep up with someone who's a gamer, "All in the Game" gives you the lowdown on the big game boxes, how to size up a new game, and what to do with old games if you switch to a new format. "Rock On: Digital Music" covers the world of music downloads and sharing. It gives you the basics of ripping and burning CDs (downloading files and recording them on a compact disk, in case you were wondering) and keeps you up to date on the legal and political developments that have made digital music such a controversial commodity. "Good Work: Research Tools" covers the serious stuff: Using e-mail and the Internet when you need to stay in touch with your doctor; handling your finances online; booking travel; and getting homework and research help on the web. And "Online Shopping: The Virtual Mall" is designed to help you transact business online without getting taken—whether you're buying the new number one best-seller or bidding at auction for a rare first edition. The chapter also includes the CONSUMER REPORTS e-Ratings of more than 100 commercial web sites.

The second part, "Systems Analysis," helps you sort through the choices you'll face when shopping for computers and other hardware, software, and digital services. You'll see buying guidance on desktop computers, laptops, and PDAs, as well as important peripherals such as monitors, printers, fax machines, cameras, and scanners. There are also sections on those pieces of home-entertainment equipment that have entered the computer's orbit: camcorders, digital cameras, CD player/recorders, MP3 music players. Other chapters give you useful information on cell phones, cordless phones, and setting up a comfortable and functional home office.

The third part of the book is a reference section with the latest CONSUMER REPORTS brand-name Ratings, plus a comprehensive glossary and profiles of the major home-computer and home-office brands.

TRENDS YOU'LL SEE IN 2003

Finding opportunities amid high-tech flameouts

It's no secret that the past two years have not been kind to dot-com startups and other technology-centered enterprises. Dozens of Internet sites that began in a blaze of glory ended with a fire sale. Companies such as Excite@Home and Global Crossing, which planned to make high-speed Internet access the norm, ended in failure, with hundreds of thousands of customers stranded.

Because such failures occurred in the midst of an economic downturn, consumers were left wary and cautious. The growth in households adopting high-speed Internet service has slowed, as have sales of desktop computers and much other digital gear.

Paradoxically, that situation can be a boon if you're shopping for new hardware. Prices for desktop computers are as low as they've ever been. And because the products continually improve (thanks to Moore's Law), you get much more computer for the dollar than you did even a year or so ago. There are also bargains to be had if you're in the market for a printer, a monitor, a scanner, or a PDA. Space-saving flat-panel monitors have dropped substantially in price, to a point at which they make good economic sense, especially for a family short on desk space. It's also easy to find a high-quality printer and scanner for less than $100 each. And $100 now buys a PDA that would have set you back $150 to $200 not long ago.

Privacy and security matter more than ever

The growth of high-speed Internet access (which can leave a computer vulnerable to invasion) and heightened concerns about terrorism have put computer security and privacy foremost in many minds, from government and business officials to law-enforcement officers to ordinary citizens.

Recent developments include the appointment of a "computer security czar" to keep tabs on governmental efforts to ward off hackers and devastating viruses. The Federal Trade Commission continues to give online privacy and identity theft a high priority. But not every action has had a positive effect. Efforts to protect children from online violence, smut, and cyber-predators have been especially flawed. In mid-2002, the U.S. Supreme Court struck down the central provisions of the Children's Internet Protection Act, which

CONSUMER REPORTS engineers gauge the clarity of computer monitors in side-by-side comparisons.

would have required public libraries to install software filters that block certain content. The law violated First Amendment rights of free speech, said the court. The Supreme Court also overturned an earlier child-protection law on the same grounds.

HOW CONSUMER REPORTS TESTS EQUIPMENT

Equipment rated in this book is tested at CONSUMER REPORTS' labs in Yonkers, N.Y. The products are bought at retail just as a consumer would acquire them. Shoppers buy specific models based on which are top sellers or innovative designs.

CONSUMER REPORTS tests are rigorous and objective, using constantly refined procedures. For home computers, benchmarks are used to assess how quickly machines can simultaneously run a number of applications, including a word processor, a spreadsheet, and a web browser. Much of the work done in the computer labs mimics how a piece of equipment would be used in the home. Testers read the owner's manual, try out all the switches, and experiment with the features. They try to answer likely consumer questions: How easy is the system to set up? Can components be replaced with industry standard parts? Are the manuals comprehensive and easy to read? If the computer is marketed for game devotees, how smooth is its 3D graphics capability?

To find the best printers, testers compare text, photos, and graphics, and they gauge the printers' speed. To assess the image clarity of monitors, testers do side-by-side comparisons. The quality of digital cameras, scanners, and other imaging equipment is assessed by comparing images created using the product. For instance, engineers inspect glossy 8x10-inch prints created by each digital camera tested, using its best-photo mode. They use the model's supplied software and output all prints to the same photo printer.

For every piece of equipment, testers carefully assess features—do they add to usability or just make an item more complicated? They check ergonomic functions—how does the camera feel in the hand?—and assess battery life.

After all these tests, testers analyze the data and results to arrive at the comprehensive Ratings that are published in CONSUMER REPORTS magazine and in this book.

Some of the products tested and reviewed in 2001 and 2002 were already being replaced by new models as this book was going to press in the summer of 2002. CONSUMER REPORTS tests computers and home-office equipment throughout the year, however, and cover how changes in technology affect your daily life. Look for the latest test results in monthly issues of CONSUMER REPORTS magazine or online at *www.ConsumerReports.org*.

PART 1

Up and Running

CHAPTER 1
Plugged in and Turned on

CHAPTER 2
Fitting Images: Photos and Video

CHAPTER 3
All in the Game

CHAPTER 4
Rock On: Digital Music

CHAPTER 5
Good Work: Research Tools

CHAPTER 6
Online Shopping: The Virtual Mall

1

Plugged In and Turned On

The Internet has profoundly and permanently changed many important parts of everyday life. People spend billions buying and selling Apple computers, zebra-striped wallpaper, and just about everything else in between. When you need information—the best route over the river and through the woods, reviews of Grandma's House restaurant, or the history of the sleigh—you turn to the Internet. You can check the latest government safety information, apply for a driver's license, pay parking tickets, order stamps, or track the progress of a package on the Internet. And when you want to send friends a quick note or a couple of snapshots, chances are that you use e-mail.

This chapter will help you find the best choices for Internet access. We will also explain the best ways to protect yourself from cyber-intrusions—companies loading you up with unwanted e-mail known as spam, companies tracking your online activities without your knowledge, hackers debilitating your computer with viruses and other infestations. We'll help you ensure that your children are protected when they go online. And we can show you the best ways to connect all the computers in your home, something that more and more households find necessary.

13
Get the right Internet access

18
Protect your computer system

23
The home network

27
Keep your private data private

29
Do your kids need an online chaperone?

GET THE RIGHT INTERNET ACCESS

Should you sign up with a big gun such as America Online with its millions of subscribers, or with a local provider? Will a dial-up account suffice, or can you benefit from a high-speed connection? Here's what you need to know.

Most people who surf the web connect to the Internet through the modem built into their computer. That approach works well enough, though it can often entail some tapping of

> **BROADBAND BASICS**
>
> To enjoy the full benefit of a broadband Internet connection, follow these pointers:
>
> ◆ Be sure the equipment is compatible if you plan to install your own modem.
>
> ◆ Obtain a printed version of any contract or terms of service; online versions can change.
>
> ◆ If you can, get a contract with a guarantee of minimum bandwidth. Also look for a contract that offers rebates in the event of outages and a back-up dial-in line.
>
> ◆ Avoid services that levy nonrefundable charges, early cancellation fees, or charges for customers who miss appointments.
>
> ◆ Watch out for contracts that come with limits on usage, the number of home computers you can connect to the Internet, or the size of e-mail messages you can send.
>
> ◆ Ask the provider if it's set up to assign you a dynamic Internet identifier, one that changes regularly so that others online can't permanently pin down your location. A connection with a fixed address can compromise security by raising your computer's hacker profile.
>
> ◆ Keep written records of service interruptions and calls to the provider's technical support service. The records may prove crucial to getting any refunds.
>
> ◆ Check the actual speed of your connection as soon as service begins and periodically thereafter. Two web sites that measure speed coming into your house at no charge are *www.dslreports.com* (click on DSLR Tools, then Speed Test) and *www.testmyspeed.com*. A speed-measuring program called DU Meter can be downloaded free from *www.hageltech.com*. If the speed seems consistently slow, contact your Internet provider. If your computer runs on Windows, you may be able to improve speed by fine-tuning the operating system. For more information, go to *www.speedguide.net*.

fingers as a web page is called up. It also requires a dedicated phone line—or the family's agreement over when the phone line can be used for calls or for web surfing.

The dial-up modem that's a standard part of every new computer, V.90, delivers data at a nominal 56 kilobits per second (56 kbps, usually shortened to 56k), but actually works at only 53k even in the best conditions. Broadband, which refers to a speed of at least 128k, is on whenever your computer is turned on, so you don't need to dial a number every time you want access. A growing number of surfers (10 million in a recent count) have adopted broadband, and they love it.

What the providers provide

By one estimate, nearly 4,000 companies provide Internet service. Some give you little more than the telephone number you need to get connected, while others make available a wealth of unique content and services. All offer web browsing, usually through Internet Explorer or Netscape Navigator. Some providers, chiefly America Online, use their own web browser. In addition, you usually get e-mail service, access to subscribers' online discussion groups, space to create your own web page, and, often, advice on crafting an attractive page.

Most families use one of the largest national or regional Internet providers. America Online has more than 25 million U.S. subscribers. Close behind are MSN (owned by the software behemoth Microsoft), AT&T Worldnet, and EarthLink. In addition to those big national Internet providers, there are thousands of smaller, local ones. You can get a list of the ones that serve your area at *www.thelist.com*, which claims to include some 4,000 providers.

The largest Internet providers can deliver one-click access to selected online shopping sites, news, instant messaging, special chat rooms, online stock trading, elaborate controls to protect children, and so on. The largest service, America Online, offers the most content. AOL dominates the field because it recognized early on people's aversion to getting their hands dirty with technology and their need to communicate with many others. Hence the popularity of its e-mail and instant-messaging services. In less populated areas, speedy access to a local access number may be more desirable than a large provider's well-developed content. But a smaller provider may not offer access numbers in other parts of the country, which you may need when traveling.

THE SMART WAY TO BUY A COMPUTER

According to a recent survey of CONSUMER REPORTS readers, it's generally better to buy a desktop computer from a manufacturer's web site or catalog than from a store. Even novices shouldn't fear ordering from a web site.

Readers said that web sites and catalogs had a better selection. Manufacturers' catalog or web-site customer-service reps were considerably more knowledgeable and helpful than retail-store clerks. The one exception: Gateway Country stores, which readers judged the same as buying from Gateway by web or phone. Among the retail-store problems that readers reported: long lines and trouble finding a salesperson.

No matter where you decide to buy your computer, always pay with a credit card. That gives you important legal protections, including the right to dispute charges for goods you didn't accept or that weren't delivered as agreed. You also gain negotiating clout with retailers.

In search of old reliable

No matter which brand of computer you buy or where you do the buying, you stand a good chance of having some trouble with the hardware. According to a recent survey of CONSUMER REPORTS readers, 5 percent bought a computer that was completely inoperable within the first month; another 11 percent said they had problems in the first month but the computer was usable. The chart at the left shows the percentage of computer brands that ever had a repair to original components.

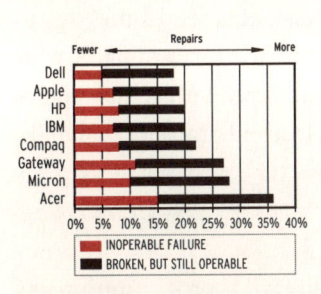

Fewer ← Repairs → More
Dell, Apple, HP, IBM, Compaq, Gateway, Micron, Acer
0% 5% 10% 15% 20% 25% 30% 35% 40%
■ INOPERABLE FAILURE
■ BROKEN, BUT STILL OPERABLE

The chart is based on 35,000 responses to the 2001 CONSUMER REPORTS Annual Questionnaire, covering desktop computers bought new between 1997 and the first four months of 2001. Data have been standardized to eliminate differences due to age and usage. Differences in score of 5 points or more are meaningful.

Our findings have been quite consistent in recent years. However, a brand's repair history includes models that may have been more or less reliable than others. Repair histories also can't anticipate design or manufacturing changes. We think you'll better your chance of getting a reliable computer if you choose a brand that has been reliable in the past.

Who provides the best help?

Subscribers to the *ConsumerReports.org* web site told us about their experiences with the manufacturers' technical-support service between January 2001 and mid-2002. Slightly more than 40 percent of the people who used tech support were highly satisfied with the service; that's lower than most other services we measure. The chart below gives the specifics.

MANUFACTURER	READER SCORE	SOLVED PROBLEM	SUPPORT STAFF	WAITING ON PHONE	WEB SUPPORT	E-MAIL SUPPORT
Apple	74	◐	◐	●	○	–
Dell	65	◐	○	○	○	○
Gateway	64	○	○	○	○	◐
HP	56	◓	○	○	○	○
Compaq	52	●	◓	◓	◓	○

If everyone were completely satisfied, the **reader score** would be 100; 80, very satisfied on average; 60, fairly well satisfied. **Solved problem** indicates how many respondents said the manufacturer solved the problem. **Support staff** represents how many said the staff on the phone seemed knowledgeable. **Waiting on phone** indicates whether respondents waited on hold too long or had other problems. **Web** and **e-mail support** indicate whether respondents had problems with those avenues of contact.

Free lemon-aid for computer owners

When nothing goes right and you buy a computer that turns out to be a lemon, you shouldn't be stuck with the bill or a huge hassle trying to get it fixed.

"Help for Problem PCs," a new free service from *ConsumerReports.org*, can make it easier to get assistance if the computer goes sour.

◆ The Action Plan lays out the most efficient and effective step-by-step procedures you need to follow in order to get retailers and manufacturers to fix a problem.

◆ The Action Library provides crucial information you need to argue your case, including the latest recalls and links to applicable consumer-protection laws.

◆ Action Communication makes it easy to contact manufacturers, retailers, the Better Business Bureau, and state and local consumer-affairs offices. You'll find names, addresses, phone numbers, and form letters you can use.

You can find our new free service on the home page of *www.ConsumerReports.org*. Click on Help for Problem PCs off the Other Features & Services top navigation bar.

Dial-up vs. broadband

COST: ADVANTAGE DIAL-UP. Monthly fees range from about $20 to $25 for unlimited dial-up access. Many providers have less expensive plans available if you go online only a few hours per month. Broadband service averages about $40 per month. (However, broadband proponents contend that dial-up service actually costs closer to $40 per month, too, once the expense of a dedicated phone line is factored into the equation.)

CONTENT: ADVANTAGE BROADBAND. There isn't one Internet for dial-up customers and another for broadband users. However, broadband gives you entrée to many new web sites and services that a 56k dial-up connection simply can't accommodate conveniently—sharing home videos with far-flung friends or family, accessing complex multimedia sites rapidly, or listening to an Internet radio station.

SATISFACTION: ADVANTAGE BROADBAND. In CONSUMER REPORTS surveys of Internet users, people with broadband are consistently much more satisfied with the connection than are those using a dial-up connection. In a national survey of some 1,500 households in April 2002, two-thirds of the broadband users said they were highly satisfied with their Internet service. But only about one-third of the dial-up users were that satisfied.

TECHNICAL SUPPORT: ADVANTAGE BROADBAND. Broadband users in the CONSUMER REPORTS survey said they had fewer problems with their Internet connection—far fewer interrupted connections or glitches that prevented them from accessing web sites or retrieving e-mail. Paradoxically, broadband users were more likely than dial-up users to avail themselves of the technical support offered by their Internet provider (69 percent for broadband, 51 percent for dial-up). More than half of broadband users (54 percent) said they were highly satisfied with that technical support. By contrast, less than half (44 percent) of dial-up users felt that way.

Switching Internet providers can be like moving to a new home. To change an e-mail address with minimal interruption, keep your old account open for an extra month or two after you start using the new one. If you have an e-mail address book, send a message to everyone in the book informing them of the change. Use automatic forwarding, if your older provider offers it, to avoid having to access the old account directly. Make sure you've complied with your old provider's rules for closing an account, to avoid problems with bills.

Broadband choices

The three main types of broadband access are these:

CABLE MODEM. The hardware uses the same cable that delivers TV programming. It's available where the local cable-TV provider has upgraded its equipment. A special modem, separate from the TV converter box, handles the Internet traffic. Cable modem now accounts for a majority of broadband connections.

Cable systems are designed like small networks, sharing the data-carrying capacity (bandwidth, as it's known) among a group of subscribers. Cable has the capacity to deliver speeds as high as 10 megabits per second (Mbps), equal to 10,240 kbps, for each channel the cable company devotes to data. But as more people go online, the less bandwidth available for each home. Depending on a neighborhood's usage pattern and its cable provider's ability to manage it, cable-modem users can experience slowdowns in web access, though they are likely to be less noticeable than with a dial-up connection.

DIGITAL SUBSCRIBER LINE. Telephone access, commonly known as DSL (digital subscriber line), uses a digital signal to transmit large amounts of information over an existing phone line, without interfering with voice calls. Voice and data move at different frequencies and so do not interfere with each other. DSL service does, however, require you to use a special modem.

DSL doesn't have the maximum bandwidth capacity of cable—it's typically 128 kbps to 1.5 Mbps, depending on the service you buy. But because DSL works on a private line, its bandwidth isn't shared with neighbors and so doesn't slow down as usage increases.

However, a DSL signal can't be used over distances more than about three miles from the telephone company's central switching office for technical reasons related to the strength of the signal on the phone line. Homes too far from that office can't receive DSL service at all. Telephone companies may expand the range in some areas.

SATELLITE-BASED SERVICE. These connections use a special dish and receiver like those for satellite TV service. Until recently, getting the Internet via satellite meant a connection only for data streaming into your house; you still needed a dial-up connection for two-way communication. Now, however, DirecWay offers a high-speed, two-way connection.

Satellite service is the most costly alternative. As of mid-2002, unlimited access from DirecWay cost $70 per month plus $380 for equipment and $200 for installation. The company says professional installation is required.

Even if you already have satellite TV service, you'll need a different antenna if you want satellite-based broadband. The data are routed through a different satellite from the one handling TV broadcasts.

In some parts of the country, however, satellite service may be the only practical way to get any broadband service at all.

Installation ins and outs

Cable installations are straightforward mainly because one company handles everything. Digital Subscriber Line (DSL) hookups can be more complicated.

Deregulation of local phone service has opened the DSL market to independent companies known as competitive local exchange carriers, or CLECs. The CLECs, in turn, contract with Internet providers, which retail the service and provide technical support. Since the local phone company is always involved because it owns the phone lines, installing DSL can mean coordinating the work of multiple companies.

Stories of installers failing to show up for scheduled appointments are legion. However, two developments promise to make it easier to get DSL.

◆ Local phone companies are now required to allow competing providers access to existing phone lines carrying voice signals. That should reduce the need for phone-company installers to visit consumers' homes.

◆ Do-it-yourself kits for DSL as well as cable are becoming more commonplace.

How to proceed

Broadband Internet access offers many advantages that a dial-up connection can't. If you take the long-range view, having broadband now puts you in the best position to take advantage of new technologies that are likely to require a high-speed connection. But, of course, not everyone needs the speed or can afford it. A dial-up connection will suffice for simple but common activities—shopping and e-mail.

What if you don't have Internet access or if you want to change Internet providers? The first step is to find out which providers can serve your home. One call to the local cable-TV company should tell you whether you can get cable-modem service. Finding out about DSL providers in your area begins with a call to the local phone company or a visit to www.dslreports.com or www.getspeed.com. For a new dial-up connection (assuming you have none now), start with America Online, EarthLink, or AT&T Worldnet. Those three are among the largest providers. AOL distributes disks for hundreds of hours of free introductory access like falling autumn leaves. For EarthLink and AT&T, call 800-EARTHLINK or 800 WORLDNET or go to www.earthlink.com or www.att.com.

If you're satisfied with your current Internet provider, give that company a call first. Staying with your provider also lets you keep your existing e-mail addresses. For information on the satellite-based service, go to www.direcway.com.

PROTECT YOUR COMPUTER SYSTEM

Hackers and computer viruses can trash your computer or use it to attack banks, insurance companies, power plants, and other institutions. Fortunately, it's easy to make your computer well protected.

If you have a broadband connection, your home computer may be probed by a hacker at any hour of any day. These hackers are seeking an entrée they can use to hide software that would allow the computer to be "zombied," or controlled remotely. And everyone who uses the Internet, even with a dial-up connection, may catch a computer virus.

"Probably every machine on the Internet is touched multiple times a day by one type of a scan or another," says Jeff Carpenter, a manager with the Computer Emergency Response Team, a federally funded research center at Carnegie-Mellon University that responds to attacks on the Internet.

Once the computer has been hacked—and chances are good that you wouldn't know until it was too late—the hacker could extract enough personal information to impersonate you or steal important financial data.

What's more, your computer could then be commandeered to help cripple major web sites, not to mention government agencies, banks, brokerages, or other businesses via denial-of-services attacks. (You aren't likely to be accused of wrongdoing if that happens, however.) Such attacks have shut down major web sites including Yahoo! and eBay. A recent business survey found that 90 percent of large corporations and government agencies detected a computer security attack.

Hackers can so freely roam the Internet because it wasn't designed for the kind of use it now gets. The Internet itself lacks effective technological, legal, and human resources to stop these incursions.

Hackers aren't the only peril to your computer. Viruses—the malicious software planted for the express purpose of causing disruption or damage—have most likely turned up in a majority of home computers in the U.S. When CONSUMER REPORTS surveyed nearly 8,000 subscribers to the ConsumerReports.org web site, 58 percent said they had found at least one virus on their home computer in the past two years. And 10 percent said the virus had caused some kind of damage.

Your computer and all the sensitive personal data stored on it do not have to be so vulnerable. Properly armored, your computer can become an important line of defense against cyberspace invaders. Readily available software can effectively block most hackers and viruses.

Firewall software: Holding off hackers

How many of the 10 million broadband users protect themselves with a firewall? Only about 60 percent, according to both ConsumerReports.org subscribers and a nationally representative sample polled in mid-2002. That would leave about 4 million computers vulnerable. Only a tiny fraction of the survey respondents said that they knew hackers had actually broken into their computer. However, many people never know that their computer has been hacked.

Following the terrorist attacks on the Pentagon and World Trade Center, government and industry tried to tighten computer security. But some developments appear to do little to identify and shut down hackers.

An anti-terrorism law enacted in the fall of 2001 stiffened some penalties for hacking, but those provisions may apply only to attacks on government, military, or commercial computers, not on private home computers. In addition, a government-industry program,

DID ANY FIREWALLS FLAME OUT?

The CONSUMER REPORTS computer experts tested the firewall included in Microsoft's Windows XP operating system, five software products, and one hardware firewall that's included in a router, a device used to connect several home computers to a single broadband connection. The vulnerability of those products was tested with both incoming and outgoing communications. For incoming attacks, the computer was poked and probed over the Internet just as a hacker would. For outgoing communications, the software's ability to filter things like instant messages was checked. That's important because instant- messaging applications and other types of file-sharing programs can be used to infect your computer with a type of software called a Trojan Horse, which performs outgoing communications. A firewall that only handles incoming threats offers no protection here.

Incoming threats. Six of the seven products tested provided excellent protection. They put a computer in "stealth mode," making it virtually undetectable and closing the software gateways technically known as "ports" (not to be confused with the ports for universal serial bus or serial cables). Either weakness can be exploited by a savvy hacker. The seventh product, though still very good, wasn't quite as effective.

Outgoing protection. Most proved effective in this regard. But Windows XP and the Linksys Etherfast Router offered no outgoing protection. If you use antivirus software and practice good computer hygiene, outgoing protection isn't essential. But if you or the kids use the computer for instant messaging and other kinds of online file-sharing, make sure the computer has outgoing protection.

Recommendations. All of the products provide very good incoming protection. But your first choice should be ZoneAlarm Pro 3.0 or Norton Personal Firewall 2002, each $50. They provide maximum protection and an extra margin of safety with outgoing protection. A good free version of ZoneAlarm is available from *www.zonelabs.com*. If your computer uses Windows XP, be sure to activate its built-in firewall unless you use another one.

STUPID VIRUS TRICKS

Most malevolent software won't infect your computer unless you open an e-mail attachment. So virus distributors use various tricks, which experts call "social engineering," to con you into clicking. A common ploy is to have the e-mail come from a family member or friend. The illustrations below show other basic types of tricks that have been used by well-known viruses and worms. Antidotes were developed for all of them. If you receive messages like these, delete them and run a virus check before you do anything else with the computer.

The infected document
Here, the subject line includes the name of the sender, probably someone you know. The message itself tempts you to open the attached Microsoft Word document ("don't show to anyone else"). The attachment is a legitimate Word file, but infected with an invisible embedded program known as a macro, which runs when you open the Word document.

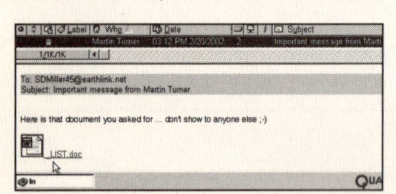

The misleading file name
If you aren't familiar with the way Windows names files, you can easily mistake the attachment's name, "LOVE-LETTER-FOR-YOU.TXT.vbs," for that of a harmless text file. In fact, the file's "vbs" suffix is the real one, which identifies it as a type of program known as Windows script. That's a rudimentary computer program an intruder writes to run on your Windows operating system. The suffix may be hidden entirely on your computer, thus appearing to be a type of file you'd willingly open, such as a JPEG image, MP3 music, or PDF document.

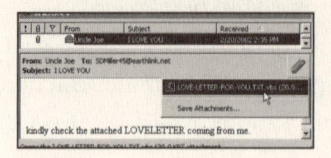

The offer you can't refuse
This example relies on your falling for a message so compelling, an offer to rid your computer of a virus, that it doesn't need to disguise the fact that the attachment is a program. Unfortunately, the program is a worm that sends itself to e-mail addresses it finds on your computer.

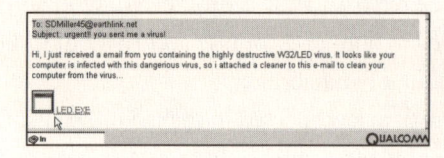

The fake web link
This example uses several tricks. The subject and message suggest that opening the attachment will take you to a web page containing party photos. The attachment's name even resembles a web address, but there's no web site involved. This is actually a program that sends itself to your friends and colleagues. This particular intrusion was designed only to tie up e-mail; it could easily have been designed to destroy data.

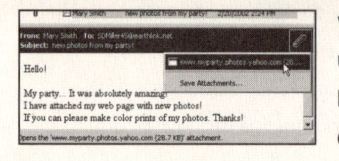

---

the National Cyber Security Alliance, launched a campaign and web site *(www.staysafeonline.info)* to educate consumers about computer security.

You can help forestall digital disaster by installing a firewall, which is software or hardware designed to block intruders, on any home computer that has a high-speed connection. A computer with a slower dial-up connection is much less vulnerable to attack because of the different way in which it is identified on the Internet.

With a dial-up connection, your computer has a dynamic Internet provider address—the string of numbers that identifies your machine and that changes every time you log on. You're harder to follow over time. By contrast, a high-speed connection typically has a fixed IP address or one that changes only occasionally. Since it rarely changes, hackers can readily track the computer for an extended period. A firewall makes your computer less visible on the Internet and helps ensure that any hacker who does find your computer won't be able to get into its programs and files.

There are three ways to equip your computer with a firewall:

◆ With Windows XP, activate its built-in firewall via the Control Panel Network.

◆ Buy a separate software firewall, an application that runs in the background to keep watch over your computer at all times.

◆ Interpose a hardware firewall between your computer and the Internet. These devices contain firewall software that operates pretty much the way a basic software firewall does.

Antivirus protection: Essential for everyone

Vast numbers of viruses have been reported over the years, and perhaps 40,000 confirmed. New ones appear constantly. Two of the most destructive—Melissa and Love Letter—caused millions of dollars in damage. But on any given day, only a few hundred viruses pose a serious threat to your computer. The number of viruses has grown because the technology to produce them is widely available and usable even by "script kiddies," as the least sophisticated perpetrators are known.

A virus can infect your computer in a variety of ways, including e-mail attachments, diskettes, or files you download from the web. Four common ruses are shown in "Stupid Virus Tricks," on page 20. The CONSUMER REPORTS survey found that Windows users encounter viruses nearly three times more often than do Mac users (62 percent vs. 23 percent). Eleven percent of Windows users reported damage; only 2 percent of Mac users did.

In the CONSUMER REPORTS survey, many who sustained virus damage said it involved lost data or expensive repairs. And only 50 percent said the computer fully recovered.

HOW ANTIVIRUS SOFTWARE FARED

CONSUMER REPORTS tested four widely available products, Norton AntiVirus 2002, McAfee VirusScan 6.0, PC-cillin 2000, and Vexira Antivirus 2.0. Prices range from $40 to $50. The products work pretty much the same way: One part of the software constantly monitors incoming e-mail attachments and new files. Another part can be used to periodically scan your entire hard drive for viruses.

Norton and McAfee are often bundled with new computers. If your computer already has antivirus software, make sure you know how to use and maintain it; don't install a second antivirus product.

The engineers tested the software by pitting each program against some relatively new actively circulating viruses. They also tested each against viruses that were circulating as far back as 1998; all antivirus products should have antidotes for viruses that old. All four products fared well against current and older viruses, though Vexira and PC-cillin missed a few.

When antivirus software has no specific way to identify a virus, it falls back on weaker technology called "heuristics" to detect unfamiliar viruses. When the engineers tested the products' heuristics, Vexira Antivirus and PC-cillin could detect only a type of infection called a "macro" virus, the type used to embed malicious programs in a word processor or spreadsheet. Vexira, which had been on the market for just a few months before the testing, was also the least capable at disinfecting viruses by reversing their damage rather than deleting them.

Recommendations. Norton AntiVirus, $50, and McAfee VirusScan 6.0, $40, get our nod because of their superior consistency and ability to detect a wider range of unfamiliar viruses. The software can't do it all, though. You must scrupulously maintain any antivirus product to be assured that you always have the latest updates. That's essential to the software's effectiveness.

COMPUTER HYGIENE 101

Regular backups of important data, plus use of antivirus software and a firewall, are the most important ways to protect your computer's contents. You can also make yourself less of a target by using applications that aren't as widely adopted as Microsoft products—Eudora e-mail, say, or WordPerfect word processing. The following measures also help ensure that important information or programs on your computer won't easily be damaged or stolen.

Essential steps

◆ Regularly update your operating system, web browser, and other key software, using the manufacturers' update features or web downloads.

◆ With a DSL or cable connection, staying online increases exposure. When you aren't using the computer, shut it off or unplug the cable or phone line.

◆ Don't open an e-mail attachment, even from someone you know well, unless you're certain you know what the attachment contains.

◆ To foil password-cracking software, make sure your passwords are at least eight characters long and include at least one numeral and a symbol, such as "#." Avoid common words, and never disclose a password to anyone online. Avoid using the same password for, say, an online discussion group and a critical task, like online banking.

◆ Run programs such as America Online's Instant Messenger only when needed. Be very careful with the file-transfer feature; a firewall won't block files sent to you this way because they piggyback on the file-transfer application itself, so you're creating an entrée for a virus.

◆ Don't forward any e-mail warning about a new virus. As many computer users have learned, the warning may be a hoax or outdated. Check for hoaxes at www.vmyths.com. The four companies whose antivirus software is rated on page 21 offer an e-mail virus-alert service.

If you've been attacked by a virus

What to do first. Unplug the phone or cable jack from the computer. Before anything else, scan your whole computer using fully updated antivirus software. If you don't have it, buy antivirus software and install it to try to eliminate the virus before you do anything else with your computer. On the other hand, if you choose to stay online, do a free scan via the web at *http://security.norton.com*. You can also download a free trial version of antivirus software at *www.mcafee.com/eval*.

What NOT to do. Don't delete files, even infected ones. Viruses can infect files your computer needs, which can often be disinfected by antivirus software. Don't reformat your hard drive or run your e-mail program until you have run an antivirus scan. If antivirus software doesn't fix the problem, contact the antivirus manufacturer.

If you've been hacked

What to do. Immediately disconnect the phone or cable jack from the computer. Run a complete virus scan on your computer to remove software such as a Trojan Horse, which hackers may have planted. A free trial version of a Trojan-cleaning utility is at *www.moosoft.com*. If you don't already have a firewall, install one. Before reconnecting to the Internet, try to find out why your computer was vulnerable.

Whom to call for help

The intruder's Internet provider. If your firewall provides the intruder's numeric Internet (IP) address, look up his Internet provider (via Network Lookup at *www.network-tools.com*) and e-mail documentation of the incident—copied from your firewall's "log file"—to the provider's "abuse" mailbox, for example, abuse@rr.com.

The authorities. Except in large cities, the chances are your local police won't be able to help. A number of state police departments or attorneys general have a computer crime unit. You can also report serious incidents to the FBI (*www.ifccfbi.gov*) or the Internet's emergency response team, CERT (e-mail: cert@cert.org), but don't expect much help.

What NOT to do. Don't try to track down hackers or get even with them. You'll merely disclose your presence and Internet address, inviting further intrusions.

To be effective, antivirus software must be constantly updated with the latest antidotes. All products that CONSUMER REPORTS tested will do that automatically via the web; older versions relied on manual updating—a serious shortcoming. In the CONSUMER REPORTS survey, 40 percent of those whose antivirus software doesn't automatically update had not downloaded an update within the past month.

THE HOME NETWORK

More and more households need to connect various computers through a network. Here's how to be sure all your computers remain on speaking terms.

If the phrase "networking your home" brings up images of goofy home automation concepts like the Internet-enabled refrigerator, you probably need to shake off the aftereffects of the dot-com marketing blitz. These days, networking your home means creating communication links between your home computers to share a high-speed Internet connection, printers, and data files.

Sharing a broadband connection is the most compelling reason to install a home network. A broadband connection is speedy enough to accommodate several users at the same time, usually without a noticeable drop in speed. A network also lets you share printers. So instead of maintaining and, eventually, replacing a separate printer for each computer, you maintain just one. Getting by with fewer printers may save you enough to justify making the one you share a more expensive model—a high-output laser printer, say, or a top-line inkjet optimized for reproducing digital photos. If you often move files from one computer to another, a network will do that in seconds.

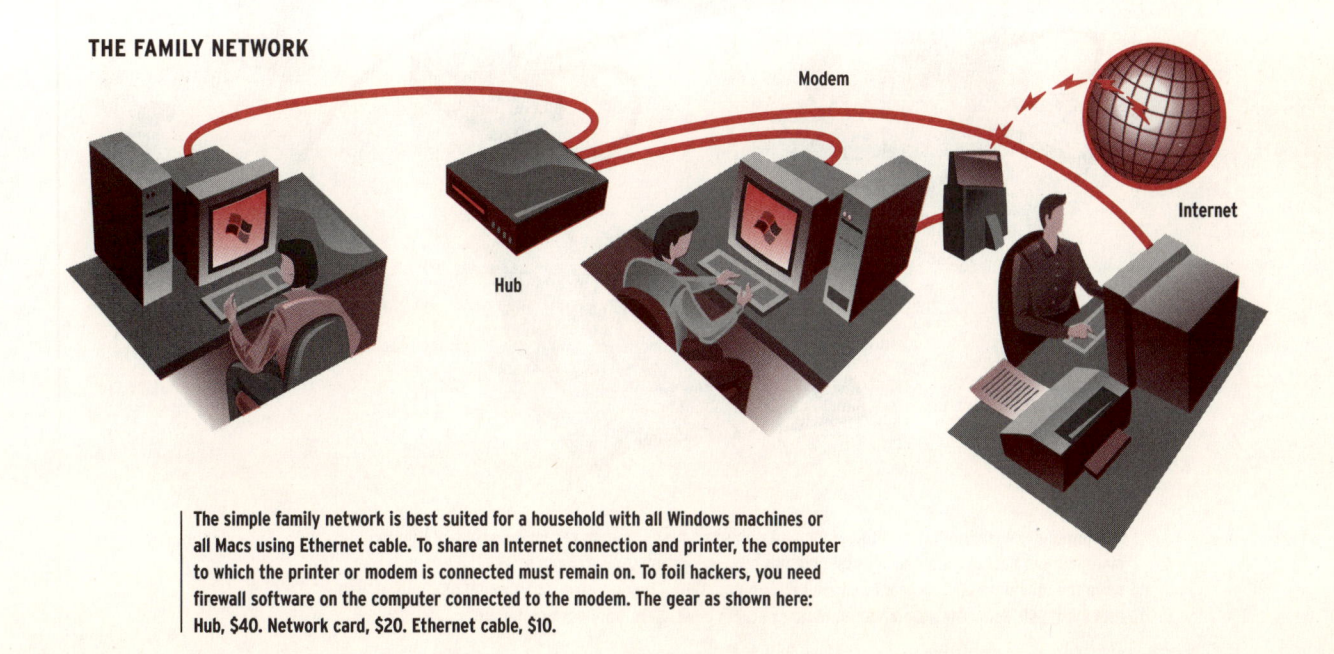

THE FAMILY NETWORK

The simple family network is best suited for a household with all Windows machines or all Macs using Ethernet cable. To share an Internet connection and printer, the computer to which the printer or modem is connected must remain on. To foil hackers, you need firewall software on the computer connected to the modem. The gear as shown here: Hub, $40. Network card, $20. Ethernet cable, $10.

The four networking options

There are four main ways to network home computers. It helps to think of the different types as building blocks that can be combined in a single network to suit your own needs. For example, you can add a wireless connection to a laptop that connects all the other computers with cables. The drawings on these pages show common networking options.

WIRED ETHERNET. The oldest of the networking technologies, this is also the one used by more than 80 percent of the people in a recent CONSUMER REPORTS survey who had a home network. It uses a special cable that can transmit data at 50 Mbps, 50 times faster than the typical broadband connection.

Ethernet boasts easy software setup and reliability at distances of hundreds of feet. Its main drawback is the cabling. You may need to drill into walls and run the cable through crawl spaces and from ceilings. If you can't or don't want to alter the house décor, you may want to consider another approach.

PHONELINE. Also called Home PNA, this approach uses existing phone wires to connect computers without affecting voice calls or any DSL connection. Each computer connects to the network via the nearest phone jack. Setting up Phoneline is simple and the installation is more flexible than Ethernet. You can relocate any computer to any room with an appropriate phone jack. For more information, go to *www.HomePNA.org*.

It's important to note that poor phone-line quality can foil this type of networking. If you normally hear crackles on the line, Phoneline isn't for you.

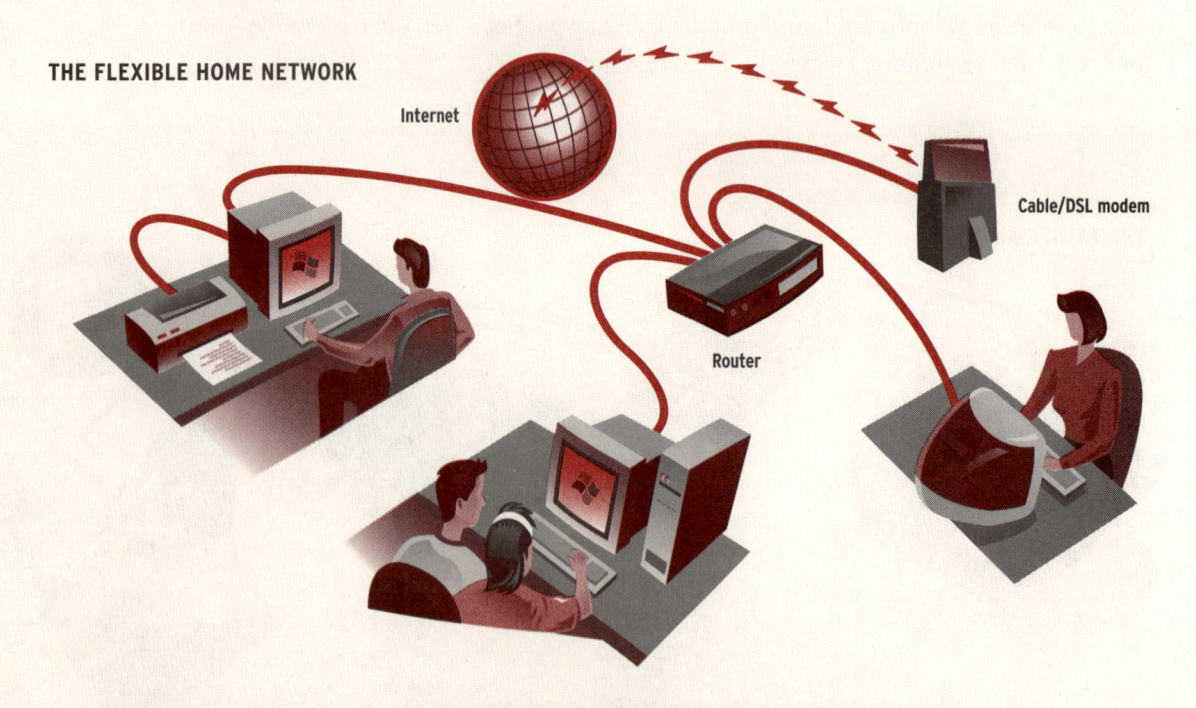

THE FLEXIBLE HOME NETWORK

The flexible home network is best suited for a household whose computers can include a mix of Windows machines and Macs. A router handles the Internet connection; any computer can access the Internet, even while the others are off. The gear as shown here: Router, $100. Ethernet card, $20. Cable, $10. Optional: Home PNA card, $60. Powerline adapter, $150. Wireless access point, $130. Wireless adapter, $70.

POWERLINE. Also known as HomePlug, this new technology uses the household electrical wiring to link computers. Each computer connects to the network via the nearest wall outlet. Setup is simple, and Powerline is flexible; you can relocate a computer to any room with an appropriate outlet. For information, go to *www.HomePlug.org*.

In CONSUMER REPORTS tests, electrical noise from appliances, power tools, dimmers, or oil-burner motors could slow network speed. Some significant drawbacks: As this book went to press, there were no routers available to let computers share a broadband connection, and no Macintosh capability.

WIRELESS. Called Wi-Fi or 802.11b (the section of the industry standard for this technology), wireless networking has provided Internet connectivity at airports, hotel lobbies, and even Starbucks coffeehouses. Wi-Fi works like a cordless phone. A base station broadcasts to a special card inside or attached to each computer. Wi-Fi is the most flexible networking approach; you can move computers just about anywhere in the house or out in the yard.

Note, however, that setting up a wireless network can involve more effort than other approaches require. The hardware is shipped with encryption turned off, we found, so you must turn it on to prevent neighbors or passersby from eavesdropping or poaching your Internet connection. You must also change the preset passwords manufacturers use and the default names that Microsoft Windows assigns to your network and work group. Hackers know those passwords.

Note, too, that heavy walls, aluminum siding, or metal pipes can block Wi-Fi

THE ADVANCED HOME NETWORK

The advanced home network is best suited for a household whose computers can include a mix of Windows machines and Macs, and wireless devices such as suitably equipped laptops in a variety of locations and configurations. A router handles the Internet connection, so any computer can access it even if the others are off. The gear as shown here: Wireless router, $175. Ethernet card, $20. Cable, $30 to $50. Home PNA card, $60. Powerline adapter, $150. Print server, $90. Wireless adapter, $70.

transmissions. You may need to relocate the base station or some antennas. Microwave ovens and cordless phones that operate in the 2.4-gigahertz band can also interfere.

Other considerations

NETWORKING MACS. If all your computers are Macs, then networking is no more challenging than for Windows computers. If you want a Windows machine and a Mac to share an Internet connection through a router, the procedure is straightforward. Just set up both computers with the router according to the router's instructions and they'll coexist nicely. But if you want to share files between a Mac and a Windows computer, you'll need special software, such as PC MacLAN ($189, at *www.miramar.com*) or DAVE 3.1 ($140, at *www.thursby.com*).

USING AMERICA ONLINE. You can't share an AOL connection over a home network because the AOL software is "session based." AOL has said it is working on a way to make the software compatible with a home network. For now, any computer in the network can use AOL's $15-per-month "bring your own access" plan, which uses a web-based interface.

HARDWARE AND SOFTWARE ISSUES. Computers that run on Windows 98 or earlier Microsoft operating systems may give you trouble. You may need to upgrade the computers to Windows XP. Most routers accept only external modems, we found. If your Internet provider supplies an internal one, you may have to fight for an exchange or buy your own. And the firewall built into some routers may conflict with firewall software running on your computers; you may have to disable the software.

How to proceed

Seriously consider a home network if your family members always contend for time on the lone broadband connection or you are planning to acquire broadband service in the first place. Wired Ethernet is the method of choice, provided you don't mind running

NETWORKING

Overall Ratings — In performance order

SYSTEM	PRICE (TWO COMPUTERS)	ADDITIONAL COMPUTER	INSTALLATION	SOFTWARE SETUP	MOBILITY	RECOMMENDATIONS & NOTES
Ethernet (wired)	$140	$30; print server, $100	○	◉	●	The system of choice for computers that won't be moved. Fast, secure, and reaches hundreds of feet. But you must be willing to wire your home. Cables are an extra $10 to $40 per computer.
Phoneline	230	60	◉	◉	○	A good choice for homes with numerous phone jacks. Demands good line quality. No print server available yet, which limits flexibility.
Powerline	300	150	◉	◐	○	Pricey, not ready for most people because of limited equipment and compatibility. Works in electrical outlets, but not with extension cords or surge protectors. Not Macintosh compatible. Line noise can slow speed. No print server or router available yet; can be connected to an Ethernet router through a $150 adapter.
Wireless	270	$80; print server, $130	○	○	◉	The best choice for laptops and computers that will be moved a lot. But covers only 50 to 150 feet. Speed drops with distance. Structures that block radio waves can interfere. Signal may reach neighbors, so encryption and passwords are a must, complicating setup.

Behind the comparison
Based on CONSUMER REPORTS tests of representative networking systems in mid-2002. **Price** is for a router (except for Powerline) and any adapters or other devices needed to network two computers. For wired Ethernet, it doesn't include cables. It excludes any labor charges. **Additional computer** is what it will cost to add one desktop or laptop to the network, excluding cables and labor. One router can accommodate a limited number of computers. If you exceed that, you'll need additional equipment. **Installation** indicates how difficult it is to set up the hardware yourself. Cabling wired Ethernet can range from simple to complex, depending on the home. **Software setup** indicates how difficult it is to make the needed changes to your computers' operating systems. **Mobility** indicates the ease with which computers can be relocated within the house while remaining networked.

cables from room to room. Wired Ethernet is also the least expensive way to network. As an alternative, consider a phone-line system, which relies on phone jacks. Wireless is best when mobility is a priority or you want network connections in rooms but you don't have phone jacks available. For more information, go to *www.HomePCNetwork.com* or *www.PracticallyNetworked.Com*.

KEEP YOUR PRIVATE DATA PRIVATE

The potential for invasion of privacy has become one of the most troubling aspects of many people's growing reliance on the Internet. But there are things you can do to keep the privacy invaders at a safe distance.

Every time you buy even an inexpensive product online or just request information from a web site, you leave behind a digital trail of valuable information about yourself that companies are eager to acquire. According to a study by the Federal Trade Commission, more than 90 percent of the online retail web sites it sampled collected personal data from consumers who visited. Yet the FTC found that only 2 percent of all commercial web sites had a comprehensive privacy policy.

As more and more people go online regularly, protecting consumer privacy is becoming a front-burner concern. Cyber-merchants routinely gather names, addresses, and credit-card numbers as they process orders. Many also ask shoppers for their e-mail address and phone number so they can send a confirmation of the transaction or contact them if there's a problem with the order. That's legitimate, but too many companies go far beyond those reasonable boundaries to solicit other information—your age, occupation, hobbies, even household income—that has nothing to do with your purchase.

The potential problem, of course, is that companies can misuse it by deluging you with solicitations to buy other products or by selling the information to other businesses. Here are some of the practices and issues you should be aware of before you double-click and send personal data across the Internet.

The cookie monster

Cookies—digital "crumbs" that are dropped onto your hard drive when you visit a web site—are the way online marketers learn about you. They contain the electronic equivalent of a Social Security number, which is used to track your movements on the web and identify you when you visit other sites; the cookie alerts the marketer that you're there so it can look up its file of your interests. Then companies deploy banner ads—or those annoying pop-up ad boxes—that are supposed to match your interests as you view sites.

A big player in the realm of cookies is DoubleClick. As soon as you visit a site affiliated with the company's network, DoubleClick enters into its private database whatever information it can get about you—your ZIP code, your area code, the organization you work for, or the type of computer you use. (DoubleClick says it doesn't collect your name and e-mail address.) At the same time, DoubleClick can also start collecting information about the actions you take online. You can "opt out" of DoubleClick's system by going to *www.doubleclick.net* and following directions to its privacy settings.

Here are some other ways to protect yourself from cookies:

DELETE YOUR COOKIES FILE. If your web browser is Netscape Navigator 3.0 or higher, you can delete your cookies file. Search your hard drive for the file "cookies.txt" and delete it. In doing so, you may lose some settings, such as web-site passwords. With Internet Explorer 3.0 or higher, cookies are not labeled as such, but you'll find them (in multiple files) in the "cookies" subfolder within the Windows operating system's "Windows" folder or, after launching Explorer, in the Preferences of Mac's Edit menu.

BLOCK COOKIES. To prevent DoubleClick or anyone else from re-creating cookie entries, choose the menu option in your browser that asks your permission every time someone tries to modify your cookie file or files. But because a cookie file identifies you as a previous visitor to that site, you'll have to retype a password and possibly reselect preferences each time you revisit a site. You need to weigh cookies' potential convenience against your own privacy concerns. A web site can't use cookies to obtain your e-mail address directly, but a cookie can associate you with an e-mail address you've volunteered.

TAKE OFFENSIVE ACTION. Install software that protects your cookie files. If you use Windows, check out *www.cookiecentral.com/files.htm*, or *www.junkbusters.com/ht/en/cookies.html*. Macintosh users can download Cookie Cutter at *www.shareware.com*. LavaSoft's free Ad Aware utility *(www.lavasoft.de)* can find and remove advertisers' cookies. In addition, AdSubtract ($30 online, from *www.adsubtract.com)* lets you block ads and enable cookies site by site.

SURF ANONYMOUSLY. A piece of software known as an anonymous remailer is a free program that alters the return address of an e-mail or discussion-group message so that your name and address are never seen. You can find such an identity-hiding program at *www.anonymizer.com*.

You've got spam

Millions of unsuspecting Americans have been spammed—sent unsolicited and unwanted e-mail, sometimes dozens of pieces a week. How does spam work? Renegade entrepreneurs spew spam to the far reaches of the Internet, millions of pieces at a time. Some get addresses by harvesting them right off Internet chat rooms and message boards. Others pirate names from membership directories of Internet providers or get customer lists from companies that do business online. Spammers also use software that generates e-mail addresses at random.

Spammers hawk get-rich-quick schemes, fraudulent deals, and pornography, among other things. It's so cheap to send spam that it's profitable even if relatively few consumers bite.

Lately some spammers have been disguising their junk e-mail in clever ways. Here are some examples:

HEY, YOU ASKED FOR IT. The message says or implies that you requested it or registered to receive "special offers from our marketing partners," or some such. The partner could be any web site you've ever visited whose privacy policy permits it to give your e-mail address to spammers. There's nothing illegal about this type of notice.

HARD TO RESIST. Among the come-ons to get you to click: A junk message from Columbia House's CD library saying, "It looks like a mistake to me. What do you think?"

WE'RE LEGIT. REALLY. Spam messages often link to web pages for an aura of legitimacy.

Some cite federal bill S.1618, Title III, with which the marketer presumably complied by providing an "unsubscribe" option. (The bill, however, never became law.)

Increasingly, Internet providers and others are successfully fighting back. The providers are working to perfect filters that eliminate spam before it hits your in box. Spam is a big deal to them because it's a financial threat. According to one estimate, 15 to 20 percent of America Online's monthly fee goes toward controlling spam. A huge volume of e-mail can overload servers, preventing desired customers from signing on. It can even crash servers, putting an Internet provider out of business temporarily. And it can turn off customers, resulting in a loss of membership.

The FTC, which gets thousands of complaints about unsolicited e-mail, has notified senders they were possibly violating federal computer-fraud and postal statutes, and has taken action against companies such as pyramid schemers. A private nonprofit group, the Mail Abuse Prevention System (its initials spell spam backward), maintains a "real-time blacklist" of spammers and tries to persuade Internet providers not to accept mail from those on the list. For information, visit *http://mailabuse.org*. You should also report spammers to your Internet provider and the FTC, at *www.ftc.gov/spam*.

DO YOUR KIDS NEED AN ONLINE CHAPERONE?
Filtering software can keep young web surfers from visiting sites inappropriate for them. Sometimes. Sort of. But don't think that a filter means you can let your guard down.

Are you concerned that your kids will encounter sexually explicit material online? Recent studies show that such content appears on just 2 percent of web sites. Even so, it's easy to reach a site with X-rated content, via a major search engine, using terms such as "Bambi" or "adult." Pornography isn't the only troublesome area. According to the Simon Wiesenthal Center, there are thousands of hate-promoting web sites. Countless other sites accessible to children promote drug use, fraud, or bomb making.

The federal government hasn't been effective at restricting children's access to sexually oriented content online. The Supreme Court struck down both the Communications Decency Act and the Children's Internet Protection Act on First Amendment grounds.

The only federal law offering explicit protection to young web surfers at home is the Children's Online Privacy Protection Act, which prohibits any web site from collecting a child's personal information without parental consent.

Who has the primary responsibility for protecting children when they go online at home? The parents of the 26 million U.S. youngsters who surf the web, that's who. According to a survey by Jupiter Research, 7 out of 10 parents handle the issue by being present when their kids go online. Only 6 percent use stand-alone filtering software, products that promise to steer kids clear of undesirable material.

The basics of filtering
Each of the products that CONSUMER REPORTS tested filters web content by interposing itself between your computer's web browser and Internet connection, then preventing objectionable content from getting through. Some filters let you decide in advance

whether to filter different types of content, such as profanity or sex information. Depending on the product and how a user configures it, a child trying to access an off-limits site may receive a warning message, a browser error message, or a partial view of the blocked site. Sometimes, the browser itself will shut down. Filtering-software designers use one of these approaches to determine whether a site merits blocking:

SOFTWARE ANALYSIS. A site's content can be rapidly analyzed by software. The filter may render a judgment at the time a child tries to access the site, or check a list of sites to block. The presence of certain phrases or images may render the site objectionable. While efficient, software analysis has its drawbacks. The software may decide to block a web site that's completely beyond reproach only because it contains a prohibited word. It may partially block a site, preventing text from appearing but letting through photos or on-screen images with embedded text. Or it may block images but not text. Most software that CONSUMER REPORTS tested blocked both words and images.

Some companies have their staff review sites individually, then place them on a list to be blocked or designated as suitable for children. This time-consuming process limits the number of sites that can be reviewed. Given the web's volatility, numerous objectionable sites can very easily remain perpetually outside the reviewer's scrutiny.

SITE LABELING. Several of the products tested incorporate a popular ratings system run by the nonprofit Internet Content Rating Association, or ICRA *(www.icra.org)*. This program, in which web-site owners voluntarily label their content, has been around for several years. It now includes labels for drugs, alcohol, tobacco, and weapons, plus the context in which words appear. Netscape's browser doesn't have the feature, but Internet Explorer can filter sites using these labels (you'll find it listed as "content advisor" under Internet Options in the Explorer menu).

CONSUMER REPORTS has found this feature in Explorer ineffective as the sole filtering technique, mainly because the many sexually explicit sites that aren't rated won't be blocked. You can set the feature to block all unrated sites, but that will block so many unrated sites as to make browsing pointless. Among the conventional sites that aren't rated are those of the White House, the U.S. Senate, the House of Representatives, and the Supreme Court.

Site labeling also depends on the honesty with which sites rate themselves. We found one site containing profanity that slipped past Explorer's filter because the site owner chose a label that didn't accurately reflect the site's content. Until far more sites suitable for children are properly labeled, labeling must be considered a complement to other filtering techniques, rather like motion-picture ratings.

How well do filters block bad stuff?

CONSUMER REPORTS' main test determined how well the filters blocked objectionable content. The engineers configured six products for a 13- to 15-year-old; they also tested AOL's Young Teen (ages 13 to 15) and Mature Teen (ages 16 to 17) parental controls, pitting them all against a list of 86 easily located web sites that contain sexually explicit content or violently graphic images, or that promote drugs, tobacco use, crime, or bigotry.

The engineers sampled web sites that appear high on lists turned up by popular search engines, thereby identifying sites that a consumer could readily encounter. The number of sites used was sufficient to allow the engineers to differentiate within the wide range of effectiveness the test found. The relative differences in performance that this test found would almost surely hold up through additional sampling of sites.

AOL's Young Teen control, the best by far, allowed only one site through in its entirety, along with portions of about 20 other sites. All the other filters allowed at least 20 percent of the sites through in their entirety. Net Nanny displayed parts of more than a dozen sites, often with forbidden words expunged but graphic images intact.

Only a few filters were able to block certain inappropriate sites. In some cases, that probably reflected differences in filtering techniques more than differences in judgment. Faulty though it may be, for example, filtering based on objectionable words apparently helped Net Nanny and Internet Guard Dog intercept a site with instructions on bomb making that eluded most others.

However, differences in judgment seem the most likely explanation for why only Cyber Patrol and both AOL controls blocked the Operation Rescue anti-abortion web site, which contains photos of aborted fetuses. Such differences raise questions about how people decide what gets blocked. According to AOL, the Young Teen control performed so well because it lets kids see only the sites on its approved list. Mature Teen blocks access to a list of prohibited sites. Kids could view an inappropriate site just because it wasn't on the Mature Teen prohibited list. (AOL considers the lists proprietary and does not disclose the sites on them.)

Do filters block good stuff?

In some cases, filters block harmless sites merely because the filtering software does not consider the context in which a word or phrase is used. Far more troubling is when a filter appears to block legitimate sites based on moral or political value judgments of those who write or sell the software.

To see whether the filters interfere with legitimate content, the CONSUMER REPORTS engineers pitted them against a list of 53 web sites that featured serious content on controversial subjects. Results varied widely. While most filters blocked only a few sites, Cybersitter 2000 and Internet Guard Dog blocked nearly one in five. AOL's Young Teen control blocked 63 percent of the sites. According to AOL, its staff and subscriber parents choose the sites kids are allowed to see using this control, with an emphasis on educational and entertainment sites. The CONSUMER REPORTS test sites may have been blocked because they didn't meet AOL's criteria, not because they were controversial.

Perhaps the most extreme example of conflicting judgments: AOL, Cyber Patrol, and Cybersitter 2000, which keep their blocked-site lists secret, blocked Peacefire, an antifiltering site that provides instructions on how to bypass filtering products. Net Nanny, which makes its list public, didn't block it.

CHAPERONING OR CENSORSHIP?

Effective filtering may well be in the eye of the beholder. In CONSUMER REPORTS tests, at least two filters blocked each of these sites:

Citizens Committee for the Right to Keep and Bear Arms. A site lobbying for gun owner's rights. Blocked by AOL Young Teen, Cybersitter 2000, and Norton Internet Security 2001.

Lesbian.org. A guide to lesbian politics and culture. Blocked by AOL Young Teen, Cybersitter 2000, and Cyber Patrol.

National Institute on Drug Abuse. A drug-information site run by the National Institutes of Health. Blocked by Norton Internet Security 2001 and Internet Guard Dog.

Southern Poverty Law Center. A nonprofit antidiscrimination law center. Blocked by AOL Young Teen and Cybersitter 2000.

Sex, Etc. Rutgers University's educational site, written by teens for teens. Blocked by AOL Young Teen, Net Nanny, and Internet Guard Dog.

What parents can do

Nearly all the filters offer some control over the disclosure of personal information, such as name and address. But the CONSUMER REPORTS test found such privacy protection too weak to rely on. Most of the products that were tested failed to block one objectionable site in five. AOL's Young Teen (or Kids Only) setting provides the best protection, though it will likely curb access to web sites addressing political and social issues.

Filtering software is no substitute for parental supervision. People who visit sites they don't want their kids to see can delete the browser's offline files, where it saves copies of recently visited web pages. Check your child's online activities by reviewing the browser's history list and bookmarks. To check for adult images your child may have downloaded, search your hard drive for images or compressed files–those with names ending in .gif, .jpg, .tif, or .zip. Two sites providing information on how to protect children are *www.getnetwise.org* and *www.safekids.com*.

2

Fitting Images: Photos and Video

Practically from their inception more than 20 years ago, desktop computers were tools for artistic, design-conscious professionals—graphic designers, magazine art directors, commercial artists, animators, filmmakers—who could afford cutting-edge hardware and expensive software. But in the past three years or so, the computer has become a convenient, readily available tool for anyone's artistic or literary expression. Today's new computers have the power, memory, and processing speed needed to quickly manipulate gargantuan graphics and image files. Just as significant, two important pieces of hardware—digital cameras and digital camcorders—have come into their own as tools anyone can use for creative expression. An Apple Computer ad showcasing the ability to transfer home video to a DVD, using software supplied with all new Macintosh computers, made the process seem as easy as point-and-shoot photography. (In truth, making your own DVD isn't quite that easy, but it's not brain surgery, either.)

Today's digital cameras and digital camcorders are easy to use. People with ample budgets and lots of ambition can look to "prosumer" products that bridge the worlds of the professional and amateur. This hardware comes with an extensive roster of features and capabilities that take dedication to master. You can expect the hardware to perform quite well. Camcorders and cameras intended for the strictly amateur consumer market also perform quite well, judging from CONSUMER REPORTS tests, but they require less dedication to master.

Point-and-shoot simplicity characterizes most digital cameras and camcorders, even those with a long menu of settings and choices. Most of the buttons and controls you often need on a camcorder fall readily to hand, so you can concentrate on the action in the viewfinder. Digital camera controls aren't always quite so handy, although the shutter button and zoom-lens control are within reach of the right index finger. Other controls, to select and

34
In the digital darkroom

38
Lights! Camcorders! Action!

39
Creativity programs

> ## HARDWARE FOR DIGITAL IMAGING
>
> **The camera is the biggest investment you'll need to make** in digital photography. It goes without saying that you already have a desktop or laptop computer. You can buy a digital camera for as little as $200 or so, or for $1,000 or more. Spending more buys literally millions more pixels, or picture elements. More megapixels yield very high quality snapshots and images with enough detail to be enlarged nearly to poster size.
>
> **Other gear includes:**
>
> **Inkjet printer.** A must for printing snapshots. See pages 131 and 174 for buying advice and brand-name Ratings. You can buy one well suited for photos for less than $100.
>
> **Card reader.** Digital cameras come with a short cable that connects camera to computer, so you can transfer images. But it can take a long time to transfer several large files that way. A separate card reader is faster. It plugs into a universal serial bus port on the computer. Readers sell for $20 and up.
>
> **Extra memory cards.** Just as you once kept a spare roll of film on hand so you wouldn't miss a good photo, it makes sense to have an extra memory card or two. Get the largest-capacity card you can afford; expect to pay around $1 per megabyte of capacity, or about $60 for a 64-MB card.
>
> **Paper.** You can buy several varieties of photo paper at office-supply and computer stores. There are papers with a matte or satin finish, as well as papers with a canvas or linenlike texture. Photo paper generally costs 40 to 50 cents a sheet. That's why it's a good idea to have a less expensive inkjet paper on hand for tests and tryouts. Ordinary copying paper will do in a pinch.
>
> **Scanner.** Necessary if you want to have digital versions of film photos and other original artwork, but not an essential. You can buy a flatbed scanner for as little as $80. See Chapter 8 for more information. There are also scanners specifically designed to scan color-film slides or negatives; they are much better suited to that task than flatbed scanners, but they're expensive.

view images already taken or to change the image resolution, aren't standardized for size, shape, or placement on the camera body.

For advice on how to shop smart for a camera or camcorder, see Chapter 8. Here, we'll help you with smart strategies for preparing, storing, and sharing photos and for editing home video.

IN THE DIGITAL DARKROOM

When the computer takes the place of the enlarger and the developing trays, you gain unprecedented control over your photos.

Digital images seem to be everywhere. Family and friends swap them across the world. Every kind of web page has them. Legions of devoted home photographers use their computers to alter images captured digitally—resizing, adjusting color and contrast, adding textures and other special effects, and so on. Many enjoy making prints, greeting cards, and T-shirt transfers on their inkjet printers, or sharing the images via the Internet. Others turn to the growing network of stores and web sites that handle digital as well as film images. Here's a rundown on the different types of software and printing services.

Software that manipulates images

Most digital cameras come with image-processing software, such as Adobe PhotoDeluxe, MGI PhotoSuite, Microsoft Picture It!, or Ulead PhotoImpact. Adobe PhotoDeluxe, a home version of the powerful professional program Adobe Photoshop, is the most common. The software lets you touch up photos or alter them in striking ways. There's often an instant-fix option to improve brightness and contrast or adjust the tint. Another common tool lets you eliminate red-eye in flash pictures. You can crop photos (change their size and shape), put them in ovals or other distinctive shapes, and straighten tilted images. You can create a mirror image or turn a photo upside-down. And you can reduce a photo's resolution, making the file small enough to send as an e-mail attachment.

Most software packages also give you a palette of creative tools. You can, for example, turn a color photo into a black-and-white or sepia-tone print or into something resembling a painting—brush strokes and all. With a steady hand, you can outline a section of one image, then electronically cut it out and paste it into another photo. You can eliminate distracting details and remove skin blemishes and other imperfections. There are ways to remove scratches and other flaws from old photos you've scanned, darken or lighten specific areas for emphasis, or throw a background into soft focus. The photos below show two simple examples of what can be accomplished.

Most image-handling software makes it easy to print images various ways—putting multiple copies on the same sheet, printing on a T-shirt transfer, or sending the photo to a web site. If you dislike the software supplied with your digital camera, you can buy one of the other packages for about $50.

Making digital images from film originals

Whether you do it yourself with a scanner or take your photos to a local photofinishing store to have them digitized, scanning lets you make digital files out of film prints or other flat pieces of artwork, such as drawings or postcards. Once digitized, you can either manipulate the images and store them on your computer, upload them to one of many online services to make prints, or post them on your own web page. You can also import an image directly into a running application, such as greeting-card software, or an e-mail or fax program, or you can save it for future use.

SCANNING IT. Adding a flatbed scanner to your computer system gives you a relatively inexpensive way of digitizing photographs. You can have individual images scanned at photofinishing shops or well-equipped copy centers, but that makes economic sense only if you do it occasionally.

Image-handling software such as Adobe Photoshop can compensate for some less-than-perfect originals, but it can't fix everything. So, when scanning originals, it's usually wise to avoid photos or drawings with noticeable flaws, unless they are part of the effect you're after. A scanner will reproduce those flaws just as a copier would.

A higher-resolution scan produces an image suitable for photo enlargement or printing, but the scanning time will be longer than at lower resolutions and the resulting file will be quite large. A resolution of 150 to 300 dots per inch (dpi) is sufficient for most tasks, including copying photographs. For copying line

Image-handling software, bundled with digital cameras or available separately, lets you make a variety of enhancements and alterations. In the photo at top right, some skiers have been "erased" to achieve an effect. The portrait on the bottom right has been improved in brightness and contrast, and some wrinkles have been removed from the face.

art with fine details or text, or if you plan to double the size of the original image later, use 600 dpi. For an image to be e-mailed, posted on a web site, or viewed on a monitor, 75 to 100 dpi is sufficient.

To get the best results, preview an image using the scanner's driver software. Use a preview scan to adjust brightness, contrast, or color, or to focus on the primary subject by cropping unwanted material.

If you want to save an image, use a resolution appropriate for the way it will be used. Scanner software typically offers you choices. From a menu, you select color photo, black-and-white image, text, and so on; the software then switches to different default settings that would be appropriate for the type of original you're working with. You're free to change those settings; see "How to Get the Most from a Scanner," below.

Resolution can be as low as 75 dots per inch, which is fine for images meant only to be viewed on a computer monitor, up to 1,200 dots per inch. Consider those higher resolutions the province of specialists who need to capture maximum detail from scanned images. Image-editing software provided with the scanner lets you make more extensive edits and prepare an image for other uses.

A scanned color photo printed as is may be perfectly acceptable to look at, but don't expect it to match the original's colors exactly. To get a closer match, you'll need to tweak the image with image-editing software. You may also want to experiment with color-rendering settings on the printer.

USING COMMERCIAL SERVICES. Drugstores and discount chains, copy shops, and service

HOW TO GET THE MOST FROM A SCANNER

Plan your usage. If you prefer to automate scanning tasks, consider shortcut buttons, which can often be customized to scan at a particular resolution or within certain dimensions, such as 4x6 inches for snapshots. And if you have an older computer without a universal serial bus (USB) port, choose a scanner that lets you connect to the parallel port.

Prepare. Avoid photos or drawings with noticeable flaws; a scanner will reproduce them flawlessly.

A higher-resolution scan produces an image that is more suitable for printing or photo enlargement, but the scanning time will be longer—two to five times longer than scanning at lower resolution—and the file produced can become quite large. Scanner manufacturers recommend, and CONSUMER REPORTS tests confirm, that 150 to 300 dpi is usually sufficient. For copying line art with fine details or text, or if you plan to double the size of a photo later, use 600 dpi. Resolution of 1,200 dpi yields little or no added benefit. For an image to be e-mailed, posted on a web site, or viewed on a monitor, 75 to 100 dpi will do.

Preview. Previewing an image using the scanner's driver software is the surest way to get the best results. Use a preview scan to adjust brightness, contrast, or color, or to focus on the primary subject by cropping the image.

Save the file. You can import an image directly into a running application, such as greeting-card software, or an e-mail or fax program. But if you want to save an image for future use, save it to the computer's hard drive in the format and resolution appropriate for the way it will be used. Photos can be saved in JPEG format to reduce file size. For images to be e-mailed, use greater levels of JPEG compression to further reduce file size. For images to be put on the web, adjust the file's resolution to alter the image's size on the screen. Uncompressed formats such as TIFF can be used if you plan to store the images on inexpensive, high-capacity media such as CDs or Zip disks. When saving successive revisions to disk, be careful not to overwrite the original file. Image-editing software provided with the scanner lets you make more extensive edits and prepare an image for other uses.

shops for professional graphic artists all offer scanning services. More and more, these companies don't care whether your snapshots exist as files from a digital camera or as files created by scanning conventional film negatives or prints. Depending on the service and your budget, you can have your film images scanned and stored on a floppy diskette, Picture CD or the higher-quality Photo CD, or uploaded to a web site. Picture CDs are $5 to $10 per roll, while Photo CDs, which can be used for superb, richly detailed enlargements, run $20 to $30.

Making prints at home or at a kiosk

With an inkjet printer, you can print photos comparable in quality to photographic prints. You can also print banners, stickers, transparencies, T-shirt transfers, or greeting cards. An alternative is using one of the thousands of freestanding photo-handling kiosks operated by Kodak, Fuji, and others in pharmacies, one-hour photo labs, and other stores. They're a handy way for you to make custom prints on the spot, without using your own computer.

Kodak's Picture Maker kiosks typify the hardware. They have a TV-style screen that displays the photo and changes you make to it, along with controls that let you choose the picture size and layout. The kiosks can read the memory card from a digital camera, a Picture CD or Photo CD, or a diskette; they also have a built-in scanner, so you can make reprints from an existing picture, a print from a diskette, or a slide. You can crop and enlarge the image or enhance it by changing the brightness or color balance, or by correcting red-eye in flash photos.

A built-in thermal dye-sublimation printer delivers prints quickly. Such prints are more permanent than those output by most inkjet printers. Prints made at a kiosk range in price from $6 to $12 per sheet.

Posting photos online

A growing roster of image-handling services and web sites will post your work on the Internet for you, let you share snapshots in online albums or through e-mail, and make traditional color prints. Some services let your e-mail recipients also order reprints printed from your original files.

With images shot on a film camera, you mail the roll to the image-handling service, which digitizes the images and, if desired, makes prints. You are notified by e-mail when the process is completed. You use the image-handling service's web site to attach the images to e-mail or include them in online photo albums. With images shot on a digital camera, you upload them to the image-handling service's web site from your computer. Kodak and PhotoWorks are among the biggest services, along with more recent start-ups such as Shutterfly.com. Some old-line photofinishers, including Mystic Color Lab, Signature, and York, also have a presence on the web. America Online offers its "You've Got Pictures" service

---

THE iPHOTO OPTION

Apple Computer offers a number of services, including the iPhoto image service, to those who use its computers.

The pros. iPhoto is a unified program that makes it easy to transfer images from camera to computer, transfer them to a file on your computer or to an Apple site, and order prints and enlargements. The prints cost as little as 49 cents for a 4x6-inch image. iPhoto includes tools for cropping and resizing images. You can also use iPhoto to arrange images in an online slide show that friends and family members can access, or even (at extra cost) to have selected images printed and bound in a hardcover book. Like many other new Apple applications, iPhoto has been designed for ease of use.

The cons. iPhoto is only available with Apple's new OS X operating system. It can't be installed on older operating systems.

with Kodak. The CVS pharmacy chain, among others, also partners with Kodak for its online service. Photofinishing sites offer a wide range of services. They may also imprint mugs, tote bags, and such with your images; store your images on their servers; or create digital versions of film snapshots when they process the original rolls.

Online companies price reprints and enlargements to be competitive with walk-in stores. Expect to pay 25 to 50 cents for a 4x6; $1 to $2 for a 5x7. (We've found that an 8x10 print produced at home on an inkjet printer costs about $1.) Many processors use regular silver halide paper and chemicals, as when printing from negatives, so reprints should last a long time.

If you upload images from a digital camera or a scanner, some processors may reduce the resolution in the original if your file does not fit their procedures. In that case, your prints might not look as crisp as you expect. Be sure the processor will use the resolution you provide.

If you upload an image that doesn't fit standard frame sizes—a long, skinny panorama, say, or a square shot—be sure to indicate how you want it printed. Some sites let you check a box to say that you want the whole image (no cropping), even if it means large, uneven margins; others may automatically crop an image's sides to force it into the frame, eliminating picture areas.

Some online photo sites are happy to store your images digitally and let you caption shots, arrange them into albums, send e-mail "postcards," and so on. Online storage can be a good backup even if you store the images on your own computer. Sellers on eBay and other online auction sites use digital images to advertise their wares. But there are limits to the amount of storage offered, on how long shots stay up (perhaps just 30 days or until you stop being an active customer), or on the image resolution (to reduce storage needs).

If you avail yourself of online storage, be clear on the privacy policy. Some sites use passwords for album access, and you can share the password with family and friends. Others have open areas, where strangers can see your snapshots; you may not want that.

LIGHTS! CAMCORDERS! ACTION!

Camcorders and newer computers with a generous amount of hard-drive space make it possible for an amateur to create video productions that are decidedly not amateurish.

With the right hardware and software, it's relatively easy to connect a digital camcorder to a computer for video editing. Your computer will need lots of hard-drive space and speed—one second of video from a digital camcorder occupies 3 to 4 megabytes—but even computers costing less than $1,000 are capacious and fast these days. You'll also need a matching input at the computer end–known as a FireWire, an IEEE-1394, or an iLink port—and 4-pin-to-6-pin FireWire cable. If your computer lacks such a port, you need to buy an adapter card and FireWire cable.

It's slightly more cumbersome to edit video shot on an analog camcorder. Instead of using a FireWire port, you'll need to have a video-capture card installed in the computer. The card will have an analog video input. Or you can use an outboard video capture device, which typically uses a USB connection to the PC.

Until recently, video editing meant either a substantial outlay for hardware and computer software or tedious dubbing of scenes. The first alternative cost too much for amateurs. The second screamed "amateur video." New software has changed that. Apple was the first to include a pro-style editing program on some of its computers. Dell and Sony also make editing software available, and there are stand-alone programs.

Many packages work this way: You connect the camcorder to the computer and patiently transfer clips, or snippets of video to the hard drive. All have some sort of onscreen staging area for the clips. Editing means using the mouse to drag a clip to a time line, trimming the length of each clip as needed. You can then add fades, dissolves, and other transitions; a voice-over; a title and credits; and music. Then you can transfer the edited version onto a recordable DVD, a video CD, or back onto tape.

The software generally requires a computer with at least 256 megabytes of RAM, a processor running at 500 megahertz, and a fast hard drive with about 40 gigabytes free. Most computers sold in the past three or four years meet or exceed those requirements.

When CONSUMER REPORTS looked at editing packages for Windows computers and the Apple iMovie program built into newer Macintosh machines, the Apple software was the easiest to figure out, with all the tools needed to create competent home videos. The programs for Windows were OK, but generally harder to use. Windows XP, the newest version of that operating system, comes with a rudimentary editing program.

CREATIVITY PROGRAMS

Programs that "paint" can help bring out your inner Picasso. You'll also see software that helps you design greeting cards, publish newsletters, touch up digital photos, and more.

Children and adults can exercise their creativity with painting programs, greeting-card designers, tools that let you touch up photographs, and more. While there are many professional-level programs available, such as Adobe Illustrator and PageMaker, there are also plenty of options for the nonprofessional.

For starters, your operating system likely includes a simple paint program that lets you draw with "colored pencils," paint with a spray can, and even use an eraser to get rid of mistakes. But you can go beyond these elementary programs with creativity and drawing programs, many of which also incorporate features for photo manipulation.

Paint Shop Pro 7 (Jasc, Windows only, less than $100), for example, includes tools for touching up photos, creating Web animations, experimenting with special effects, and more. Painter 7 (Corel, $370) is an advanced painting program for the Mac.

If you've been hearing about Adobe Photoshop but fear it is beyond your capabilities, try Photoshop Elements (Adobe, Windows and Mac, $99). Designed specifically with the novice artist in mind, it lets you work with both digital and traditional photos, cropping pictures, removing red-eye, repairing overexposures, and more. Adobe Photo Deluxe 2.0 Mac (Adobe, Mac only, $49) helps you import photos into a desktop machine, organize them into photo albums, and touch them up.

With Microsoft's Picture It! Publishing Gold (Microsoft, Windows only, $44.95), you can create your own greeting cards, and touch up photos before adding them to your creations.

Greeting-card packages allow you to create impressive greeting cards using personalized greetings and your own or prepackaged art. Some programs also include video and audio clips, which you can incorporate into the card and send via e-mail. Others give you the tools to set up web pages to post a baby or wedding announcement or share other special moments with faraway family members. Greetings 2001 (Microsoft, Windows only, $29.95) gives you plenty of design choices, with more than 4,000 templates, 12,000 images, and 500 animations to get you started.

For a do-just-about-everything package, there are PrintMaster Platinum 12 (Learning Co., Windows only, $39.99) or Print Explosion Deluxe (Nova Development Corp., Mac only, $59.99). You can create invitations, banners, place cards, and even party hats. More than 200,000 images give you plenty of material to work with.

Computer, electronics, and office-supply stores all carry some creativity software. For more information, go to *www.cnet.com* or do an Internet search for "creativity software."

3

All in the Game

Want to slay a dragon, slam a Randy Johnson fastball over the fences, pilot a Jedi spacecraft, explore the Amazon, or build a virtual civilization from scratch and reign supreme? You can when you're immersed in the eye-catching fantasy worlds of video and computer games. Here's how to get in on the action or keep up with an avid player.

Video and computer games, like movies or TV, offer an enjoyable escape from reality. But game players aren't couch potatoes: They participate in their entertainment by continually influencing and shaping the game's outcome with their decisions and actions. That ability to control and even master a world no matter how unreal is the main appeal of gaming. What's more, playing games may relieve stress. It's fun, too.

Video and computer games present challenges and obstacles. To be adept, you need logical-thinking and problem-solving skills, plus hand-eye coordination. Success, even in small increments, gives gamers a sense of accomplishment that brings them back for more. Parents and educators may worry that the pastime breeds anti-social behavior in its youthful fans or that the games expose players to excessive amounts of violence, but games aren't only about shooting and slugging. Sports, racing, and role-playing depend on strategic thinking. Simulations involve critical thinking, and casino games and puzzles sharpen problem-solving skills. Video gaming can also be a popular social activity. It engenders camaraderie and good-natured competition among family and friends. And, even with an initial outlay of a few hundred dollars, video gaming can deliver a good entertainment value. It's not uncommon to spend 50 hours on one game.

This chapter will introduce you to the big names and special language of video games, so you can help youngsters get started in the best way, or keep up with a friend or family member who's gaming big-time. And who knows? This may even persuade you to try something more challenging than the version of solitaire that came with the computer.

42
Getting started with video games

43
Outmoded games: They aren't obsolete

48
Gaming online

GETTING STARTED WITH VIDEO GAMES

Here's a brief rundown of the game-controller options and the accessories to consider.

If you're a newcomer to this pastime, video gaming is the easiest entrée. A video-game system's plug-and-play setup (simpler than setting the time on a VCR), near-instant game-loads, and lower equipment costs make it the more sensible choice for the novice interested in pure gaming. Installing computer games requires some technical know-how, familiarity with add-ons such as video cards, and perhaps more patience than most itchy-fingered gamers have. Playing fast-paced, reflex-action flying, driving or so-called "quick twitch" games on a computer will require an additional controller.

For a video game, you'll need a game-playing machine (also called a console, system, or platform) and a TV set to display the action. The newest, most powerful video-game systems are Microsoft's Xbox, Sony's PlayStation 2, and Nintendo's GameCube. They boast three-dimensional graphics, excellent sound, and absorbing game-play that approaches arcade quality. Xbox and Playstation 2 can also double as DVD players. For specifics, based on CONSUMER REPORTS tests, see below.

A console comes with one game controller and cables to link to the audio/video inputs of your TV. If your TV doesn't have those inputs you'll need an RF adapter; expect to pay $10 to $20. Count on buying at least one additional controller, for $20 to $40. Nearly all games can be played in one-player mode; many allow two or more people to play simultaneously or against each other. Gimmicky controllers that vibrate or that resemble steering wheels or flight yokes may add verisimilitude, but are not a gaming necessity. Games, which cost around $50 new, are sold separately.

To begin play, you pop a game disk into the console. Within a minute the game will load. By scrolling through a series of screen prompts, you select gaming parameters and optional settings, such as the difficulty level and background music. To maneuver characters through the game, you push "joysticks" (actually knobs that rotate full circle), directional

WHICH IS BEST: GAMECUBE, PLAYSTATION 2, OR XBOX?

The following shopping tips are based on the evaluations of CONSUMER REPORTS experts and of 19 testers ages 9 to 15:

♦ Each system has spectacular graphics and special effects, and loaded our games in less than a minute. Those weren't determining factors in our tests.

♦ Make sure the system you're considering offers the games you like. For example, the Mario family of games is available only for Nintendo systems such as the GameCube, not for Microsoft's Xbox or Sony's PlayStation 2.

♦ PlayStation 2 will play the games you bought for your PlayStation One. The GameCube is not compatible with Nintendo 64 games, however.

♦ Assess the features you want. When you're not playing video games, PlayStation 2 and Xbox allow you to use the console to listen to your music CDs or to play a DVD movie. With the Xbox, you can also record songs from CDs onto its built-in hard drive. The GameCube doesn't have audio CD or DVD capabilities.

♦ Be prepared for add-on costs for extra controllers and memory cards. The Xbox requires a memory card only if you want to take settings with you – if, say, you take the game to a friend's; its hard drive otherwise saves settings. To use the Xbox's DVD feature, you'll need a $30 playback kit.

♦ If your kids are beginners or don't play video games very much, you may be just as happy with a Nintendo 64 or PlayStation One; they cost a lot less and can be used with hundreds of titles still for sale or rent.

NEX-GEN GUIDE: WHAT'S NEW, WHAT'S NOT IN GAMES

Home video gaming has been around since the 1970s. But it wasn't until the mid-'80s, when Nintendo ushered in the modern era of video gaming with the Nintendo Entertainment System, that the hobby captured our imagination. It hasn't let go since. In 2001, video- and computer-game sales topped $6 billion for the third year in a row.

Every few years, game-console companies battle each other for those dollars by rolling out new, heavily promoted systems. Today's PlayStation 2 replaced Sony's original Playstation (1995). Nintendo's N64 (1996) replaced the Super Nintendo (1991), which, in turn, replaced the original Nintendo (1985). Sega, manufacturer of the popular Genesis machine in the late '80s and early '90s, outsold Nintendo for a while, but faltered with the Saturn (1995). The company failed to make a comeback with Dreamcast, the first "nex-gen" machine introduced in 1999 and discontinued in 2001. Many other video-gaming systems, notably Atari, have come and gone.

WHAT'S AVAILABLE

NEW	OLD	PORTABLE
Xbox 100+ games	Nintendo 64 (N64) 200+ games Also plays Game Boy games	Game Boy Advance (GBA) 300+ games
PlayStation 2 (PS2) 350+ games Can also play PSX games	PlayStation (PSX) 800+ games	Game Boy Color (GBC) Being phased out, but dozens of games still available
Game Cube (GC) 150+ games	Dreamcast (DC) 300+ games	PSOne with LCD screen 800+ games
	Super Nintendo (SNES) 700+ games	
	Nintendo (NES) 700+ games	

arrows, and various buttons on the controller. You'll need two hands to hold the controller and, until you get the hang of what to press, you'll think you need a few extra thumbs.

Accessories worth considering

Accessories from independent companies cost less and generally work just as well as gear bearing the console makers' names.

MEMORY CARD. This lets players save a game's settings or progress so they can pick up where they left off. Consider buying one memory card for each serious gamer in the household, or to store data from multiple games. Cards typically cost $10 to $30, depending on their capacity.

CABLES. If you have a high-end TV you may want to make full use of its capabilities by replacing the A/V cables that come with the game system. Component video or S-video cables help reduce video distortion (the fuzzy lines that run across the set) and sharpen picture quality. An optical cable will take advantage of a Dolby Digital sound system.

OUTMODED GAMES: THEY AREN'T OBSOLETE

Older games don't have to be consigned to a box in the back of the closet.
A brand-new Xbox, PlayStation 2, or GameCube are sure to top a gamer's wish list. But an older system may be the right choice for a new or budget-minded gamer. PlayStation and

Nintendo 64 can still dazzle. Where graphics are concerned, Dreamcast is nearly on a par with the current systems. More importantly, there are hundreds of titles to choose from for these older systems. All it takes is a handful of games that are played over and over to make any system worthwhile. Here are you options if you don't want to go for new gear.

Buy a used system

Although Nintendo 64 and its ilk are no longer made or sold at mainline retailers, you can find "pre-played" (used) systems at gaming specialty stores and websites for $30 to $170. Used games generally cost $1 to $50. New games aren't being made for old systems. You can also rent games at video stores.

GameStop and Electronics Boutique, two national gaming-specialty chains, sell refurbished and used equipment and games, as well as the newest gear. A refurbished console, one that's been repaired by the manufacturer, sells for about 10 percent less than a new one and carries the same warranty. Used systems sell for even less. A one-year warranty from the store costs $5 to $30, depending on the system. Because the screen may freeze up when playing a dirty or scratched game, it's important to check the shiny, reflective side of the disk for scratches. Be sure you know the retailer's return policy before you buy and, if possible, test a used game before handing over money. GameStop will give you a refund or issue a store credit if you return a game within seven days; Electronics Boutique will issue a store credit if you return a game within two weeks.

Trade in an older system to upgrade

Gaming emporiums accept trade-ins from gamers eager to upgrade. They offer store credit for a working system with connecting cables and one controller. Trade-in value, however, may be just one-tenth of the original price. The chart on page 45 gives price comparisons.

A used game's trade-in value depends on its popularity and condition. Game stores may deduct half the value if the box or instructions are missing, or if the game disk is scratched.

Sell the old system

If you want cash for your old systems, place a classified ad in the local paper or hold a garage sale. You can post sale items at Amazon.com; or, try your luck at an online auction (see Chapter 6).

These brick-and-mortar retailers specialize in new and used games and equipment.

GAME RATINGS: KNOW THE CODE

Playing a video game is like being inside an animated big-budget movie packed with adrenaline-pumping thrills, spills and, quite often, violence ranging from the comic-cartoony to graphic realism. How do you know whether a game is appropriate for your child? Know his or her interests, reading level, and problem-solving ability. Then check the bold letters on a game box for its ESRB (Entertainment Software Rating Board) rating:

- EC – Early Childhood. For ages 3 and up.
- E – Everyone. For ages 6 and up.
- T – Teen. For ages 13 and up.
- M – Mature. For ages 17 and up.
- AO – Adults only. For ages 18 and up.
- RP – Rating Pending. The product has been submitted to ESRB and is awaiting a final rating.

Such small-print phrases as "comic mischief" and "strong language" under a game's ratings are the ESRB's Content Descriptors. They help explain why a game earned its classification. For more information on the ESRB and a detailed explanation of its guidelines, call 800-771-3772 or go to *www.esrb.org*. The web site lists more than 7,000 games by title, system, ratings, and descriptors.

According to the Interactive Digital Software Association (IDSA), sports, action, role-playing, and racing games were the most popular in 2001. More than half of the video and computer games released in 2001 carried an "E" rating. One in four earned a "T" and one in ten an "M."

A rating, of course, is someone else's opinion. The best way to know whether a game suits your needs and interests is to play it.

GAMING-STORE PRICE COMPARISONS

The table shows what GameStop and Electronics Boutique, two leading game retailers, were charging for new (and not-so-new) game controllers and a widely sold game in mid-2002. Prices change daily, so treat the numbers here as guides, not gospel.

SYSTEM	NEW	REFURBISHED Game Stop	REFURBISHED Electronics Boutique	USED Game Stop	USED Electronics Boutique	TRADE IN VALUE* Game Stop	TRADE IN VALUE* Electronics Boutique
PS2	$200	$180	$180	$170	$170	$120	$125
Xbox	200	180	180	170	170	120	125
GameCube	150	140	140	140	140	90	100
Nintendo 64	–	–	–	35	60	15	10
Sega Dreamcast	–	–	–	50	60	20	15
Playstation	–	–	–	30	35	5	20
Playstation One	50	–	–	40	40	25	20
Super Smash Bros. (GameCube)	50	–	–	45	45	30	25

GAMESTOP www.gamestop.com. Operates under several names, including FuncoLand, Software Etc., and Babbage's. The web site includes a store locator.

ELECTRONICS BOUTIQUE www.ebgames.com. Operates under several names, including EB Gameworld, EBX, EBKids, Stop-N-Save Software. Call 800-800-5166 to find the nearest store.

Other gaming-speciality web sites include:

CHIPS & BITS www.cdonline.com. This site is associated with Computer Games Online and Computer Games magazine. To get a mail-order catalogue, call 800-699-4263.

GAMESPOT www.gamespot.com. Includes a shopping bot that compares prices and links to online sellers.

GEXPRESS.COM www.gexpress.com. This is a source for games, DVDs, action figures, and the like.

To buy or sell used games and equipment online, try one of these sites: www.amazon.com, www.ebay.com, or www.half.com.

Game time

Be sure the system you want offers the types of games you like or want for young gamers. If possible, try a game before buying, get suggestions from like-minded players, and check out game review-magazines and web sites.

Although gaming is becoming more and more popular with adults, it's still considered a kid's activity. Nearly half of all video-gamers and one-third of computer gamers are under 18. Unfortunately, most games don't carry suggested age ranges. For guidance in selecting age-appropriate titles, check the game's ESRB ratings (see the box on page 44). Use your own judgment as well and make time to play alongside young gamers.

Depending on your level of play and the type of game, it can take half an hour to become familiar with a new game and considerably more time to become skilled enough to attain higher levels. Racing games are usually a good choice for a beginner who wants to become adept at using the controller. (Button placement differs on each system's controller.) Simulation games don't require fine motor skills, but take more advanced reading and thinking skills.

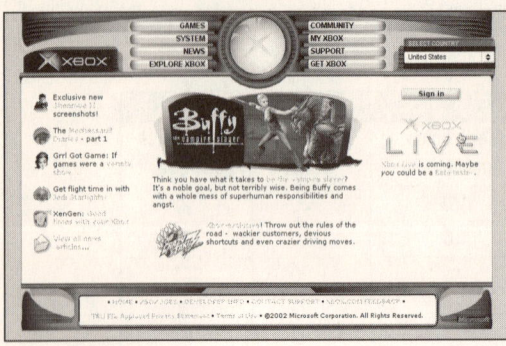

Game types

Dozens of independent publishers produce games for more than one system. Console makers also publish games, some of which are proprietary for their system. Games usually fall into one of the categories listed below, but they're not mutually exclusive: You may have to solve a puzzle to advance in a role-playing game, fly a plane in an action/adventure game, or fight crosstown rivals while skateboarding.

Web sites for game systems, such as the Xbox screen shown here, preview new games and help owners diagnose problems.

ACTION/ADVENTURE. A character must overcome obstacles and defeat bad guys through dozens of increasingly difficult levels of play. Game-company mascots Sonic the Hedgehog (Sega), Crash Bandicoot (PlayStation), and Nintendo's well-known "Mario" family of games fall into this category, as do most games based on popular TV shows and movies.

CLASSIC/TRADITIONAL. Play souped-up versions of board, card, trivia, and arcade games, and puzzles such as Tetris and Pac-Man.

FIGHTING. You control one combatant intent on knocking the stuffing (or gorier innards) out of another. Pokémon and Virtua Fighter are examples.

FIRST PERSON/SHOOTING. You are inside the body of an armed figure peering down the barrel of a weapon and bent on wiping out the enemy. Halo and Quake are among the many games of this type.

RACING/FLYING. Steer from behind the wheel or drive as you would a remote-control car. Popular titles in this category include Gran Turismo and Star Fox.

ROLE PLAYING/STRATEGY. A character on a quest in unfamiliar lands must collect items, interact with the locals, and prove his mettle. Includes such titles as Final Fantasy and The Legend of Zelda.

SIMULATION. Build and manage a civilization or business, as in The Sims and RollerCoaster Tycoon.

SPORTS. Enter a field of dreams for any major, minor, or extreme sport. Includes such titles as Madden NFL and Tony Hawk's Pro Skater.

WAR. Reenact an historical battle or mastermind an assault against a new enemy. Titles include Medal of Honor and Wolfenstein.

Try before you buy

IN STORES. Most gaming-specialty stores will let you give a game or two a whirl, but they're not arcades. Go at off hours, when they won't be crowded. Develop a relationship with a sales associate and get

---

FOR GAMING NEWS AND REVIEWS

These web sites, maintained by game-devotee and software magazines, are useful places to visit for the most up-to-date information:

Electronic Gaming Monthly www.egm.gamers.com
GamePro www.gamepro.com
Game Informer www.gameinformer.com
PCGamer www.pcgamer.com
Computer Games www.cgonline.com
Children's Software & New Media Revue
www.childrenssoftware.com

Game System Company web sites
The places to go for specific information about the game system you have:

Nintendo. www.nintendo.com
PlayStation. www.us.playstation.com
Xbox. www.xbox.com

gaming recommendations. Toy and electronics stores often set up stations or interactive kiosks where gamers can sample parts of pre-loaded games. Xbox Odyssey, a mobile arcade, is scheduled to roll into more than 30 cities by the end of 2002.

RENT OR BORROW. Video retailers and some grocery stores rent video games, often for a few dollars for several nights. They often sell used games as well. Check your local school or youth center for game-swapping clubs. Borrow from friends and neighbors. Public libraries may lend computer games.

DEMOS. Some gaming magazines come with a CD that contains playable sections of upcoming games. Computer games will need to be installed onto a computer; Xbox and PlayStation games will only work on their respective systems. (No GameCube demos were available when this book was prepared.) Demos also feature "trailers"—clips promoting other new releases.

ONLINE DEMOS. Check gaming web sites for an even larger selection of video-game trailers and computer-game demos. They can be downloaded, usually for free. Some web sites may ask you to register online before downloading, others may charge a fee to copy a downloaded game onto your own CD.

APPROACH DOWNLOADING WITH CAUTION. File sizes for computer games usually range from 50 to 150 megabytes (MB). Downloading can be slow, depending on your computer and Internet connection, this is frustrating especially when you get a server time-out message or the computer crashes. And unless you're familiar with the web site where the game resides, you risk downloading a potentially destructive computer virus as well.

> **GAMING ON THE GO**
>
> **A portable gaming system** such as Nintendo's Game Boy Advance (GBA), about $70, is an even easier way to get into gaming. The GBA, like its predecessors the Game Boy Color and black-and-white Game Boy, has a small, built-in screen and runs on batteries. Games run $30 to $40 each and are generally not as complex as console games. Still, they're engaging enough to help quell restless kids on car trips and elsewhere.
>
> Sony introduced a new portable gaming concept in 2000 with a redesigned, sleeker version of its original PlayStation, now dubbed PSone, $49.99. The size of a portable CD player, the PSone works in tandem with a TV but can also attach to a $100 battery-powered LCD screen. In mid-2002, Nintendo and Sony came out with similar LCD screens for their GameCube and PS2 systems, each $150.
>
> Our advice: Consider one of these portable systems only if you're a serious on-the-go gamer who already owns a library of games.

Game news and reviews

PRINT. A cottage industry of gaming magazines keeps enthusiasts abreast of developments, reviews the latest releases, and previews what's coming up. Reviews typically show shots of the game in action and assign a numerical score for key gaming attributes: graphics, sound, playability (controller responsiveness), concept/creativity, fun, and replay value.

Most gaming magazines adopt an in-your-face attitude to appeal to the industry's primary audience: male teenagers and young adults. Reviewers' personalities and interests shine through intentionally; find one whose gaming tastes and style mirror your own. Parents looking to scope out games for their kids may want to consult the Children's Software Revue, whose editors are educators and child-development experts.

Gaming magazines also supply a host of playing tips and "cheat" (secret access) codes. Push a series of buttons on the controller in a certain sequence to get additional powers, do special moves, and jump to higher levels of play. To learn how to win a game or uncover hidden levels, consult strategy guides and other specialty publications and web sites dedicated to a favorite title or game series.

ONLINE. Gaming-fan web sites also offer a slate of news, reviews, and playing tips, plus more in-depth information about new and old games. You can sign up for e-mail newsletters and get recommendations from like-minded players in chat rooms, bulletin boards, and fan sites. Gaming-company web sites, though promotional in nature, can be a useful resource for searching games by category or replacing a manual.

GAMING ONLINE

The Internet has transformed electronic gaming from something you do alone or with a few friends into a herd activity. Computer gamers logged onto the Internet can compete against people from all corners of the earth at all times of the day or night.

A hugely popular "MMORPG" (Massively Multiplayer Online Role-Playing Game) such as EverQuest may have tens of thousands of devotees logged on at the same time, for hours at a time. You may have to pay an additional monthly fee of $10 to $20 to play online computer games through a separate server. A broadband connection helps speed up play.

At this writing, the makers of Xbox and PS2 announced plans to debut online video gaming through their systems in the fall of 2002.

Gamers looking for a quick-twitch fix can log onto a growing number of gaming web sites such as Pogo.com that offer hundreds of arcade-type action and sports games, word games, card games, board games, trivia games, and more to appeal to gamers of all ages and both sexes. Download and install a free software application such as Macromedia Flash to play, compete against others, and win prizes. Free, of course, has its price. You may have to register an e-mail address. Ads frequently pop up while games load. Name-brand products may crop up in the background or as part of the plot.

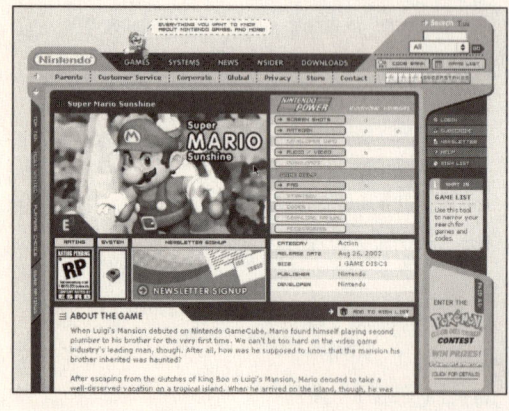

How many Mario games can you handle? The Nintendo web site gives details on them all.

Rock On: Digital Music

Ripping. Burning. Once, those words described onstage shenanigans at a heavy-metal rock concert. Now, they describe activities that even classical music devotees practice in the privacy of their own homes—downloading and recording music. Here's what you need to know about the technical and legal issues.

49
The ABCs of MP3

50
Do-It-Yourself CDs

THE ABCs OF MP3

Recorded music is no longer the exclusive province of shiny discs sold in plastic cases. It's now possible to pluck individual songs from the Internet in a form that can be used in a variety of ways.

Instead of using discs or tape cassettes, portable MP3 players store digital music in their internal memories or on removable storage media. (MP3 is the common shorthand for digital audio of every stripe, even though it refers to only one of the formats used to encode the music.) Unlike portable CD players, standard MP3 players are solid-state devices with no moving parts, which eliminates skipping, even on a bumpy road. The amount of music you can store varies. A player with 32 megabytes (MB) of memory will hold about half an hour's worth of MP3 files with nearly the sound quality of a CD; it sells for about $100. Players with 64 MB of capacity are becoming more common and affordable. A few players have 128 MB of storage. High-capacity players, with storage capacity measured in gigabytes, can hold hundreds of selections: "1,000 songs in your pocket," in the words of the slogan for Apple's iPod player. High-capacity players store music on a hard drive, similar to the one on a computer; these players sell for $200 to $500.

There's another major distinction: You don't buy prerecorded tapes or discs, but instead create your own digital MP3 files. Using music-management software often supplied with the player, you can convert audio CDs to MP3 files on your computer—a process known as ripping. Then you transfer the MP3 files from the computer to the portable player. You can also download songs from the Internet (see the box on page 51), then use the music-management software to burn a CD: transfer the songs to a recordable compact disc.

If you don't care about having music-to-go, you don't need to buy a player. You can download free software for playing MP3 files, then leave the music on your computer for listening at your convenience.

Clearly, listening to MP3 music is more involved than, say, popping a CD or tape into a player and pushing a button. If you don't know your way around a computer, you may need help from someone who's more technically savvy.

Tuning up

To use an MP3 player, you start by installing the software that comes with the player onto your computer. Players that have a universal serial bus (USB) connection are plug-and-play; you don't have to fire up some software first. Almost all players are compatible with computers that run Windows 98 and later versions of Windows. There are many Mac-compatible models on the market.

There are two software components: The PC-to-player interface and the music-management software. While the player and management functions are separate on a few players, most models integrate them into one application so you can drag and drop files from the computer's hard drive to the player's memory, or record tracks from a CD in your CD-ROM drive onto your computer as MP3 files. The software also keeps track of MP3 files and lets you organize music into categories and customize your own playlists. RealJukebox and MusicMatch are among the most common music-management applications. If you don't like the software supplied with the player, you can download different software, including a limited version of MusicMatch and Windows Media Player, from the Internet at no charge.

Once the software is installed, you can record tracks from audio CDs by inserting them in your computer's CD-ROM drive. You start the music-management software, hit Record, and the tracks are converted to MP3 format and stored on your computer's hard drive. You then transfer the MP3 files to the player, which connects to the computer via a USB or, less often, through a high-speed interface such as FireWire.

THE ALPHABET SOUP OF FORMATS

MP3 is the name of an audio-file format—a way of digitally encoding music. MP3 stands for Moving Pictures Expert Group 1 Layer 3.

Other formats, such as WMA (Windows Media Audio) also exist. Music-management software provided with new MP3 players—or available free online—is more versatile than before, able to convert a variety of formats from one to another. That's a benefit as new formats are introduced. The players also can play more formats than before.

DO-IT-YOURSELF CDS

Whether you use a computer or a separate audio component, it's now easy and affordable to create your own digital music mix on a CD.

With the computer, you use a CD-burner disc drive and software, which now come standard with all but the least expensive desktop computers. (You can buy

A HITCHHIKER'S GUIDE TO MP3

Even though Napster declared bankruptcy and essentially vanished in mid-2002, there is still a robust traffic in online music for listening, sharing, downloading—and, above all, purchasing. Burning music is another matter. Not every site lets you create a copy of the songs you download. Here's a highly selective guide to web sites devoted to digital music. You can easily find dozens of others with an Internet search. These are commercial sites, so expect ads everywhere.

www.emusic.com A subscription site that's linked with mp3.com, and that claims to have 35,000 subscribers. It says it gives access to 200,000 songs in every genre from 900 of "the world's best independent musicians." Translation: No major artists or major recording labels. You can burn the music you download, and you get unlimited downloads for a fee of $9.99 to $14.99 per month.

www.fullaudio.com Has partnerships with record companies and music publishers. Claims to have some 50,000 songs available. Charges $7.49 to $14.99 per month, for unlimited previews and 50 to 100 downloads. But only songs from Warner Records can be burned to CD.

www.listen.com Has licensed the catalog of the five major record labels. Uses the Rhapsody digital jukebox. Its $9.95 monthly full service gives access to more than 27,000 tracks and lets you burn up to 10 tracks per month. Its "all access" option gives full access to more than 169,000 tracks but doesn't allow burning.

www.music.lycos.com/downloads This area of a leading search engine lets you search for artists.Music.lycos.com/rhapsody gives you access to software that combines what Lycos terms the world's largest on-demand music collection. It costs $9.95 per month.

www.mp3.com This longstanding site is owned by Vivendi Universal, a major record label. The site says it offers access to more than 1.2 million songs by some 200,000 artists, with links to *www.emusic.com, www.getmusic.com,* and other sites. You can get recommendations by e-mail and categorize the songs you download.

www.mp3grandcentral.net The brash, frenetic home page of this music-searching site appeals openly to those who once used Napster. In its own words, the site "guarantees you'll be able to find what you're looking for and have the ability to download as many songs as you want. It costs $18.99 for a one-year membership, or $4.45 for the first 30 days, $3.99 for subsequent 30-day periods.

www.musiccity.com Created by StreamCast Networks, this site is "dedicated to helping level the playing field for independent musicians to help them distribute their content to the world and be compensated." It works with the Morpheus User Network (a file-sharing program that's somewhat similar to Napster). Downloads become an application that can only be opened inside of Morpheus. Artists get 70 percent of gross sales, and the artists make the rules for the number of times you can listen to a song before you have to pay for it, and what you pay. Musiccity.com recommends 99 cents per single, $8 per album.

www.musicmatch.com This site sells a proprietary media player known as Jukebox. Jukebox 7.2 lets you burn custom CDs from MP3s, record music into MP3s, and play MP3s, CDs, and Windows Media. The player costs $20; for an additional $39.99 you're entitled to all future versions. You can try the player free for a week.

www.musicnow.com A joint venture of RealNetworks, AOL Time Warner, Bertelsmann AG, and EMI Group Inc. Provides access to more than 75,000 songs from three major recording labels. The MusicNow site was under development when this book went to press. You can access the music service at *www.real.com/realone/services/music.html.* This service costs $9.95 a month, for up to 100 downloads and 100 audio streams.

www.pressplay.com Owned by Sony Music Entertainment and Universal Music Group, this subscription service claims 70,000 songs available from Sony, EMI, and Universal. Charges $9.95 to $24.95 per month, depending on the specific download site selected and the number of downloads and copies you wish to make. The basic $9.95 plan, for example, lets you stream 500 songs, download 50, and burn 10 onto a CD.

www.top-mp3-music.com This is a kind of dedicated search engine-cum database. It provides links to what it calls "the busiest and best MP3 web sites on the Internet."

www.winamp.com This site offers a proprietary digital music player and has a minibrowser that gets you to the Shoutcaststream homepages.

a drive and software for an older PC for about $200.) Alternatively, you can add a CD player/recorder to your stack of audio components. It has one to three trays holding CDs for listening or copying, along with a drive that holds a blank CD for recording. (For more on the hardware, see Chapter 9.)

Both methods allow you to copy entire discs or to dub selected tracks from multiple discs to create your own CD compilations. Both will record to CD-Rs (discs you can record on only once) or CD-RWs (rewritable discs that can be erased and rerecorded repeatedly). CD-Rs play on almost any CD player, while CD-RWs generally play only on new disc players configured to accept them. The sound quality is the same with either type of disc.

Computers vs. CD player/recorders

Here's how burning CDs with a computer compares with making them on a CD player/recorder:

RECORDING QUALITY: NO DIFFERENCE. Both methods copy music with little or none of the degradation that occurs when making recordings on tape. In CONSUMER REPORTS tests, the recordings from the computer and component CD player/recorders were audibly (and even electronically) indistinguishable from the original CD. That's true even when we recorded at high speeds.

SOURCES FOR MUSIC: ABOUT EVEN. The computer lets you burn CDs from MP3 files downloaded from the web. You can't do that with a component recorder. Otherwise, both types of recorder handle the same music sources—LPs, cassettes, or even TV or radio sound. Some models have a microphone input, offering a low-cost way for home musicians to make digital recordings of their performances. With a computer, you can connect almost any music source (except perhaps a turntable) directly to the sound card.

COPYING ENTIRE CDS: ONE SMALL EDGE FOR THE COMPONENT RECORDER. To copy a CD on your computer, you load it and follow the onscreen menus. With two drives, you insert the source CD and simply copy it to a blank disc in the other drive. If your computer has only one drive, you first copy the CD onto the hard disk, then remove it, load the blank disc into the tray, and follow the menu directions to burn the CD onto the blank disc. Most CD recorders have separate trays for the blank and recorded CDs; you use the remote control or console to quickly complete copying.

MAKING COMPILATION CDS: A BIG EDGE FOR THE COMPUTER. A computer provides maximum flexibility for assembling a CD from several prerecorded discs. When you insert a CD into the drive, the track list is displayed on your screen, letting you drag the desired tracks into another panel. As you insert successive CDs, you can see the playlist for your CD-to-be and change the order of the tracks. With a CD recorder, you program selections from up to three discs in the changer, a process familiar to anyone who's programmed a multidisc CD player. If there are only two trays (one for record, one for play), you must swap discs in and out. Most units show only a running total of the time as you program tracks, but no other details for a playlist.

RECORDING FROM ANALOG SOURCES: AN EDGE FOR THE COMPONENT RECORDER. Using a CD player/recorder to record from an LP or cassette tape is much like making an audiotape with a cassette deck. You select an analog external recording mode, pause the recorder, and set the recording levels (a task the recorder does automatically when recording from a digital

DIGITAL DILEMMAS: WHAT'S LEGAL, WHAT'S NEXT

With digital recording evolving rapidly, there are several developments that complicate decisions on buying and using equipment:

Is it legal? The controversy centers on the legality of downloading copyrighted music from the Internet. When the Internet service Napster was in its heyday, hundreds of thousands of people swapped millions of songs every day. Napster's software acted as a clearinghouse, allowing one user to go directly to another person's computer and copy as many songs as they'd like. Some artists and record companies contend this amounts to stealing. Similarly, the software for "burning" CDs warns that users "may be violating copyright law."

Napster is now defunct—ironically, bought out by one of the world's largest record companies. But there are still plenty of places to go for online music (see "A Hitchhiker's Guide to MP3," on page 51). Most charge a monthly fee for the ability to download music files.

The music industry's trade association, the Recording Industry Association of America, is reportedly moving toward filing copyright-infringement lawsuits against individuals who offer the largest number of songs on a Napster-style peer-to-peer basis. Up to now, the industry has taken legal action mainly against the companies operating file-sharing services. And some record companies are reportedly spreading bogus or tainted versions of popular songs around popular song-sharing sites on the Internet, apparently in an effort to drive disaffected surfers to the record companies' for-pay sites.

A 1998 law, the Digital Millennium Copyright Act, makes it unlawful to circumvent anti-copy encryption codes embedded in CDs and DVDs, as well as other digital controls on access to files. Some CDs and DVDs already have such codes. They make it impossible to fast-forward through portions of a prerecorded movie, for example, or they cause your computer to crash if you try to rip the CD.

Other legislation being considered by Congress would further restrict consumers' freedom to hear music, see films, and read digital books when and where they want. The Consumer Broadband and Digital Television Act would require manufacturers of computers, DVD players, and other hardware to embed in their devices the software that would automatically follow the electronic restrictions imposed by publishers, studios, and music labels. So if a music producer didn't want you to copy any tracks from a CD, you wouldn't be able to burn it at all. Older MP3 players might not be able to store and play newer recordings.

The Secure Digital Music Initiative, known as SDMI, is among those promulgating standards to protect copyrighted music from unauthorized distribution. The encryption technology could make some MP3 players sold today unable to accept new music in the near future unless they can be upgraded to comply with new standards.

Many legal experts believe copying music only for use on your own MP3 or CD player is covered under the "fair use" provision of copyright law and under the federal Audio Home Recording Act, which legalizes such home-taping activities as taping CDs to play in the car. And while the legality of sharing MP3 files online without permission from the copyright holder is before the courts, it is legal to download music from web sites that offer files with the full permission of copyright holders.

Buy now or wait? Several new music formats said to work better with encryption technologies—including Windows Media Audio and Advanced Audio Codec—have emerged as alternatives to MP3, and others are likely to follow. Look for MP3 players that have upgradable firmware (the player's built-in instructions).

While the debate rages, Consumers Union has urged caution about the adoption of encryption technology that might unduly restrict the free flow of public information. Libraries, for instance, can use MP3 files to make audio materials available over the Internet, just as they now lend CDs, cassettes, and videotapes.

Clearly, digital music technology is not yet mature, so it's likely we'll see a stream of less expensive, more capable equipment. Today's players may not be state-of-the-art for long, but prices are low enough and, our testing shows, performance good enough that some folks may want to invest now.

source). Once recording is under way, you generally insert track numbers between selections, using the remote—another step the recorder does automatically when recording from CDs. A few tested models inserted track breaks between songs recorded from cassettes, but most in analog mode ran songs together into one long track.

To record from cassettes using a computer drive, you connect the cassette deck to the computer's sound card. To record from LPs, you need to connect the turntable to a preamplifier (found in most receivers) to boost its signal strength to a level the computer can read; the preamp is then connected to the computer. While CD player/recorders usually capture every flaw in an analog recording, the computer's burning software often includes sound processing that will reduce defects such as the snap and crackle of a vinyl LP.

Most recorders also come with the optical digital inputs that allow another digital audio component—say, a digital audiotape player—to be connected to the unit directly. Some also have the coaxial inputs that some older digital devices use.

COST OF BLANK DISCS: AN EDGE FOR THE COMPUTER. Computers and components use different types of discs. The CD-Rs for a computer cost less than $1 each when purchased in quantity. Computer CD-RWs are about $2, while music CD-R or CD-RW discs configured for use in a CD player/recorder are slightly more expensive. The higher price for music discs is due mostly to a surcharge imposed to reimburse musicians and other copyright holders, who feared a loss of revenue from unauthorized home recording. To tell if you're buying a music disc, look (carefully—the box designs are frustratingly alike) for the words "For Digital Audio Recordings" or "Recordable CD for Music Use."

Blank discs also differ in their recording capacity, which ranges from 74 minutes to 80 minutes. Also, some cannot accept certain recording speeds (look for words such as "All Speed Recordable" on the box). Unlike some tape recording (videocassette recording, for example), the speed at which you record a CD doesn't affect capacity or quality, only how long you have to wait for the recording process to be completed.

5

Good Work: Research Tools

One of the most accommodating features of a computer system is its adaptability. When the fun is over, the hardware is ready to help you take care of business. This chapter can help with guidance for using a computer and the Internet to best advantage for financial planning, family health care, travel arrangements, parenting advice, and homework help.

SHOULD YOU BANK ONLINE?

The answer is a qualified yes. We'll help you decide where to point and click, deposit and withdraw.
Almost one in four American households has given up checking for clicking, choosing to do their banking electronically. Customers who take their accounts online discover that they can operate practically paper-free. After typing in account information for each creditor (which the bank stores), customers merely enter the amount they wish to pay. The bank then either transfers funds electronically or issues a check and mails it. ATM withdrawals and debit-card purchases are reflected on a customer's computer instantly or by the end of the day. Regular checks are recorded when they clear.

Don't think you'll be giving up paper checks completely, however. The bank will send you a checkbook and ATM card that you will want to use for the spur-of-the-moment contribution you make to a political candidate or that objet d'art you pick up at a local crafts fair. And you may still need to mail some deposits or make them in person.

To find out how well online banks perform, CONSUMER REPORTS evaluated those that Jupiter Media Metrix, a New York e-commerce research company, ranked as having the largest clientele. Staff members opened accounts at 15 different banks, and the magazine surveyed 300 subscribers to its web site, ConsumerReports.org, who said they bank online,

55
Should you bank online?

60
Using the internet to manage your health

63
Beyond E-mail for good health information

64
Buying travel online

69
Hitting the (virtual) books

BEYOND BANKING: FINANCIAL PLANNING AND INVESTMENTS

Even if you decide not to bank online, you can still use the Internet to enhance your family's financial planning and investment strategies, using services like the ones listed here to do your research. Keep in mind how a site makes its money—if it's selling a service, even the most helpful feature may have an underlying propositional aspect. Because you have to give information to do business with a bank, pay close attention to privacy policies. Beware of false tips and phony news stories in chat rooms. Don't trust solicitations inviting you to invest in various financial schemes.

Personal planning

Many sites offer planning help. Examples: Charles Schwab *(www.schwab.com)*, Fidelity *(www.fidelity.com)*, Merrill Lynch *(www.merrilllynch.com)*, Prudential *(www.prudential.com)*, T. Rowe Price *(www.troweprice.com)*, and Vanguard *(www.vanguard.com)*.

The Securities and Exchange Commission, the government's overseer when it comes to stocks and other investments, is also there to help the average consumer. Click on its interactive tools section *(www.sec.gov/investor/tools.shtml)* for a Mutual Fund Investment Calculator, which helps you estimate and compare the costs of mutual funds. The SEC also provides links to a retirement fund calculator, Social Security planner, and quizzes.

Bloomberg's web site *(www.bloomberg.com)* tracks current market activity and business news. Bloomberg's Tools icon helps you track your portfolio, get stock quotes, and crunch numbers with one of eight calculators.

The editors of SmartMoney magazine *(www.smartmoney.com)* offer several tools, including an asset allocator, a broker meter that measures the speed of your broker's web site, and a mutual fund finder and analyzer. An online bill-paying center lets you receive, review, and pay all your bills online. The cost is $8.95 per month.

Investment research

Fund managers are profiled in detail at Brill's Mutual Funds Interactive *(www.fundsinteractive.com)*. FundLink connects you to the home pages of more than 100 mutual funds, while Funds101 takes novices through a lesson plan on mutual funds. The Toolshed includes stock charts, prospectuses, corporate earnings, and SEC filings.

Hit the Research & Tools button at CBS MarketWatch *(www.cbsmarketwatch.com)*, and you're taken to a page stuffed with trackers, indexers, and analyzers. You can look up the best and worst performers, get information on IPOs, and check out a variety of stock screeners. CBS runs this site in conjunction with Data Broadcasting Corp.

The web site of Morningstar *(www.morningstar.com)* lets you set your own criteria and choose stocks and mutual funds based on those parameters. The site gives information on company performance, valuation, and stock performance to aid in your decision making.

Standard and Poor's Select Fund *(www.standardandpoors.com/productsandservices/funds/index.html)* lists mutual funds that meet its criteria. The Mutual Fund Investors' Center *(www.mfea.com)*, a site sponsored by the Mutual Fund Education Alliance, a group of no-load mutual-fund companies, lists 12,000 funds in its database. A chart can help you select funds by identifying your objectives, such as capital growth or high current income.

An "off-center view" of the mutual fund industry is what the editors of FundAlarm *(www.fundalarm.com)* say you'll get at their site. FundAlarm's mission is to help its readers decide when to sell, rather than buy, a fund. To that end, FundAlarm identifies 3-Alarm Funds—those that have "consistently underperformed."

Portfolio tracking

Most Internet portals offer portfolio tracking. Yahoo! Finance *(http://finance.yahoo.com)*, for example, lets you track up to six stocks, by name or ticker symbol. You can view daily, weekly, monthly, or yearly charts summarizing the Dow, Nasdaq, Standard and Poor's index, and more.

The Motley Fool *(www.fool.com)* tracks portfolios with a touch of humor: Fool's 13 Steps to Investing Foolishly, Investing Basics, Choosing a Broker, and Mutual Fund Basics.

You don't have to own Quicken software to track your portfolio on the Quicken web site *(www.quicken.com)*. The site lets you add or remove dozens of criteria from your portfolio, including Morningstar Overall Grade, Category P/E, Industry ROE, and more.

and consulted more than two dozen industry experts.

Although all the banks tested paid a bill well enough (few survey respondents had complaints), there were big differences in fees and levels of service, with Etrade and Citibank coming out on top. Even if you already bank online, the Ratings (see page 58) may lead you to discover that you could do better elsewhere. Most banks promise to process bills within 3 to 5 days, for example, but some said they might take as long as 10 days. Only six banks promised to pay penalties if a payment arrives late. Then too, opening an account at some banks can be an ordeal, particularly if you aren't already a customer of one of the bank's brick-and-mortar branches.

Online banking has some potential drawbacks, though they should not stop you from trying it out. For starters, there's the increasing risk of identity theft, as more and more banking information surges across the Internet. Another problem: Privacy policies at some web sites are so difficult to understand and act on that you will be hard put to escape a marketing blitz. Online banking may add to your costs. Some banks will assess a monthly charge merely for having an account unless you meet a specified balance requirement. On top of that, you could pay another monthly fee for bill paying. Learning this isn't easy because some sites bury the information.

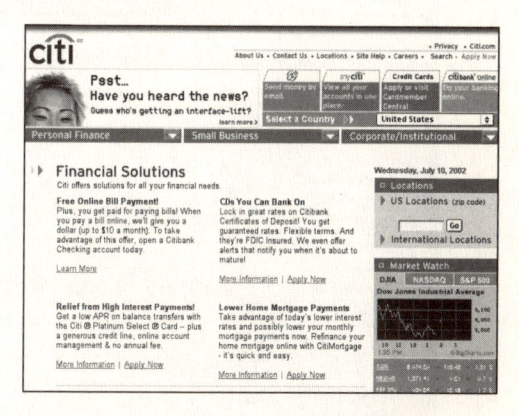

Citibank has one of the highest-rated online banking services.

Security leaks

Uppermost in consumers' minds these days is security. Two-thirds of the survey respondents said they were concerned that a hacker might disrupt their bank's web site. In reality, the money in your bank account is safe. As part of its contract with you, your bank will replace cash swiped by a cyber-crook just as it would if the loot were stolen by an armed robber. The bank can't do much about the theft of personal information, however. Once hackers have your Social Security number and date of birth, both of which may be attached to your bank account, they can open credit cards in your name, run up bills, and wreak havoc with your financial life. Fortunately, security breaches have been rare.

Indeed, if there's anyplace on the Internet you can feel secure, it will be at a bank web site. Banks have years of experience storing customers' personal information. All the banks we rated use 128-bit, Secure Sockets Layer (SSL) encryption, which scrambles data in transit between your web browser and your bank's web server. (A web site using SSL technology will have an address preceded by "https," and you'll see a closed lock icon at the bottom of your screen.) Customers must submit user IDs and passwords before gaining access to accounts. And the banks have firewalls and virus-detection programs to keep outsiders from pilfering accounts.

Of course, hackers may find holes in such protections. But information may be most open to manipulation not during transmission, but at the bank, where an employee could make off with it, or on your own computer, where your name and account number may be available for all to view.

About 60 percent of those surveyed said they were concerned that their online bank would share their personal information. Legislation passed in 1999 allows all banks to market many investment and insurance products or to partner with companies that do. The law prohibits financial institutions from selling information, but it allows them to share it with

ONLINE BANKS: HOW THE LARGEST COMPARE

Overall Ratings   In performance order

Excellent ● | Very good ◗ | Good ○ | Fair ◐ | Poor ●

BANK WEB ADDRESS (WWW.)	OVERALL SCORE 10 30 50 70 90	STATES WHERE AVAILABLE	MINIMUM BALANCE	COST FOR BILL PAYING	ACCT. SETUP	SITE NAVIGATION	PRIVACY	CONTENT	COMMENTS
Etrade etrade.com		All	$1,000*	No charge	◗	◗	○	◗	$10 monthly fee. 10,000 ATMs available to customers. Deposits must be sent via U.S. mail.
Citibank citibank.com		All	1,500	No charge	◗	○	○	◗	$7.50 monthly fee. Can send statements via e-mail.
NetBank netbank.com		All	None	No charge	◗	◗	○	○	Deposits must be sent via U.S. mail or can be made at 18,000 ATMs after account has been open 120 days.
JPMorgan Chase www.chase.com		All	3,000	No charge	○	○	○	◗	$9.50 monthly fee. Requires consumers to wait three to five days before conducting transactions.
Bank One bankone.com		All	500	$6.45	●	◗	○	○	$5 monthly fee. Opting out of marketing solicitations requires customer to phone a toll-free number.
Bank of America bankofamerica.com		All	500	5.95	●	◗	○	○	$6 monthly fee. Bill paying free to customers with more than $5,000 on deposit.
Fleet Bank fleet.com		All	None	4.50	◗	○	◗	○	$3 monthly fee. Easy to use and navigate.
Key Bank keybank.com		All	None	4.95	◗	○	○	○	Guarantees all payments to arrive within five business days or bank will pay late fees and finance charges.
Washington Mutual wamu.com		All	None	5.00	○	○	○	◗	You must print form and mail it to avoid sharing personal information.
Firstar Bank firstar.com		Ariz., Ark., Ill., Ind., Iowa, Kan., Ky., Minn., Mo., Ohio, Tenn., Wis.	None	4.95	◗	○	◗	○	Took weeks to send out ATM cards.
Wells Fargo wellsfargo.com		All	None	6.95	○	○	◗	◗	One of the easiest sites to navigate.
U.S. Bank usbank.com		All	None	4.95	●	○	◗	○	Unsatisfactory privacy policy. Account history is limited to last 180 transactions.
PNC Bank pncbank.com		All	100	5.00	●	○	○	○	$12 monthly fee. Confusing organization, with one account for banking, another for bill paying.
Sun Trust suntrust.com		Ala., D.C., Fla., Ga., Md., Tenn., Va.	None	5.95	●	◐	○	○	No search feature available.
Fifth Third Bank 53.com		Fla., Ill., Ind., Ky., Mich., Ohio, W.Va.	None	7.50	●	●	◐	◐	Unsatisfactory privacy policy: Site offers no direct way to opt out of sharing your personal information.

Required deposit to open an account.

Behind the Ratings

To find out how well online banks perform, the CONSUMER REPORTS personal-finance staff selected 15 that Jupiter Media Metrix, a New York e-commerce research company, ranked as having some of the largest client bases. The staff closely examined each bank's web site, set up accounts, and paid a bill to Consumers Union. The data in the chart was current as of mid-2002; fees and charges are always subject to change. **Overall score** is based on the web site's privacy and security policies, ease of opening an account, efficiency of navigation, and bill-paying cost. **States where available** shows where the banks do business **Minimum balance** is the amount required to escape the monthly fee that some banks assess each month if the balance drops below t1he minimum. **Cost for bill paying** is the total monthly charge for a customer who writes 25 checks a month. **Account setup** tests how easily a consumer who is not already a customer of the bank can set up an account. **Site navigation** assesses how easily customers can move through the site. **Privacy** reflects the clarity and prominence of a site's information-sharing practices. Banks that do not share customer information with third parties received a higher score. **Content** evaluates the quality and completeness of product information, including loan applications and brokerage services.

affiliates, either related companies or a ring of marketing partners. The law says banks must give you a copy of their privacy policy and a way to opt out of sharing information with nonaffiliated firms.

Online extras

About 80 percent of the survey respondents said that online banking is easy and quick. Many bank web sites have added a number of helpful services to banking and bill-paying functions. Some issue e-mail warnings when your account drops below an amount you specify or if you have insufficient funds to pay a bill. All allow you to set up automatic recurring payments for regular monthly bills, such as mortgage and car loans.

A couple of banks have introduced services that could revolutionize money handling. They issue cash vouchers via e-mail that can be sent like checks or deposited into any account that accepts wire transfers. A few banks also allow you to receive your bills online, letting you view and pay them all in one place.

Some glitches remain

Even though Internet banking has been around since the mid-1990s, it still has snags. If you don't already have an account at the bank, signing up could take hours. While we attempted to fill out an application, a web site would repeatedly time out, forcing us to start from scratch.

Curiously, some banks with an online option weren't equipped to send application forms over the Internet. We've found others that fail to specify that they will accept customers only from certain states. The CONSUMER REPORTS staffers learned this only after trying to sign up from New York and being rebuffed. And even after establishing the account from other locations, staffers had to wait weeks for an ATM card and checks.

Once the accounts were working, some nifty services turned out to entail some hassles. For example, minor changes to payee information, such as a new address, required deleting the account entirely and listing it again from scratch. It was also easy when setting up a recurring payment to unknowingly include other billers under the same payment plan or to schedule more frequent payments than we desired.

Banks that exist solely online, such as Etrade and NetBank, have a built-in disadvantage —no local branches. Although you can access national ATM networks like Cirrus and NYCE with cards from Internet-only banks, you will incur a fee. You will also have to mail in deposits the old-fashioned way.

Online fees

All banks allow you to view your account activity online at no charge. If you want to add an extra, like bill paying, you will generally pay a monthly fee; it's about $7 as of this writing. But you may have to dig to find out what the fee is. Most banks make you hunt for the information in Customer Service, FAQs, or a site map. Some banks offer free trials for online bill paying. Some add per-check charges after a specified limit. High fees are offset by savings on stamps and time spent addressing envelopes. JPMorgan Chase or Citibank offer bill-paying free to their account holders regardless of balance.

How to proceed

Online banking is a tempting convenience and one we think you should use, but with caution. The first bank to check out is your own. Then take these precautions:

◆ If you don't want an avalanche of solicitations, study your bank's privacy policies, usually linked at the bottom of the site's home page. You may want to consider another bank if you can't opt out easily.

◆ If you can't locate information about your bank's fees, try the site map or FAQs. Figure out how much you would pay to write 25 checks a month, what a very active account might issue; then compare the total to the banks that are rated. (On average, Americans write 15 checks a month.)

◆ If you decide to move to another bank, try its demo, which will show you how the site works before you go to the trouble of moving all your accounts.

SOFTWARE TO HELP MANAGE YOUR MONEY

Financial software is designed to give you a clear snapshot of your spending, savings, tax situation, and investments. There are several different categories, some focused on specific areas (such as online banking or saving for retirement) and others offering comprehensive planning tools. Most financial software now has direct links to the Internet, allowing you to access your investment portfolio, check current interest rates, download your credit-card transactions, and pay bills online.

You could track financial information in a spreadsheet program, but specialized financial programs do a lot of the setup work for you.

Intuit and Microsoft dominate the personal finance space with Quicken 2002 Deluxe from Intuit (Windows and Mac, $45) and Money 2002 Deluxe from Microsoft (Windows only, $45). These programs help you manage your money, from planning a budget to saving for college to paying bills electronically. You can balance bank accounts, calculate loan costs, and bank online.

Among Quicken's features: 30 performance indicators for your investments; missed bill reminders; capital gains estimator; and improvements in its statement reconciliation functions. Money 2002 includes an asset allocation wizard that helps you distribute investments among various options. It takes you through a detailed setup process, and the Account Register provides real-time feedback.

You can import data from your financial software into your tax software if you buy compatible packages. Microsoft's Money integrates with H&R Block's Kiplinger's TaxCut (Windows and Mac, $29.95), while Intuit's Quicken works with its own TurboTax (Windows and Mac, $29.95). A preinterview in TaxCut gets users started, while a tax-planning function helps you figure out how to save on next year's taxes, plan stock purchases or sales, increase deductions, and more. When you buy TurboTax Deluxe, you also get one free state-tax download. Access is provided not only to official IRS publications for help, but to live tax experts. If your employer and financial institutions are signed up with TurboTax's program, the software will automatically retrieve W2 and investment data for you.

◆ Be sure you have firewall security and virus-protection software for your home computer, especially if you use an Internet connection that stays on all the time, like a digital subscriber line (DSL) or a cable modem. For specifics, see Chapter 1.

USING THE INTERNET TO MANAGE YOUR HEALTH

E-mailing your doctor has potential benefits, but you need to know the pitfalls. And you need to know how to wrest essential facts from the mass of medical information and misinformation on the Internet.

When Chris Olney, of Wenham, Mass., learned that he had a thyroid disorder, he was already home when he thought of the question he most wanted to ask his doctor. So he asked via e-mail. Within a day his doctor answered his question and referred him to relevant web sites.

Beth Segel, of Dana Point, Calif., developed a rash in her ninth month of pregnancy. Instead of driving 25 miles to the doctor, she had her husband take a digital photo and e-mail it to her doctor, along with a very detailed description of her history and symptoms. The doctor was able to identify the rash as an apparently minor food reaction and said she could wait for her scheduled appointment in two days unless the rash spread or appeared to get worse.

E-mails are part of the growing reliance on computer-based communications that is changing the way many patients relate to their doctors. "Online communication offers so many potential benefits—convenience, cost savings, even improved care—it's almost inevitable that patients and doctors will do more and more business by e-mail," says Tom Ferguson, M.D., a University of Texas researcher who is investigating the Internet's effects on health care.

A report from the Institute of Medicine, an independent group that advises the federal government, concluded that many patients "could have their needs met more quickly at a lower cost if they had the option of communicating with health professionals through e-mail."

But along with the likely benefits come potential risks. Many people fear that their messages could end up in the wrong hands. Improper e-mail use could further depersonalize doctor-patient relationships already strained by pressure from insurers to curtail office visits. And patients and doctors could take the practice too far, using it to diagnose and treat problems that require in-person contact.

There's far more good than harm in medical e-mails. But you need to know how often and how many to send, when you can safely communicate with a doctor at a distance, and when you should be seeing one face to face.

Privacy and etiquette

People's biggest fear about e-mailing their doctor is that other people might read the messages, according to a survey from the California HealthCare Foundation. E-mail can go astray when users click on the wrong address or when systems malfunction. Moreover, e-mail can be intercepted fairly easily; in some states, employers can do that legally without telling you. But the reality is less worrisome than the theoretical risks. None of the sources that CONSUMER REPORTS medical reporters contacted knew of any cases of medical snooping. Most people should be able to adequately protect their privacy by taking a few commonsense precautions.

In a 2001 nationwide survey from Harris Interactive that involved some 1,000 adults with Internet access, roughly 80 percent said they would like to communicate by e-mail with their doctors. That may lead some doctors to worry that they'll be overwhelmed by "cyberchondriacs," but the record so far doesn't support that concern. One family practitioner says he used to spend at least an hour a day returning phone calls, but got beeped at home anyway. E-mail lets him respond more quickly and when it's convenient.

Joseph Scherger, M.D., dean of the College of Medicine at Florida State University, says that e-mail increased his out-of-office communications with patients by 50 percent. But much of that came from contacts he initiated. The total time he spends communicating with patients has been cut in half.

To use e-mail to best advantage with your doctor, follow these guidelines:

◆ Before you start firing off messages, find out whether your doctor is willing to communicate by e-mail. If the answer is yes, ask how quickly the doctor typically responds.

◆ Ask whether your doctor's e-mail system has features to safeguard privacy. If not, ask if he or she would consider switching to a system that does.

◆ Determine how much sensitive information to include in your messages by asking your

> **ONLINE HEALTH: COMING SOON**
>
> **Here are three innovations that are now available or may be available soon.**
>
> ◆ **Virtual house calls.** In several small-scale experiments around the country, patients can now undergo fairly complete physical exams via devices installed in their homes. As the patient and doctor see and talk with each other through a teleconferencing system, the patient can use common medical devices—a stethoscope, scale, blood-pressure cuff, spirometer (to measure breathing capacity), and oximeter (to measure blood-oxygen level)—all connected to a monitor that transmits the readings to the doctor.
>
> ◆ **Online medical records.** Having access to your medical records might be useful if you are actively involved in managing your own care. With your permission, online records also let doctors view your medical history anytime, anywhere—a possibly lifesaving benefit in an emergency. To prevent snooping, such records should be available only at secure sites and should have tracking programs that record who looks at them.
>
> ◆ **Online second opinions.** Most people can obtain a second opinion from a nearby specialist. But individuals who can't find an expert locally or who want one from a prestigious institution can now ask their physician to visit the web site of three top hospitals—Massachusetts General, Brigham and Women's, and Dana-Farber/Partners Cancer Care, all in Boston—and request an "e-consult." Their doctor mails, faxes, or e-mails their medical information to a doctor chosen by the hospital, who e-mails back an opinion. (Note that the consultation fee, $600, is not reimbursable.)

doctor whether anyone else in the office might read them and whether they'll be included in your medical record.

◆ Consider sending health messages only from home, not work, and avoiding e-mail altogether for very sensitive topics.

◆ Ask whether your doctor's e-mail system automatically acknowledges receipt of your e-mails and tells you when the doctor is gone for more than a day or so. If not, ask whether the office could program the system to do so.

◆ Limit messages to important matters and keep them short.

◆ In the subject heading of the e-mail, state your name and your concern, such as prescription, medical advice, or billing.

◆ Acknowledge your doctor's messages.

When to e-mail your doctor

E-mail is ideally suited to many tasks that doctors or their staffs often do over the phone. Those include routine matters such as making appointments, obtaining test results or prescription refills, and asking follow-up questions to office visits.

But two less-routine matters can probably also be handled by e-mail—monitoring chronic diseases and prescribing drug refills for minor recurrent health problems.

However, don't let e-mail updates replace periodic office visits, which can be especially important if you have a chronic disease. For example, people with diabetes need to have their eyes and feet examined frequently. Be prepared for possible objections if your doctor has been monitoring your disease during office visits and thus charging for that service. Unless you're one of the few people whose insurer reimburses physicians for e-mail visits, you may have to negotiate a modest out-of-pocket fee with your doctor.

E-mail can also be used for prescription refills, provided you have readily identifiable symptoms that your doctor has previously diagnosed; such problems include recurrent urinary-tract infections, sinus and yeast infections, and backaches.

Many other acute problems, even familiar ones like a headache or sore throat, sometimes require a physical exam or more questioning than e-mail typically allows. If the problem is recurrent, ask your doctor whether it's sufficiently simple and identifiable that you can diagnose future bouts on your own. If not, don't expect the doctor to prescribe treatment via e-mail.

Some doctors are experimenting with web sites that guide patients through questions designed to diagnose acute problems. Patients should use those sites only if they've seen their doctor about the same problem within the previous six months, according to guidelines from a collaborative group of major medical societies and insurers.

BEYOND E-MAIL FOR GOOD HEALTH INFORMATION

Although web sites such as DrKoop.com succumbed to dot-com fever, there are still many good sources of information on the Internet. Here's our prescription for healthy surfing.

The web offers an abundance of information on health. Experts give insight and advice, tools help you track bad allergies, and calculators set weight-loss and exercise goals. You can also test the protection afforded by your health plan and keep an eye out for products recalled because of safety issues. But how can you find accurate and appropriate health information? That's difficult. Many health-oriented sites have a financial stake in selling particular products or therapies, which may taint their objectivity and expose you to intrusive commercial messages. For example, when CONSUMER REPORTS researchers typed "sleep disorders" into the search box of CBS HealthWatch, an ad for zalephon *(Sonata)*, a sleeping pill, appeared on the top of the screen, complete with information provided by the pill's manufacturer on insomnia. Meanwhile, sites aimed at health-care professionals are often too technical and too abundant for consumers.

To find dependable information, follow these tips:

♦ Avoid general search engines such as Yahoo! or Google, which often yield excessive or questionable information. For example, when the CONSUMER REPORTS researchers typed "Lyme disease vaccine" into the Yahoo! search engine, the first 10 references included links to "Cheryl's Lyme Disease Site," "Dawnie's Lyme Site," and "Jean's Lyme Page." Those sites contained individuals' personal experiences with the disease. While such accounts may provide some useful insights, they're hardly authoritative sources.

♦ Start at respected general-health sites. The best is Medlineplus *(www.nlm.nih.gov/medlineplus)*, the National Library of Medicine's consumer-health site. It has numerous tools—including a medical encyclopedia and a drug-reference guide—produced by reliable government or nonprofit groups. Other good starting points: HealthWeb *(www.healthweb.org)*, which has links to sites chosen by medical librarians; and the Centers for Disease Control and Prevention *(www.cdc.gov)*, which has information about public-health issues.

♦ For more detailed information, look for a reliable, noncommercial organization that specializes in your particular concern. Medlineplus has a comprehensive list of such organizations, as does the Directory of Health Organizations *(dirline.nlm.nih.gov/)*.

♦ Other reliable sites that can get you started include Oncolink *(www.oncolink.upenn.edu)* for cancer information; ClinicalTrials.gov *(www.clinicaltrials.gov)* for ongoing trials; the U.S. Food and Drug Administration *(www.fda.gov/cder/drug)* for latest information on new drugs and recently identified risks; the site of the National Center for Complementary and Alternative Medicine *(nccam.nih.gov/nccam)* and Quackwatch *(www.quackwatch.com)*, which concentrate on identifying dubious alternative health-care claims; and Medwatch *(www.fda.gov/medwatch/safety.htm)*, which contains the latest information on new drugs and recently identified risks.

These commercial sites can be helpful:

CBS HEALTHWATCH (www.cbshealthwatch.com). This site offers a number of interactive sections. You can have a detailed look at the USDA's food guide pyramid, or calculate your body mass index in the "Diet and Nutrition" section. "Eye on Health" features separate areas on heart disease, cancer, AIDs, and antibiotic use.

For the most part, this site has numerous links to health-related articles, which in turn have links for more information on specific topics. For instance, a piece on Staph infections linked to articles on antibiotic use.

INTELIHEALTH (www.intelihealth.com). This site is produced by a subsidiary of Aetna, the health-insurance company. Among the sources for InteliHealth's information are the Harvard Medical School and the University of Pennsylvania School of Dental Medicine. InteliHealth articles emphasize the "how-to" aspects of health care, with tips on preventing injuries, maintaining nutritional excellence, and controlling diseases such as asthma. There's a Drug Resource Center and an Ask the Pharmacist column, as well as a poison control resource center and a prevention fact sheet. A physician locator from the American Medical Association lets you find a doctor by name or specialty.

KEEP KIDS HEALTHY (www.keepkidshealthy.com). Founded by a Texas pediatrician, this site helps parents deal with health issues of every kind. A detailed asthma section, for example, offers a peak flow calendar, a tool for tracking peak flow zones, treatment options, and lots more. The breastfeeding center doles out advice on nutrition, weaning, frequency, and milk production. The main site can also be browsed by age, from newborn to adolescent. Growth charts, a vaccine schedule, and product recalls keep your kids' health on track. And a baby-naming guide helps you decide whether he's a Noah or a Christopher or whether she's a Jennifer or a Marlena.

SAFECHILD (www.safechild.net). Among other things, it has an archive of recalled products, news, and a setup for e-mail notification of recalls. It's a project of the Consumer Federation of America Foundation.

It's been said often, but it's worth repeating: If you go to web sites for medical information, be sure to follow up with a doctor before undergoing any treatments. There are many factors to consider with any illness or injury.

Web sites such as SafeChild.net can be a very useful source of information about safety recalls and news about child products.

BUYING TRAVEL ONLINE

A world of travel deals can be had with a few clicks of a mouse. The challenge for "book-it-yourselfers" is recognizing when the web is a useful tool and when it's not.

The Internet has changed the way people research and pay for travel. By going online, you now have access to the systems that were once exclusive to travel agents and airline reservations clerks. Early on, the main travel-related attraction of the web was cheap airline tickets. Now people are spending millions online buying vacation packages–trips that integrate several travel components into one price.

To meet the demand for online travel information and bookings, a large number of travel sites has sprung up. You'll see two major types: "branded" sites that are produced by specific airlines, car-rental companies, hotel chains, and the like; and "integrated" sites where you can comparison-shop for low airfares, car-rental deals, and the like.

The six largest sites are: Cheap Tickets (www.cheaptickets.com), Expedia (www.expedia.com), OneTravel (www.onetravel.com), Orbitz (www.orbitz.com), TravelNow (www.travelnow.com), and Travelocity (www.travelocity.com). They differ in their look and in other details, but they have features in common. They are all robust, rich sites supported in part by advertising revenue, in part by fees for processing reservations, and in part through various forms of compensation from airlines. They have varying degrees of independence. Travelocity, for example, is owned by Sabre, the leading computer-reservations system used by travel agents. Orbitz is owned by a consortium of airlines. The sites also differ in their ease of use, their privacy policies, and in the degree of neutrality they appear to show to the airlines whose fares and itineraries they show.

> **TRAVEL-BUYING TIPS**
>
> These tips can help you get the most out of shopping for travel online:
>
> ◆ Compare results from different sites against each other, and against outside sources, such as travel agents or airlines. Call a hotel directly to see how the price on the web compares with their direct quote.
>
> ◆ Don't confuse web-site ads with actual listings (even though some web sites and advertisers make that hard to do).
>
> ◆ The earlier you book, the better: Sites offer better options weeks in advance. You can also secure web-only discounts for busy travel periods from car-rental sites and others.
>
> ◆ If you often book the same route, it helps to check timetables from the airlines serving it (available online, in ticket offices, or at the airport).
>
> ◆ Flexibility is essential; try a range of times and alternative airports (airline timetables and Internet sites provide the airport codes).
>
> ◆ Try not to book electronic tickets on short notice; if you input a misspelled name, there may not be a record of your e-ticket, and you could be out of luck.
>
> ◆ Note that airlines do not treat all passengers equally. For rebooking or canceling flights, compare the fees charged by web sites, travel agencies, and airlines.
>
> ◆ Write down (or print out) confirmation numbers when you book online. Take these with you to the rental-car counter, hotel, or airport.

Which travel sites are best?

To find out how those six sites compare, the editors at Consumer Reports Travel Letter (CRTL) joined forces with Consumer WebWatch. (CRTL is the CONSUMER REPORTS monthly newsletter on travel news and bargains; Consumer WebWatch is a grant-funded project at Consumers Union, publisher of CONSUMER REPORTS, that's dedicated to establishing standards for online commerce.)

CRTL ran exhaustive tests seeking airline reservations from the sites—540 flight queries in all. The tests looked at five key factors: ability to provide the lowest fares, the ability to provide viable flight itineraries, ease of use, customer service, and privacy and security policies. CRTL asked for the lowest economy-class fare on 19 busy domestic nonstop routes throughout the U.S. The itineraries included routes frequented by vacationers as well as business travelers. Also included: a variety of trips with advance bookings ranging from same day to 105 days in the future. There were nine test sessions in all, run at various times of the day and days of the week. As a check on the web sites, CRTL simultaneously requested identical information from Sabre, the computer-reservation system. In every case, we took the first displays returned by the sites.

Two clear winners emerged. Expedia beat its competitors in providing the greatest

> **ONLINE TRAVEL TOOL KIT**
>
> **If you book travel online, you'll encounter some or all of these web-site tools:**
>
> **Airfare comparisons.** These deliver quotes of the lowest fares on all major airlines to most destinations worldwide.
>
> **Destination guides.** Most major sites have online destination guides that cover the major tourist cities. You may have to do some extra digging to find information on out-of-the-way locales.
>
> **Fare minders.** Plug in a few cities to which you'd like a good airfare, and the site will notify you via e-mail when a low fare becomes available.
>
> **Flight tracking.** If you have a flight number and a date, you can check the arrival and departure status of flights on major carriers. Most large travel sites as well as airline web sites offer this function.
>
> **Hotel finders.** The rate comparisons are handy, but listings may skew toward budget and tourist hotels or those in the first-class and deluxe category—but rarely both.
>
> **Last-minute deals.** If your schedule is flexible, you can grab some great travel deals.
>
> **Loyalty-program tracking.** Many sites let you track frequent-flier miles or cardmember reward points in one place. You'll need to register for this service.
>
> **Rental-car finders.** Just plug in your destination, arrival/departure details, and car class, and you'll get a breakdown of the best rates from the top companies in the business.
>
> **Weather reports.** Most major sites link to a major weather Internet site, where you can often get three- to five-day forecasts for most destinations around the world.

number of lowest fares. Travelocity offered the best array of low fares coupled with the best ease-of-use features and viable flight choices (no six-stop puddle-jumpers to get from Philadelphia to Louisville). Expedia and Travelocity offered the best customer service, and they had the tightest privacy and security policies.

However, while those sites excelled in certain areas, none outshone all the others in all aspects. There is no single site that's always best. To get the best fares, comparison shop.

Orbitz performed well at providing the lowest fares and viable flights, but it was edged out in most tests by either Expedia or Travelocity. What's more, the technological divide between those three sites and the others that were evaluated is so considerable that CRTL editors can't recommend using the also-ran web sites at all, unless you're looking for deeply discounted nonrefundable airfares.

The bottom line for booking air travel online? Search for fares among Expedia, Orbitz, and Travelocity; when you find a good fare, check the airlines' own sites for deals on the route you want to travel.

Are the sites biased?

In earlier CRTL evaluations of independent web sites, there appeared to be a relationship between the airlines that advertised on the sites and the order in which flight choices were listed. That's particularly important because flights listed first are booked more often.

The latest tests also raise questions about potential bias and the way flight information is displayed. The promotional considerations, banner advertising revenue, and other kinds of compensation from airlines have muddied the waters. The CRTL study looked specifically at what happened when the lowest-fare flight offered on Sabre was operated by a smaller carrier, one not among the owners of the Orbitz travel site. In the 18 cases when Sabre's first pick was a small carrier, Orbitz offered a higher fare in 11 cases, or 61 percent of the time; the other five travel sites offered a higher fare from 5 to 50 percent of the time. However, we couldn't detect a pattern of Orbitz favoring major carriers over smaller ones.

Are such omissions or reordering of fares the quirks of a complex pricing mechanism or examples of bias? It's impossible to know. Nevertheless, it's reasonable to conclude that the relationships between the travel sites and their airline advertising and marketing partners have raised reasonable doubts.

Do the sites offer viable flights?

Getting the lowest fares can require routes that don't make much sense to many travelers. That's why CRTL used the following standards to determine if a flight is viable: a single-airline itinerary; a departure time no more than one hour prior to or four hours later than that requested; no more than one connecting flight, but with a preference for nonstop flights; a connection time of no more than three hours; and a connecting airport no more than 700 miles from a straight-line route between origin and destination.

The standout for generating viable flights was Travelocity. It offered the highest percentage of first-listed flights that were viable (59 percent). Travelocity (owned by Sabre) did very well at providing viable flights that matched Sabre's fares (40 percent), while Orbitz outpaced the other sites in providing viable fares that beat Sabre's fares.

Are the sites easy to use?

There are four things you should be able to do on a travel site:
- Broaden or narrow airport search parameters.
- Specify the number of stops en route.
- Select a seat.
- Re-sort search results by price, departure time, or total flight time.

Travelocity is the only site of the six tested with all those functions. Expedia and Orbitz are close behind. The other three have holes in their lists of capabilities.

Several of the sites have features that are likely to be helpful when you're booking a flight. Expedia, for instance, provides on-time percentages for specific flights after you make a selection but before you're asked to pay. Travelocity has a handy feature: If you've confined your search to a specific airport, the site processes your search and then alerts you if there is a lower fare available at another airport in the metropolitan area. Cheap Tickets offers both an Express Search and a Power Search. The latter is better suited for more flexible travelers, since it lists an airline's lowest fare even if seat availability doesn't exist for the time and date you select.

How to use the travel sites to best advantage

Travelocity or Expedia (and to a lesser extent Orbitz) are good places to begin an online fare search. But keep this important advice in mind, whether you're using them to book or just to look:

COMPARE RESULTS ON SEVERAL SITES TO FIND THE BEST DEAL. Keep in mind that bookings are in real time and could change before you pay. In this respect, we like Expedia and Travelocity best, because they allow you to create an itinerary and hold the reservation. Although they don't guarantee the price, you can still return to the reservation if you decide to book the flight. And once you find a low fare for a specific airline, go to the carrier's own web site to see whether you can find an even lower fare.

BE SURE YOU UNDERSTAND THE SITE'S FEE STRUCTURE. Once again, we like Expedia and Travelocity because neither one charges a flat fee for all transactions regardless of the airline. But such fees often vary according to the airline's agreement with the site—and those deals are often in flux.

Orbitz is one of the most useful travel sites on the Internet.

BE FLEXIBLE. You may find a lower fare if you can choose alternate travel dates, flight times, or airports.

PAPER TICKETS COME AT A PRICE. There can be a difference between the price of an e-ticket and the price of a paper ticket, particularly if you book online.

IF YOU'RE USING A TRAVEL AGENCY, FIND OUT IF IT CAN BEAT AN ONLINE DEAL. Inquire about preferred-supplier deals an agency may have with specific airlines and see if those arrangements can provide you with any benefits. Also ask if the agency is adding on a booking fee; nearly all agencies now do.

IF YOU'RE FLEXIBLE, USE A SITE THAT LETS YOU BOOK CHEAP, NONREFUNDABLE TICKETS. We found some real bargains on Cheap Tickets, OneTravel, and Travel Now for those willing to accept a restricted fare.

ALWAYS TRY TO BOOK SEVERAL WEEKS IN ADVANCE. You'll have a better chance of securing low-priced seats, which often sell out first.

TRAVEL SECURITY UPDATE

Virtually all travelers—not just flyers—have been subjected to new security measures since the terrorist attacks on Sept. 11, 2001. The changes mean more identity checks, more security searches, and higher fees. Airline passengers pay a $2.50 per flight surcharge, up to $10 per round-trip, to help pay for security upgrades.

You can help ensure a smooth trip with some advance planning. Check the news about your destination before you leave home. A government alert could hamper your ability to get around. Ask your carrier about check-in times.

Above all, understand these new realities:

◆ **Your personal belongings—and bare feet—may be displayed before strangers.** Avoid wearing items that can set off detectors: belts with metal buckles, heavy jewelry, shoes with buckles, or even bras with metal underwires. You may be asked to take off your shoes, so select footwear that's easy to remove and put back on.

◆ **Airplane security is being stepped up.** JetBlue, for example, has installed video cameras, giving pilots the ability to see what's going on in the cabin. As of this writing, there are efforts at the federal level to arm pilots. The Transportation Security Administration has earmarked $100 million for cockpit-door modifications, although cockpit doors won't be made fully bullet-proof for another year.

◆ **The passenger sitting next to you may be a sky marshal.** The government is training thousands of men and women to carry guns and fly anonymously in the passenger cabin. But the number of marshals still isn't enough to cover the more than 25,000 commercial flights in the U.S. each day.

◆ **Disobeying an order from the flight crew could mean trouble.** Crews are now instructed to rigidly enforce rules that might have been relaxed in the past. A belligerent passenger could cause a plane to make an unscheduled landing.

◆ **Traveling by ground transport may be faster than flying.** If your flying time is less than two hours, you could spend more time at the airport than in the air. That has prompted many to travel by car, once the overall time spent in transit has been considered.

◆ **No more breezing through North American borders by car.** Even when driving between the U.S. and Canada, expect long lines, especially at peak times. You should carry your driver's license and birth or naturalization certificate or a passport. Mexican border officials require a driver's license and proof of citizenship.

◆ **For cruises, allow more time to embark in the home port.** All passengers and crew are now required to pass through metal detectors. Officials are inspecting all carry-on and checked baggage.

◆ **Prepare for inspections at some theme parks and museums.** Visitors are now required to open their belongings for inspection. That means everything from diaper bags to coolers will get a thorough going-over, so expect delays.

HITTING THE (VIRTUAL) BOOKS

Here's a well-chosen list of sites that can help you and your children with the research you need for work or school—and maybe have some fun in the process.

The Internet has become the ultimate research library. Indeed, many of the best research libraries have an online presence. This list gives the CONSUMER REPORTS favorites for homework help, school research, and all-purpose curiosity browsing.

ASK DR. MATH *(www.mathforum.com/dr.math)*. It's not the most attractive site, but Ask Dr. Math can be useful. From the home page, you can search the archives for a specific math topic, look through the FAQ, or cull the archives by class level (elementary, high school, etc.). If you can't find the answer to your question in the archives, you can write Dr. Math directly.

ASK JEEVES FOR KIDS *(www.ajkids.com)*. Like its "mother" site, Ask Jeeves for Kids allows you to type in straightforward questions—such as "What is Denmark's major export?"—and then provides you with a number of choices to narrow your search for information. There are also "study tools" for general knowledge gathering. You can use the thesaurus, world atlas, dictionary, and almanac, or click on the buttons for math, history, science, biography, or links to more information.

BRITANNICA.COM *(www.britannica.com)*. Considering that Encyclopedia Britannica in book form consists of 32 volumes, it's no surprise that the web site is rich and multifaceted. You pay $9.95 per month or $69.95 per year for access to the full text of any article. The opening paragraphs of the articles can be read for free.

FEDERAL REGISTER *(www.access.gpo.gov/su_docs/aces/aces140.html)*. Access government documents both executive and legislative at the official Federal Register site. You can search by type of document (such as presidential papers), or for laws and bills, by year and by specific date. You can also look for federal regulations, laws, and other documents at the National Archives and Records Administration *(www.nara.gov)*.

HOW STUFF WORKS *(www.howstuffworks.com)*. "Stuff" can be just about anything at this site, founded by the author Marshall Brain (his real name). You'll learn how animal camouflage works, how to pick a lock, how your kidneys operate, and more. Once you've viewed the detailed articles, you can join in the forums to post a question or continue the discussion. You can also receive a free e-mail newsletter summarizing new features.

INFO PLEASE *(www.infoplease.com)*. Dream up an almanac and you'll probably find it here—world, U.S., biography, sports, weather. You can search any or all of the almanacs; links take you to related sections or move you to adjacent entries in each book.

MERRIAM-WEBSTER *(www.m-w.com)*. Free thesaurus and dictionary lookups are available at Merriam-Webster's site, where you can also play word games, get a word-of-the-day sent to your inbox, and use the Barnhart Dictionary Companion's update of new words.

NATIONAL GEOGRAPHIC *(www.nationalgeographic.com)*. Video features, multimedia maps, and of course National Geographic's reporting characterize this site. A database with abstracts of more than 100 years of National Geographic publications is available. There's also a homework help area with multimedia information on dozens of topics.

The Internet is tailor-made for research in any subject area.

REFDESK *(www.refdesk.com)*. There's so much information on the home page of RefDesk, you almost don't know where to begin. But if you're looking for answers, you've come to the right place. You'll link with one click to reference tools such as Ask the Experts, Fast Facts 2002, search engines, almanacs, maps and atlases, medical information, postal rates and currency-conversion charts, and Homework Helper. Monitor airline traffic around one of the nation's airports, find out who's leading which country with ChiefsofState.com, and do some spying with the CIA's World Factbook 2001.

Online Shopping: The Virtual Mall

While it can't duplicate the experience of strolling down Rodeo Drive, shopping on the web does deliver considerable rewards. At its best, online shopping is quick, efficient, fun, and informative. Easy searching by author, title, genre, or other categories makes the web a good place to shop for products such as books, music, and videos, which are small and light and easy to ship. Computers and home-electronics equipment are also easy to find. Online auctions open the door to rare or hard-to-find items. While online sales account for just a tiny portion of the trillions spent annually on retail, e-tailing has demonstrated that it's definitely here to stay.

CONSUMER REPORTS' regular evaluations of online shopping sites show that web merchants nearly always deliver the goods—as ordered and on time. The shopping experience, however, can be another matter. Among concerns are sites that are difficult to navigate, product details that are hard to decipher onscreen, items that are disappointingly not available, and security and privacy issues. For e-Ratings of online shopping sites, see page 83.

71 Smart e-tail sites

77 Online auctions: Going...going ...dot-gone

83 Consumer Reports e-Ratings

SMART E-TAIL SITES

Beyond matters of taste and budget, certain key elements should be in place to help ensure a pleasant and secure web-shopping experience.

An appealing e-tail site is many things. Of course it has merchandise that matches your taste level and budget, and it may be a subsidiary of a brick-and-mortar retailer that is familiar to you. Other fundamentals include ease of use, clear policy statements regarding privacy and credit-card security, and appropriate breadth and depth of product choices. Individual attributes may be judged more or less important for different product categories.

For example, images of products are more important when shopping for clothing than when shopping for books or CDs, although the book or CD cover should be shown once you have selected a title for a closer look.

Policies to look for

All policy information should be easy to find. Ideally, it will be available by clicking on a link from any page on the site. At a minimum, policy information should be found on particularly relevant pages (for example, security information should be easily accessible when you're placing an order) and on a site's home page.

SECURITY. A clear security policy statement describes the strategy employed by the web site to ensure the safety of a customer's credit card and other information. Make sure any web site you're shopping on has a security mode that encrypts credit-card numbers. When you switch from browsing to buying, the merchant should issue a prompt that tells you the transaction is being switched to a secure system. A safe site will display a symbol of an unbroken key, a picture of a closed lock, or a web address that begins https:// (note the "s" added to "http").

PRIVACY. A clear privacy-policy statement describes the type of personal information collected from a customer, the reason that information is collected, and who will have access to that information. In general, merchants should make it very easy for customers to "opt out" of being placed on any third-party lists. Some sites use a conveniently placed check box or radio button to indicate a lack of consent. The merchant should not ask for extra information beyond what is needed to place an order (name, address, phone number, e-mail address, billing information) without having a clearly stated purpose.

If the extra information is to be used for personalization, the site must offer an easy way to opt out of such personalization.

The best sites do not share any information with third parties unless the customer gives explicit consent. Customers should have to "opt in" rather than having to "opt out." The best sites also say they won't change their information-sharing policies without notifying their customers.

SHIPPING AND HANDLING. A clear shipping and handling policy statement describes shipping costs and how many days it will take for the item(s) to arrive. In general, sites should offer regular and express shipping, and the least expensive option should be the default. Shipping fees should be reasonable (we compared them with shipping fees of companies in the same category), and shipping and handling costs should be disclosed before the ordering process begins.

The better sites have relatively low shipping costs and no additional charge to ship items with different availability separately (for example, back-orders).

RETURNS. A clear policy statement includes the who, what, where, how, and how much of returning items. Look for a 100 percent satisfaction guarantee that allows customers to return any item for any reason (unless prohibited by law) in a reasonable amount of time (a minimum of 30 days). Sites should meet the industry standard for returns. The standard may be less than a complete satisfaction guarantee if it has a reasonable basis (for example, music CDs and software can only be returned unopened, unless they arrive damaged).

Sites should offer a full refund, rather than just a credit or exchange, and restocking fees should be paid by the merchant. The better sites, as applicable, allow items ordered online to be returned to local retail stores; exceed the industry standard for returns; and pay return shipping fees if the wrong or a defective product was shipped. (Ideally, the merchant would always pay return shipping fees.)

CUSTOMER SERVICE. A clear customer-service policy statement describes how and when a representative may be contacted. For instance, customer-focused services should be provided to enhance the shopping process, including a toll-free phone number, an e-mail address, and a "snail mail" address. Service should be available seven days a week, 24 hours a day, preferably with a live person and not an e-mail screen; better sites do offer this. A

THE EIGHT HABITS OF SMART E-SHOPPERS

According to the federal government, online retail sales now total more than $9 billion a year, and e-commerce is growing at a double-digit pace. Any time you venture online to shop, CONSUMER REPORTS suggests that you set a budget, keeping these things in mind:

1. Play to the web's strengths. Web shopping excels in several areas. It gives unparalleled access to product information and exposure to web merchants that offer a wider selection than any one store. Comparison shopping is easy, and you don't need to brave crowds or trudge from store to store. But web shopping won't help if you need an item right away. You're also better off shopping at a brick-and-mortar store if you're after a product you need to see, hear, touch, or try on. Returns and exchanges can also be more of a hassle online than at a local store.

2. Check out the merchant. When you visit online merchants, get in the habit of reading the company's privacy and security policies. They do change from time to time. Look for the TRUSTe symbol or a Better Business Bureau Online seal, both indicating that the merchant's business practices have been independently audited as consumer-friendly.

You can log on to the BizRate.com site evaluations (at *www.bizrate.com*), where you'll find compilations of other consumers' shopping experiences. You can also use ConsumerReports.org's e-Ratings, on page 83 or online (*www.ConsumerReports.org*).

3. Be organized. Have a few backup ideas in case you cannot easily find your first choice. The more information you have, such as a model number, the easier it is to find sites that sell your selection.

4. Give yourself enough time. Even if you know precisely what you want and where to buy it, you still need to factor in ample time for delivery—and for dealing with problems that may arise, such as the belated discovery that an item has been back-ordered. Unfortunately, during the holiday shopping season, you need to leave even more time than you think is reasonable.

5. Bookmark searches to compare products. If you've found an item you like but are not sure you want to buy it, place it in the site's virtual shopping basket. Then bookmark the page in your browser so you can easily return after you've considered other possibilities; to find the carted items still there later, you'll need to have cookies enabled in your browser software. You can also open a new window on your browser to shop on other sites.

6. Use available comparison tools. If you've zeroed in on two or three models, use a shopping bot that allows you to compare features and prices. A bot is a price-comparison web site that automatically scours the Internet looking for the product name or model number you've entered. Many bots specialize in selected categories, such as music or computers. You can find bots by using a search engine such as Google (*www.google.com*), looking for "shopping bots."

7. Look for sales. If it's a bargain you're after, try running sales at *www.shoppinglist.com*. The site lets you search by ZIP code, category, brand, or store.

8. Know when to cut your losses. When shopping online, it's easy to get sucked into a time warp. If you're having trouble finding a particular item, it may be better to log off and try again later—or perhaps head for the mall.

"Help" or "Frequently Asked Questions (FAQ)" section should be available. Merchants should send an e-mail confirmation of an order and notification of when items will ship. The better sites, as applicable, have special services, such as including batteries at no extra charge with all products requiring them, and features such as online order tracking.

What makes a site easy to use?

The information on each page of an easy-to-use site is designed and structured so that customers can easily understand it and find what they need. It's simple to navigate from one part of the site to another. Ordering should be simple and sensible. Sites advertising products from businesses other than their own should ensure that those ads are small, out of the way, and clear as to their purpose.

DESIGN. Aside from basic aesthetics that make shopping more enjoyable, look for pages that are designed and structured so customers can easily comprehend the information presented and just as easily find what they need.

The better sites are designed with simplicity and consistency. The best designs are those that don't draw attention to themselves. They have uncluttered, easy-to-read pages, use moderation in color and typefaces, and avoid the use of distracting animation.

Pages should be organized so that important information is emphasized, and all information is grouped and presented in a logical, predictable fashion. You should see everyday language and consistent organization across pages.

NAVIGATION (BROWSING AND SEARCHING). Whether customers want to browse through all products, look at a specific category of product, or search for a specific item, they should be able to do so easily.

The better sites have consistent, well-placed menus and submenus (tabs or button bars) with meaningful labels that lead to key pages on the site (for example, Home, Shopping Cart, and individual product categories). They also have clear navigation aids—button bars, consistent icons, highlighted icons, page-specific cursor shapes, etc.—on every page that allow customers to know where they are on the site at all times. Clear navigation will also make it easy for customers to go where they want to go and find their way back to where they've been.

It's often better to buy electronic gear online rather than at a brick-and-mortar store.

Shopping sites should be organized so that customers can move around with the fewest number of mouse-clicks (three to four clicks should be the maximum). They should also list relevant product categories with meaningful labels for sensible browsing. Finding items should be at least as simple as zipping through a dress rack at a store. So, within browsing categories, product listings should have enough pertinent information (price, description, and/or picture) to help the customer quickly select items to examine in more detail.

Look for a search engine that lets customers quickly find items by product category, brand name, product name, model/item number, and price, as well as other relevant criteria for that particular category. The search should be well cross-referenced and flexible enough to tolerate minor misspellings, missing hyphens, or partial product names. Matches, or "hits," should be sensibly prioritized. Ideally, the search feature should be accessible from every page, with no extra clicking required.

A good site will offer options to sort, screen, and compare lists of products, and have links that work—and no dead ends.

ORDERING AND CANCELING. The overall process should leave customers feeling confident that they ordered the item they wanted at the price they intended to pay.

The better sites offer a "cart" or other way to collect and hold items while shopping, without a customer's having to register. The cart information should track product names, numbers, and prices, and keep a running subtotal (including shipping and handling costs).

Sites should indicate up front when an item is out of stock, and make it easy to change the quantity of each item ordered and to remove unwanted items. You should be asked to fill out a simple, clear, short order form (one to two screens). If you inadvertently leave out any information from the form, the site should alert you and clearly identify and pinpoint what needs to be filled in. Also, it should be clear when an order will actually be placed and how to cancel an order both before and after placing it.

ADVERTISING CLUTTER. This is applicable only to sites advertising products from businesses other than their own. The better sites are ad-free, have ads that are not "hidden" or disguised as editorial content, or have ads that are minimally intrusive (no animation, pop-ups or rolling text; ads located off in a corner).

Hallmarks of excellent content

Here is what CONSUMER REPORTS looks for when it rates online shopping sites. For a look at our e-Ratings, see page 83.

At the better sites, merchants should offer a breadth of product categories and a depth of product choices appropriate to their business. There is a lot of useful information about individual products to help the customer make purchasing decisions. There are special features that take advantage of interactive technologies and make shopping online easy and satisfying.

BREADTH OF PRODUCT CATEGORIES. The range of product categories offered is appropriate to the type of merchant. Keep in mind that specialty sites tend to have a more limited range of product categories. Larger, mall-type sites usually offer an expanded range of categories. When relevant, the site describes how its product offerings online compare with its company's retail-store and print-catalog offerings, and what's available from other e-tailers.

DEPTH OF PRODUCT CATEGORIES. The number of product choices within a category should be suitable to the type of company/merchant. Specialty sites are expected to have a more limited number of products, while larger, mall-type sites, department stores, warehouse-type stores, and so on should offer an expanded number of products. When relevant, the site compares its product offerings online with its company's retail-store and print-catalog offerings, and those of other e-tailers.

PRODUCT INFORMATION. Pertinent, descriptive product information is provided in a concise way. The better sites clearly describe each product and what is included with it, to differentiate it from other choices. They offer additional useful information, such as professional or customer reviews, links to related products, links to information about authors and artists,

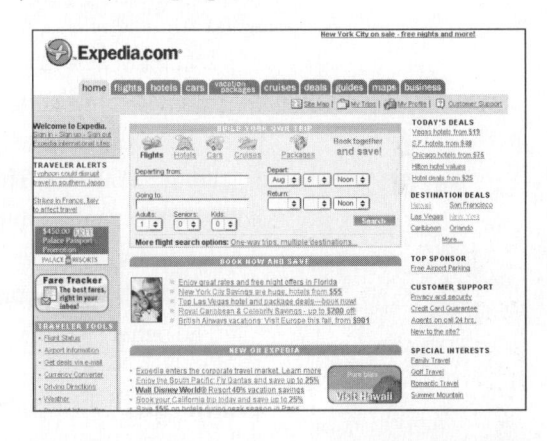

Look for clear booking and cancellation procedures when making travel plans online.

and more, as appropriate. Good sites also show a good-quality picture of the product, and list prices clearly.

PERSONALIZATION/CUSTOMIZATION. There are features that personalize the site for individual customers and that make the shopping experience (and especially subsequent shopping experiences) more efficient, effective, and perhaps more fun. The better sites make it easy for customers to use personalized/customized features, but also offer an option for customers to easily opt out of these.

Good sites make sensible product suggestions in an unobtrusive manner, based on what the customer is looking at or has previously purchased. They keep records of previous purchases or "favorite products" for easy reordering. In addition, they make it easy for customers to set up a personal account to store billing information for easier ordering next time.

Sites should also offer an address book, gift registry, and/or reminder calendar when appropriate. And customers should be able to search for products based on their own criteria when applicable.

SPECIAL SERVICES. These are helpful services that aid the customer. The best sites ask if the purchase is a gift, and offer gift-wrapping and gift cards either free or at a reasonable price. They also offer to hide the price of a gift on the invoice.

UNIQUE FEATURES. These are distinctive features that take advantage of interactive technologies and make shopping online a worthwhile experience—for example, music sites that let customers hear music samples, book sites that let customers read book excerpts, and clothing sites that provide a representative body model to "try on" clothes.

The better sites offer useful, not gratuitous, features that work.

Online gift shopping

Shopping for gifts online can be quick, easy, and convenient. Many sites handle returns and exchanges as well as any brick-and-mortar store. Here are some of the services you'll see when shopping for gifts online.

GIFT REGISTRIES. Many sites offer special gift registries for easy browsing and item selection. Gift givers are usually required to enter a special registrant number or simply the name and address of the registered recipient. When selecting a gift for big occasions (baby showers, weddings, etc.), this feature can save a time-consuming trip to the store.

Signing up with a registry can help gift receivers avoid duplicates or unwanted gifts (provided gift givers check the registry) and even get you money-saving offers. But it does compromise your privacy. Information you may want to keep private is readily exposed to the world. And the information can be sold to other companies for direct sales or other market purposes. Check online gift registries' privacy policies.

SHIPPING-TIME ESTIMATIONS AND SHIPPING OPTIONS. To ensure on-time delivery, look for sites that can estimate how long an order will take to arrive at its destination using standard shipping. Many of the best sites provide that information and offer two-day express or overnight delivery (helpful if you wait until the last minute to order a gift).

GIFT WRAPPING AND CARDS. Look for free or low-cost gift cards (beyond the standard gift message printed on the packing slip), so you can include a personal greeting with your gift. Some sites offer low-cost wrapping or special gift boxes, while others will wrap or box your gift free of charge with a minimum total purchase.

GIFT CERTIFICATES OR "GIFT MONEY." These features are offered by many sites. Make sure the gift certificate or money will remain valid for at least six months from date of purchase, so your gift recipient has plenty of time to make a decision. Many sites offer specially wrapped or boxed gift certificates and will enclose a card bearing your personal message.

EXCEPTIONAL RETURN POLICIES. In the event your gift isn't perfect, you'll want the recipient to be able to return it easily. Look for web sites that let you return anything, for any reason, within a minimum of 45 days. Also, look for sites that include postage-paid, pre-addressed envelopes or address labels with all orders for easy returns, or that allow on-line orders to be returned to brick-and-mortar counterparts for exchange or refund, with no questions asked.

OMISSION OF GIFT PRICE ON THE PACKING SLIP. A few sites will omit the price of your gift on the packing slip enclosed with the item; that's a nice touch.

INTERACTIVE GIFT FINDERS. Some web sites have cool interactive gift finders that help you pick the right gift for that special person. They inquire about your gift recipient (usually based on what's offered at the site), let you indicate a price range, and then suggest a few gift ideas based on that information.

Protecting your credit

If your credit-card number is stolen online, you have the same protections you do if it's stolen offline: If you report the theft soon after you discover it, you are liable for only $50, even on international transactions. Although not required by law, some web merchants will reimburse that $50, with the credit-card company paying the rest. (Check buying or ordering information on individual sites.)

But what if you think a web merchant has misrepresented a product? For example, that cordless phone you ordered was advertised as a digital spread-spectrum model, but it isn't. Your protection and recourse are the same as if you ordered by catalog. Unfortunately, if the merchant, web or otherwise, is not in your state or within 100 miles of your home, some protections won't apply. For example, you may not be able to withhold payment to your credit-card company if you have a dispute with this merchant over the quality of the phone. But in practice, many credit-card issuers will try to mediate, or will at least credit your account until the dispute is settled. If that doesn't work, you'll have to contact your state attorney general's office or local consumer-protection office to file a complaint.

ONLINE AUCTIONS: GOING . . . GOING . . . DOT-GONE

Online auctions can be a bargain-hunter's paradise. Playing safe and bidding smart can help you avoid misrepresentation and fraud.

Online auctions represent a potent marriage between technology and shopping. eBay, which got its start selling Pez dispensers in the mid-1990s, now handles some 170 million auction sales, exchanging $9.3 billion worth of goods in 18,000 categories. Little wonder that Newsweek recently dubbed the site "the Internet's hottest marketplace." By 2003, it has been forecast, total online-auction revenues will jump to nearly $20 billion.

Yet for all the hoopla, the fraud and misrepresentation that plague real-world auctions are also common online. The National Consumers League, a nonprofit watchdog group that independently logs online-auction abuses, reports that the most common problem plaguing this new shopping medium is that buyers fail to receive items they bought and paid for. The nonstop auction action is also taking a human toll. According to the Center for On-Line Addiction, an organization that counsels people with compulsive disorders related to Internet overexposure, some 15 percent of clients seeking treatment are online-auction junkies.

Sizing up the seller

Big online-auction sites, such as Amazon, AuctionAddict, BidBay, eBay, and Yahoo!, operate what are arguably the world's most democratic commercial venues. Anyone with something to peddle—from upscale retailers and purveyors of rare collectibles to amateur pack rats and lowly liquidators of discontinued or distressed merchandise—is welcome to list his or her wares. But if everyone can play, how can you know who's not playing fair?

Both buyers and sellers operate behind a veil of anonymity that the auction sites are scrupulous to preserve. Sellers identify themselves by a screen name. To date, the courts have upheld the right of the auction sites to be held harmless for misdeeds committed by sellers. But there are steps you can take to protect yourself.

CHECK THE SELLER'S FEEDBACK RATING. Each of the major third-party auction sites maintains a forum where buyers can rate and post comments about their experiences doing business with a given seller (and vice versa). The comments, usually grouped by positive, negative, and neutral, are aggregated over the most recent 7-day, 30-day, and 180-day period, giving potential new buyers an opportunity to detect improvement or deterioration in the seller's recent performance. While a record of experience can be helpful, it's hard to know just how much credence to give the assessments of other strangers.

Harder to gauge is what a buyer might expect from a seller who has no feedback ratings at all. When CONSUMER REPORTS informally surveyed the feedback scores of 125 sellers at five top online-auction sites, 30 percent had no buyer ratings.

To help lend credibility to new sellers, eBay has initiated a voluntary program that includes identity verification by Equifax Secure, a division of the credit-reporting firm. Sellers who pass muster get to display an ID Verify icon on their feedback profile.

CONTACT THE SELLER. Auction sites collect e-mail addresses for all users when they register. They make that information available to potential bidders, usually by a direct link from the web page where the seller's goods are displayed. While intended chiefly to allow bidders to question the seller about the terms of sale and the condition of the goods being sold, direct e-mail contact may be a good way to begin sizing up the seller's trustworthiness.

Taking stock of the goods

At a real-world auction, you can normally preview the items being offered for sale and scrutinize possible buys for telltale details that the auction catalog may not fully disclose. Online auctions give you no such advantage. Indeed, some of the most popular merchandise categories—antiques, collectibles, and consumer-electronics gear—are particularly difficult to appraise from a brief description and a thumbnail photo.

READ DESCRIPTIONS CAREFULLY. Sellers are legally bound to describe their wares accurately, but that still leaves them lots of wiggle room to fudge inconvenient facts. Obviously, the more unique and costly the item being offered, the more painstaking you should be in verifying the seller's claims. At the very least, you should expect a full explanation of the object's physical dimensions, construction materials, and condition, including complete details on any physical or operational flaws.

For electronics gear, office equipment, or household appliances, expect the seller to supply specifications on any critical performance features and a full product pedigree, including manufacturer, make, and model number. If you cannot find the information you need, contact the seller and have him or her put the details you need in writing before you bid.

Especially when bidding on appliances or consumer electronics, watch for anything that suggests the product is not new. Online auctions are a favorite venue for companies to unload "reconditioned" or "like new" merchandise. "New" products come unopened in the manufacturer's original packaging and carry a full warranty. If you do bid on a reconditioned item, make sure that it has at least a 30-day warranty on all parts and labor and that you have the option to return it if it does not meet your full satisfaction.

LOOK FOR INDEPENDENT AUTHENTICATION. The potential for you to overbid based on an incomplete or erroneous understanding of an item's origins or condition is greatest for collectibles. Minor flaws—even something as small as a poorly positioned image on a rare baseball card—can cut deeply into the object's value. Fortunately, there are price guides for nearly all genres of collectibles, and they're worth consulting before you bid. In addition, look for sellers who have had their wares independently rated by a recognized appraisal group (for more on appraisers, see page 82).

Beware of bidding shams

Auction sites have a vested interest in maintaining a fair and open bidding process. All the big sites reserve the right to monitor sales and look for bidding irregularities. But they do not guarantee that problems will be caught, and with thousands of simultaneous auctions under way round-the-clock, the volume of activity greatly exceeds even their best intentions to spot violators. That leaves it up to you to be alert for common bid-rigging tricks.

SHILL BIDS. Acting in concert with cronies (or even alone using an alias), a seller will raise bids entered by legitimate buyers to up the ante. Naturally, shill bidders will drop out of the competition before the auction ends, but not before they've artificially pumped up the final sale price.

SHIELD BIDS. This scheme is most often a conspiracy among buyers attempting to ensure that auctioned goods can be purchased at a low price. One bidder bids low, while a compatriot enters an unrealistically high bid in an effort to scare off potential rivals. As the auction is about to close, the high bidder withdraws his offer, enabling the accomplice to win by default. One effective foil to this tactic is to closely monitor the closing minutes of the auction and enter a late bid after the high bidder withdraws. It's also possible to enter a proxy bid, allowing you to boost your bid automatically in the event that a previous high bid is retracted.

Some sites, like BidBay and Yahoo!, let sellers "blacklist" buyers who have engaged in unethical bidding in past dealings. But the best defense is for vigilant buyers and sellers to report violations to the auction site; the Federal Trade Commission *(www.ftc.gov)*; and the Internet Fraud Complaint Center *(www.ifccfbi.gov)*, a joint initiative of the Federal Bureau of Investigation and the National White Collar Crime Center.

Tips for buyers

No matter where you decide to poke around, here's how to make your online-auction experience productive, efficient, and fun:

CUT THROUGH THE CLUTTER. Finding what interests you from an auction site's mountain of wares can be frustrating. If you're in a mood to prowl the online-auction halls, give yourself a few broad goals—looking in on the baseball memorabilia listed on eBay, for example—and set a time limit for your scouting expedition. If you have your eye out for a particular item (a digital camera, say, or Wedgwood dishes), look for an auction site that showcases a deep inventory in that specialty. Most sites list the number of items being offered in each category. Then click through to the subcategory where you're likely to find the item you seek, and type the name of the object you want in the search field to zero in on the auctions most relevant to you.

eBay, by far the leading online auction site, is moving into regular retail sales.

USE ALERTS. Most auction sites will also let you create a personal page that can track all of your bidding activity, alert you when items you want become available, and even bid automatically on your behalf. That's more efficient than jumping from auction to auction in pursuit of a rare bauble.

CHECK PRICES BEFORE YOU BID. In the fluid, seesaw competition to outbid rivals, it's easy to overpay. Auction hounds responding to CONSUMER REPORTS' invitation to share their online-bidding experiences warned especially about the dangers of paying too much for items sold as new. To improve your chances of getting a good deal, it's important to research prices carefully before you bid. Comparison-shopping sites can provide a quick reality check on most common consumer products that show up in auctions. Use those prices as the upper limit for your bidding. For collectibles, check a price catalog that specializes in the goods you are considering.

USE PROXY BIDDING. Online auctions can run as long as several weeks, so it hardly makes sense to hang around until the virtual gavel falls to see if your bid prevails. Fortunately, the auction sites make it easy to stay in the action by offering a proxy feature that does your bidding for you.

Called Bid Butler at uBid.com and Bid-Click at Amazon.com, proxy bidding lets you enter an initial offer for an item you want and, at the same time, set an upper limit for how much you'd be willing to bid. Your maximum bid is kept confidential throughout the sale. As other bidders raise the ante, your bid is automatically boosted by the minimum amount needed to remain top bidder. Your bidding ends when your limit is reached, so you'll never pay more than you want or than is absolutely necessary to win.

By putting your bidding on cruise control, you can avoid falling prey to a common—and legal—online-auction ruse called sniping. As an auction reaches its end, snipers zero in to outbid the current leader by entering a last-minute offer that's just high enough to win.

Doing your bidding

While most sites offer the traditional highest-bid-wins auctions, many sites also offer variations on the basic theme. Whichever format you face, your best bidding strategy is to enter the minimum price required to get started. Then take advantage of the proxy-bidding capability auction sites offer to register incrementally higher bids up to your predetermined maximum.

RESERVE-PRICE AUCTIONS. These allow the seller to set a minimum acceptable bid that must be met for a sale to occur. Potential buyers are alerted to the existence of a reserve price, but the amount remains confidential. If no one meets the reserve, there's no sale. However, you can contact the seller when the auction closes to try to negotiate a sale. Although many visitors to ConsumerReports.org said they find reserve-price auctions frustrating, they're worth considering for items you believe have measurable monetary value as opposed to more elusive collector value.

DUTCH AUCTIONS. With these, sellers are given a quick way to dispose of large batches of identical items. The seller lists a minimum price and the number of units for sale. Bidders specify a price and the number they're willing to buy. All winning bidders pay the same amount per item, which is the lowest successful bid. Here's how a scenario might play out: A seller has 10 computers for auction at $1,000 each. Ten people bid the $1,000 minimum for one computer each. In this case, all 10 bidders are winners. Now, suppose five people bid $1,250 for one computer each and 10 others bid $1,000. Because demand exceeds supply, the higher bidders are guaranteed a computer. The others will go to the earliest $1,000 bidders. The final price for each computer will be $1,000, since all winning bidders pay the same amount.

PRIVATE AUCTIONS. The identity of bidders remain anonymous. At the conclusion of the sale, the identity of the winner is revealed only to the seller.

REVERSE AUCTIONS. These put bidders in control by enabling them to indicate the maximum they're willing to pay for goods like home electronics and services ranging from airline fares, hotel rooms, and rental cars to home-equity loans, mortgages, and long-distance phone service. The seller then decides whether to go ahead with the deal. Priceline.com is synonymous with the "name-your-own-price" concept for plane tickets and other travel arrangements. But others, such as iOffer.com, bring together businesses that also want you as a customer, too.

EXPRESS AUCTIONS. Following the typical highest-bid-wins format but often lasting an hour or less, these are popular because they create a sense of immediacy.

FALLING-PRICE AUCTIONS. These resemble a department-store clearance. The seller sets the price for multiples of the same item, and the bids get lower over time until all the items are gone. If you bid early at the opening price, you win. If you watch and wait for the price to drop, there are fewer items available. The deeper the discount, the greater the risk of ending up empty-handed.

Avoiding auction pitfalls

Online auctions require discipline and attention to detail. Here is a strategy:

START SMALL. Whether buying or selling, take time to learn the rules and customs before you venture into any big-money transactions. With a few small purchases or sales under your

WHERE TO TURN FOR HELP

There's no end to the objets d'art people collect. Trouble is, you don't always know how much that oil painting you just inherited is worth, whether it's real or fake, or where to post it for sale. We searched the Internet for useful information sources that can help you determine value and authenticity, find auctions that cater to your interests, and simplify payment. Here are some sites we found useful:

Appraisal services. The American Society of Appraisers (*www.appraisers.org*), the Appraisers Association of America (*www.appraisersassoc.org*), and the International Society of Appraisers (*www.isa-appraisers.org*) are three of the most authoritative organizations. You'll find expert referrals for dozens of categories, including antique furniture, ceramics, clocks, coins, fine art, gems, glass, guns, jewelry, militaria, rare books, rugs, watches, and so forth. The sites provide a list of members and their areas of expertise.

Authentication services. An appraiser might not be qualified to authenticate an item but can sometimes provide a referral. Museums often are a reliable source of identification, too. Another option: Contact a reputable trade association, such as the American Numismatic Association (*www.money.org*) for coins and paper currency or the American Philatelic Society (*www.stamps.org*) for stamps. For sports cards and autographs—areas where authentication, grading, and valuation are extremely important—there's Professional Sports Authenticator (*www.psacard.com*). To obtain reliable authentication, you'll at minimum need to submit photos of the item; more likely, you'll have to bring or mail it in.

Escrow services. For a fee, these independent businesses can minimize the risk of fraud by holding a buyer's payment until that individual receives and approves of the merchandise. One of the better known services is Escrow.com. Before using any escrow service, investigate its reliability by checking with the Better Business Bureau and state and local consumer-affairs agencies.

Auction search engines. These portals will pore through dozens, sometimes hundreds, of online auctions for the items you like, based on the search criteria you enter. One we've seen with a wide reach is *www.auctionsa-z.com*.

belt, you can establish a solid feedback profile that will give other auction fans confidence in your reliability as a buyer or seller.

NEVER BID BLIND. However artfully a seller describes an object, a buyer can't form a reliable judgment of quality or condition unless it is accompanied by photos and, in the case of collectibles, independent authentication. For a collectible or unique object valued at $100 or more, insist on an unambiguous, detailed description; multiple thumbnail photographs that display the object from several angles; and independent authentication by a recognized authority.

KNOW HOW TO CONTACT THE SELLER OFFLINE. E-mail may be a sufficient way to get more information when bidding, but it's not an adequate way to resolve the complicated issues that can arise after your bid is accepted. At the very least, you'll need a confirmed address and phone number.

WATCH SHIPPING, HANDLING, AND INSURANCE CHARGES. These can turn a bargain into an expensive transaction. Be sure to factor in all the supplemental costs you'll incur if your bid is accepted, and decide whether it's still a good deal.

Sealing the deal

Even the best auction purchase can unravel if you fail to take the right steps to ensure that your treasure arrives safely before the seller pockets your payment.

PAY BY CREDIT CARD. The simplest and generally the safest way to pay for your auction winnings is with a credit card. The card issuer will credit your account if you don't receive your merchandise or if the goods received are damaged or not as described in the original listing.

USE AN ESCROW SERVICE. Many sellers who lack merchant accounts that let them accept charge cards insist that payment be made through personal check, cashier's check, money order, or cash on delivery. That's a poor choice for buyers paying more than a few dollars for their auction winnings.

There is now a better payment option that can protect the interests of both parties. Independent escrow services, such as Escrow.com and Tradenable.com, accept credit-card, check, or money-order payments from the buyer. The money is released to the seller only after the buyer receives and approves of the merchandise shipped from the seller. Fees usually run no more than 5 percent of the item's selling price.

Similar services, including Amazon.com Payments, and Yahoo! PayDirect, allow buyers and sellers to send and receive money online from an account that draws upon the buyer's credit card or bank account. eBay recently purchased the PayPal service and has announced plans to fold it in with its eBay Payments service. With any escrow service, registered users can send payments by e-mail simply by keying in a dollar amount on an online form. The service is generally free to buyers; sellers pay a modest fee. Another nice feature: When you use one of the proprietary payment systems, the sponsoring site may provide free fraud insurance up to a specified limit.

CONSUMER REPORTS E-RATINGS

CONSUMER REPORTS regularly evaluates online shopping sites. Complete findings are posted at *www.ConsumerReports.org*. The Ratings here were current as of July 2002. Here is an overview:

Sites are selected based on sales volume, site traffic, and popularity or relevance in a particular category. Some sites are included simply because they are of particular interest to consumers. To rate each site, we follow a consistent shopping technique—browsing for products, looking for specific items and features, placing an order, and so forth. All site URLs have the www. prefix.

We give an overall score that sums up the excellence of a site's policies, usability, and content, and how these elements combine to create an efficient and productive online shopping experience. The overall score is not necessarily an average of the site scores for policies, usability, and content. If one characteristic of the site is exceptional, the site may receive a higher overall rating, and if one of the components is far below standard, the site may receive a lower overall rating.

The policies judgment reflects our evaluation of the quality and clarity of a site's explanation of security, privacy, shipping, return, and customer-service policies. At the minimum, all sites are expected to process customer information by using secure servers and to permit customers to easily keep their names off mailing lists. Companies receive higher scores if they have relatively inexpensive shipping charges; promise to cover the first $50 of any fraudulent charge resulting from a site transaction; do not share customer information with third parties unless the customer agrees; and offer a 100 percent satisfaction guarantee with a full refund.

The usability judgment evaluates how easily and efficiently a shopper can browse the site for products, search for certain items, and place an order. The content judgment evaluates the extent of product categories and choices within those categories; the quality and amount of product information given; and the availability of useful personalization/customization, special services, or unique features.

E-Ratings in this section

Products, p.85
- Apparel
- Baby gear
- Books, music & videos
- Computers
- Electronic gear
- Health & beauty
- House & Home
- Office & mailing supplies
- Pet supplies
- Small appliances
- Software
- Sports & camping
- Toys & games

Services p.92
- Auctions

Travel sites p.93
- Airlines, domestic
- Airlines, foreign
- Airlines, lowfare
- Car rentals
- Cruise lines
- Hotels, moderate
- Hotels, upscale
- Railways
- Theme parks

PRODUCTS

SPECIAL SECTION E-RATINGS

Better ◐ ◑ ○ ◒ ● Worse

Apparel

WEB SITE	OVERALL SCORE	POLICIES	USABILITY	CONTENT	COMMENTS
Bluefly bluefly.com	◑	◐	◑	◑	Bluefly prides itself on being a "virtual company" and has no retail stores. The web site focuses on off-price designer apparel and home accessories. With very good privacy, security, and return policies, this site offers a satisfying shopping experience.
Eddie Bauer eddiebauer.com	◑	◑	○	◑	This company offers women's, men's, and children's apparel; footwear; and accessories online. This site has a very good privacy policy and offers live chat with a customer-care representative.
Gap gap.com	◑	◑	◑	◑	This site has a very good privacy policy. Helpful features include an address book, a reminder service, and a gift finder. Well-organized, sensible product categories and constant menus make browsing especially efficient.
JCPenney jcpenney.com	○	○	○	◑	This site has very good security and return policies. There's a large selection of clothing, and special features like an address book and gift finder.
J. Crew jcrew.com	◑	○	◑	◑	Good organization and a clear, contemporary design make it very easy to browse through the clothing here. There are clearance and weekly sales sections, and a helpful gift guide. Sensible suggestions are made for related items.
L.L. Bean llbean.com	◑	◑	◑	◑	It's easy to browse and search for clothing and other products, but pictures tend to be blurry. You can have a live chat online with customer-service reps for help. Links to information, such as details about product materials, add interest.
Lands' End landsend.com	◑	◑	○	◐	The Lands' End site features women's, men's, and children's apparel; footwear; accessories; luggage and home furnishings. This site has many useful and entertaining features, including a virtual model to demo outfits.
Macy's macys.com	○	◑	○	○	The search feature needs some improvement, and duplicate items appear in many product categories. The depth of product choices is limited, compared to other similar sites. Online orders can be returned to local Macy's stores.

Baby gear

WEB SITE	OVERALL SCORE	POLICIES	USABILITY	CONTENT	COMMENTS
BabiesR'us babiesrus.com	◑	○	◐	◐	This easy-to-use site offers a wide selection of baby products. Lots of extras, including a gift registry, gift finder, check lists, advice, and more make this site a standout. Affiliated with Amazon.com
Baby Depot babydepot.com	●	◒	◒	◒	This site has a number of shortcomings. There is only a limited selection of baby products, the search feature needs improvement. Information about shipping charges is not provided until after the ordering process begins.
babystyle.com babystyle.com	○	○	○	◑	There is a fairly wide range of information and advice on this site, with celebrity features and much information oriented toward keeping a new mom feeling stylish. The search works well.
buybuyBaby buybuybaby.com	◒	○	○	◒	A limited product selection, inefficient browsing, and a somewhat cumbersome ordering process are just a few of the sites drawbacks.
RightStart.com rightstart.com	○	◒	○	◑	This site has less-than-satisfactory policies. There is a large selection of baby products with thorough descriptions. Product Watch provides information about product recalls.

CONSUMER REPORTS DIGITAL BUYING GUIDE • 85

PRODUCTS *continued*

Books, music & videos

WEB SITE	OVERALL SCORE	POLICIES	USABILITY	CONTENT	COMMENTS
Amazon *amazon.com*	◖	○	●	◉	This site has a huge selection of books and music, including eBooks. There are author biographies, links to other books by the author, professional reviews, and recommendations for related books. The search feature is good, and the ordering process is clear-cut but lengthy.
Barnes & Noble *bn.com*	◖	○	◖	◉	An impressive search engine, an especially large selection of out-of-print titles, and numerous links to useful information make for a satisfying shopping experience. But the policies are not as consumer-friendly as other merchants in this category.
Borders *borders.com*	○	○	●	◉	There is a huge inventory and a very good search engine at this site, but shopping here is generally unexceptional. We couldn't find a way to browse for books in much depth.
CDNOW *cdnow.com*	●	●	○	◉	This site provides a very satisfying shopping experience, as long as you are searching for specific music titles and artists. There is a wealth of product information and special features like personalized recommendations are offered.
EMusic.com *emusic.com*	○	○	○	○	This site has a lot of music offerings, but a very limited selection of artists, many whose names may be unfamiliar. The main categories for browsing are sensible, and the search feature is flexible.
GetMusic *getmusic.com*	◐	◐	○	◐	GetMusic.com provides exposure to various types of music and also has an online store. There is a huge selection of CDs here, but compared with other sites in this category, there are few special features to enhance the shopping experience.
Half.com *half.com*	○	○	○	○	Half.com is an online marketplace where previously owned books, CDs, movies, and video games are bought and sold at discount prices. The main categories for browsing are sensible and are broken down in useful ways. Prices and inventory levels are updated every 20 minutes.
J & R Music and Computer World *jandr.com*	●	●	○	◉	The shopping experience here is enhanced by a generous amount of useful and interesting product information, including a glossary of technical terms. Live Help is fast and informative.
MP3.com *mp3.com*	○	○	○	◉	This site allows users to organize and access CD and MP3 collections on the Internet. There are some useful customization features and lots of music news and related information.

SPECIAL SECTION E-RATINGS

Better ● ◐ ○ ◑ ● Worse

Computers

WEB SITE	OVERALL SCORE	POLICIES	USABILITY	CONTENT	COMMENTS
Apple *apple.com*	●	○	●	●	Easy to navigate, this site has a sleek design and helpful descriptions of Apple products, with direct links to purchase them. There is a very good shipping policy, with no charge for ground shipments. But the return policy is very strict: Some items can not be returned, and others must be returned within 10 days.
Compaq *compaq.com*	○	◐	○	●	This site is fairly easy to navigate. Individual product descriptions are easy to grasp, but the limited information they offer may prove insufficient for customers who want detailed specifications. Somewhat confusing privacy policy and a restrictive return policy are two drawbacks.
Dell *dell.com*	○	○	○	●	This site offers a large selection of Dell and third-party products. Clear-cut browsing categories make it easy to know whether you want to look further. Fairly extensive support for Dell products is available. A visit offers a satisfying shopping experience.
Gateway *gateway.com*	●	○	●	●	Easy to navigate, with a lucid design, this site is notable for its large selection of Gateway and third-party products. User-friendly features include a comparison tool to evaluate similar products side by side. There is plenty of helpful buying advice as well as useful links to customer and magazine reviews, related products, and accessories.
Hewlett-Packard *shopping.hp.com*	○	○	○	○	With a simple sleek design, a visit here offers a satisfying experience. But some sections do not appear to be fully integrated, making it confusing to navigate at times.
IBM *ibm.com*	○	○	◑	○	A very good security policy. Unlike all the other sites in this category, computers in the consumer-oriented section could not be customized.

Electronic gear

WEB SITE	OVERALL SCORE	POLICIES	USABILITY	CONTENT	COMMENTS
Amazon *amazon.com*	●	○	●	●	There is a large selection of products here, as well as product information and links to order the appropriate batteries.
BestBuy *bestbuy.com*	○	◐	○	○	This site offers a fairly wide selection of electronic gear, but its privacy policy is confusing. Searching and ordering are clear but the design is cluttered and hard to read.
Circuit City *circuitcity.com*	●	●	●	●	A large selection, helpful product information, and side-by-side comparisons are offered at this site. Items purchased online can be returned to a local store.
Crutchfield *crutchfield.com*	●	●	●	●	This site has consumer-friendly policies, including free shipping for returns. There is a helpful tool to select car audio components, and many useful features that incorporate interactive technology.
J & R Music and Computer World *jandr.com*	●	●	○	●	This site has easy to locate policies, a price matching offer, and a huge selection of products. There is also a useful glossary of terminology for those who are less familiar with today's high-tech jargon. But the design is busy and some text is difficult to read.
Radio Shack *radioshack.com*	○	◐	○	●	A poor privacy policy. The site offers a moderate amount of electronic gear compared to others in this category, but it does offer a specialized selection of electronic components not offered elsewhere.
The Sharper Image	○	○	●	○	The site offers easy to locate policies, a price matching offer, efficient browsing, and some fun interactive features—but only a moderate amount of electronic gear compared to others in this category.

PRODUCTS continued

Health & beauty

WEB SITE	OVERALL SCORE	POLICIES	USABILITY	CONTENT	COMMENTS
Drugstore.com drugstore.com	○	○	○	◐	This site has a very large selection of brands and products, customer reviews, and ingredient lists for some products. There are interactive worksheets for personalized health advice, and a shopping list for storing and reordering favorite products. The browsing and search features need improvement.
ibeauty.com Ibeauty.com	○	○	◐	○	You'll find a limited selection of high-end beauty brands and products. Its excellent shipping policy is offset by inefficient and incomplete browsing and searching features.
Sephora.com sephora.com	●	●	○	●	Very good shipping and return policies, easy browsing, product-ingredient lists, and a huge selection of high-end beauty and personal-care lines make this site stand out. There are also interactive features, such as a gift adviser and wireless shopping with a web-enabled cell phone.
Vitamin Shoppe vitaminshoppe.com	○	○	●	○	An excellent search feature and sensible browsing categories make this site easy to use. A large selection of health and nutritional products is available, but there aren't many extras.
Walgreens walgreens.com	○	○	◐	●	Although this site offers a large number of brands and products as well as many helpful extras, the privacy policy, search feature, and ordering process could all use improvement.

House & home

WEB SITE	OVERALL SCORE	POLICIES	USABILITY	CONTENT	COMMENTS
Chef's Catalog chefscatalog.com	○	○	○	○	This site has thorough product descriptions, and is easy to browse. But the search engine isn't always smart.
The Company Store thecompanystore.com	●	○	●	●	Good organization makes it easy to browse and search for products at this site. A Comforter Guide and other useful features enhance the shopping experience.
Crate & Barrel crateandbarrel.com	●	○	●	●	This site is organized well, product descriptions and information are thorough, and browsing is easy. There are some useful special features, including a gift planner (that inclues a reminder service and address book), a gift finder, and a gift registry, that enhance the shopping experience.
Domestications domestications.com	○	●	○	○	There is a very good security policy on this site. Browsing for bedding by theme is a useful option, but the search feature has some glitches.
Lillian Vernon lillianvernon.com	○	○	○	○	The categories for browsing are sensible and easy to navigate. The search engine is adequate, with matches that are generally sensible, making for an efficient shopping experience.
Martha Stewart marthastewart.com	○	○	●	○	This site is organized well with easy navigation and browsing. Product descriptions and information are thorough and include a small photo that can be enlarged. There are no special features to enhance the shopping experience.
Target.com target.com	○	○	●	○	Easy-to-find policies, thorough product descriptions and information, easy browsing and navigation, and a few special features make for an efficient shopping experience.

Office & mailing supplies

Better ◐ ◑ ○ ◒ ● Worse

WEB SITE	OVERALL SCORE	POLICIES	USABILITY	CONTENT	COMMENTS
FedEx fedex.com	○	○	○	◑	A very good privacy policy, a clear-cut design, and sensible browsing categories make this an efficient site.
Levenger levenger.com	○	○	○	◑	Aside from the fact that this site offers a larger inventory than any single Levenger catalog, the shopping experience is generally unexceptional.
Office Depot officedepot.com	○	○	○	◑	A large selection of office supplies, interactive features, and links to business services, make for a satisfying office experience. Browsing is well organized.
OfficeMax officemax.com	◑	◑	○	◑	This site offers a very good security policy and a low-price guarantee. A large selection of office supplies, a variety of business services, buying guides, free e-mail, and more make for a well-rounded shopping experience.
Staples staples.com	◑	○	◑	◑	Easy navigation and a clear-cut ordering process make shopping this site's large inventory a stress-free operation. Special features include links to business services, a business community, an online business forum, and dividend programs for small businesses.
USPS.com usps.com	○	◒	○	◑	The online arm of the United States Postal Service has confusing policies and no search feature. However, the design is clear-cut and browsing is well organized. For buying stamps or other postal products, this site provides a satisfying experience.

Pet supplies

WEB SITE	OVERALL SCORE	POLICIES	USABILITY	CONTENT	COMMENTS
allpets.com allpets.com	○	◑	○	○	A very good privacy policy, helpful resources for pet owners, and a lively community section can be found here. On the downside, this site can be tedious to search, and the product selection is not as large as other sites in this category.
J and J Dog Supplies JandJdog.com	○	○	○	○	A very good privacy policy. This site offers a small, specialized inventory of dog-training equipment that is generally not found on other sites reviewed in this category. There is not much offered in the way of interactive web technologies.
Petco Petco.com	◑	◑	○	◑	Very good privacy and a wide variety of products make this site stand out. There's also an enourmous amount of pet-related information, including articles on grooming, nutrition, training, and more. The site features a community section with pet-specific message boards and clubs.
PetFoodDirect.com petfooddirect.com	◑	◑	◑	◑	A flexible search feature makes it easy to find your pet's favorite brand of food among the many that are offered here. The large selection of pet supplies and helpful information for pet owners, including a discussion on holistic pet care and the free Ask the Vet e-mail service, also make this site stand out.
Pet Planet petplanet.com	○	◑	◒	○	This site can sometimes be confusing and tedious to navigate. Interesting features include a pet care library and a calendar that lists local pet-related events, but a potentially useful local business search returned very few results when we tried out the feature.
PetSmart petsmart.com	◑	○	○	◐	Despite a busy design, this site is fairly easy to use, with a wide range of pet supplies offered. There's an enormous amount of pet-related information and advice, including a food calculator and comparison tools that allow customers to determine how much to feed their cats and dogs, as well as to compare the ingredients in food products.

SPECIAL SECTION E-RATINGS

PRODUCTS *continued*

Small appliances

WEB SITE	OVERALL SCORE	POLICIES	USABILITY	CONTENT	COMMENTS
J & R Music and Computer World *jandr.com*	◐	◐	○	◐	Although usability needs some improvement, a large selection of products, the ability to sort products by price and product name, and links to appliance accessories make this site worthwhile.
Kmart *bluelight.com*	○	○	○	○	Kmart's site on the Internet offers a respectable selection of small appliances, and provides a description of key product features. The main categories for browsing are generally sensible and the search feature is adequate.
Sears.com *sears.com*	○	○	○	○	This site offers a low-price guarantee and most items purchased online can be returned to local Sears stores. There is useful product information, as well as cleaning and maintenance tips.
Wal-Mart Online *walmart.com*	◐	◐	◐	○	Efficient browsing, good product information, and special features such as an address book, personal shopping list, and a photo center make for a satisfying shopping experience.

Software

WEB SITE	OVERALL SCORE	POLICIES	USABILITY	CONTENT	COMMENTS
Adobe.com *adobe.com*	◐	◐	○	◐	Adobe's web and print publishing software are available at this site, accompanied by thorough product descriptions. There are also technical guides, tutorials, and some free downloads, including the Adobe Acrobat Reader.
McAfee.com *mcafee.com*	○	◐	○	◐	The McAfee web site has a very good security policy and is fairly easy to navigate. Virus protection and PC security software are available, as well as a support center, message boards, manuals, and detailed product information.
Microsoft *microsoft.com*	○	○	○	◐	This site offers a selection of Microsoft software, hardware, and books. Although you can have a generally satisfying shopping experience here, it's unexceptional compared with other sites in this category.
Symantec.com *symantec.com*	○	○	◐	○	This site has a very good security policy and is fairly easy to navigate. Virus protection and Internet security software are available, as well as the latest news on computer viruses.

SPECIAL SECTION E-RATINGS

Sports & camping

Better ● ◖ ○ ◐ ● Worse

WEB SITE	OVERALL SCORE	POLICIES	USABILITY	CONTENT	COMMENTS
Cabela's *cabelas.com*	○	○	○	◖	This site has an extensive selection of hunting and fishing gear, a web bargain area, and useful links. It's easy to browse through products, and the privacy policy is very good.
Fogdog.com *fogdog.com*	○	○	○	◖	Fogdog.com offers a lot of useful product information, including buying guides, feature articles, customer reviews, and athlete's advice. It has a return policy.
Orvis *orvis.com*	○	○	○	○	This site sells clothing, home items and sporting goods with a focus on fly-fishing. Browsing for products is tedious and the search feature needs improvement.
Patagonia *patagonia.com*	○	◖	○	○	Patagonia specializes in high-tech sports clothing, and the site provides extensive product description. There is a very good privacy policy, but there are few special features to enhance the shopping experience.
REI *rei.com*	◖	◖	○	◖	This site has a vast selection of clothing and equipment for numerous sporting activities. It has easy-to-find policy statements and sensible browsing categories.
theSportsAuthority.com *thesportsauthority.com*	○	○	◖	○	There is a large selection of sporting goods offered here and an outlet for discounted items. But, not a lot of extra features to enhance the shopping experience.

Toys & games

WEB SITE	OVERALL SCORE	POLICIES	USABILITY	CONTENT	COMMENTS
eToys *etoys.com*	◖	○	◖	◖	This site offers a very large selection of toys but not a lot of detailed product information. Browsing can be somewhat cumbersome, but the detailed search and sorting features are good. Online orders can be returned to local K-B Toys stores.
Kbkids *kbkids.com*	◖	○	◖	◖	This well-organized site offers a rather efficient shopping experience, along with some special interactive features. Toys can be sorted by price and other criteria, and online orders can be returned to local K-B Toys stores.
Nintendo of America *nintendo.com*	○	○	○	◖	This site offers replacement parts and accessories for all Nintendo games and systems. The ordering process is straightforward, but subcategory lists can be quite lengthy, with no helpful way to sort products.
Toys "R" Us *amazon.com*	◖	○	◖	●	There is a wide selection of toys here, with helpful categories for browsing, and good product information. There are many useful interactive features that enhance the shopping experience.
Wal-Mart Online *walmart.com*	◖	◖	◖	○	This site has a large selection of toys. Efficient browsing, good product information, and special features such as an address book, personal shopping list, and a photo center make for a satisfying experience.

SERVICES

Auctions

WEB SITE	OVERALL SCORE	POLICIES	USABILITY	CONTENT	COMMENTS
STANDARD AUCTION SITES These sites operate as an intermediary between independent buyers and sellers. Transactions are undertaken at your own risk; the site will not intervene in disputes.					
Amazon.com Auctions amazon.com/auctions	◐	○	◐	◐	This site provides a very satisfying and secure auction experience. There are many features that make bidding and listing items quite easy, including a tutorial for new users and tips for sellers.
AuctionAddict.com auctionaddict.com	○	○	◐	○	Although initially frustrating to navigate, this site offers a wide range of auction listings and several helpful features, including free e-mail and a community center for auction news and discussions.
Biddington's biddingtons.com	○	◐	○	◐	Biddington's specializes in contemporary art, antiques, and fine-arts auctions. The policies are difficult to find and confusing, but the site is fairly easy to navigate and offers a large number of auction listings.
eBay ebay.com	⊙	⊙	⊙	⊙	Reasonable policies and very well-organized listings, as well as many helpful features, make eBay the outstanding site in this category. Navigation is easy, and there are discussion boards, news, articles on collecting and various auction categories, and many more features too numerous to list.
Sothebys.com sothebys.com	◐	◐	⊙	◐	This site specializes in traditional fine and decorative art, jewelry, and books. The policies are very clear and the site is very easy to use. Lots of informative articles and guides make this one of the most interesting sites in this category.
SportsAuction.com sportsauction.com	◐	◐	◐	◐	This site specializes in sports memorabilia, including trading cards, sports art, and autographed collectibles. There are very good privacy and return policies. Navigation is easy and there are many helpful features.
uBid.com ubid.com	○	○	○	◐	Consumer Exchange Auctions, Vendor Exchange Auctions, and UBid's own auctions make up the majority of those available on this site. However, these auctions are not well integrated, making browsing somewhat inefficient.
Yahoo! Auctions http://auctions.yahoo.com	◐	◐	◐	◐	This site offers a large number of items in a wide range of categories. The site is easy to use and has very reasonable policies. It also offers charity auctions, a black-list feature, category clubs, and more.
RETAILER SITES These sites feature an auction option for purchasing new or reconditioned merchandise, and they usually have a return policy.					
JCPenney auction.jcpenney.com	○	○	◐	○	This site features merchandise from JCPenney overstock, and includes women's, men's, and children's clothing and accessories, as well as home and leisure products. The site is easy to use and has a very good security policy.
The Sharper Image http://auction.sharperimage.com	◐	◐	○	◐	This site offers a selection of overstocked Sharper Image products, including gadgets for the home, garden, and office, and personal-care products. There are also one-of-a-kind items and collectibles. The site is easy to use and has several useful features for placing bids.
AUCTION SEARCH ENGINE This site pores over dozens of online auctions simultaneously to locate desirable items.					
AuctionWatch.com auctionwatch.com	○	○	○	◐	This unique site allows registered users to efficiently search and/or set up auctions at several sites at once. AuctionWatch.com is fairly easy to use and provides much helpful information.

CONSUMER REPORTS DIGITAL BUYING GUIDE • 93

TRAVEL SITES

Airlines, domestic

Better ◐ ○ ◑ ● Worse

WEB SITE	OVERALL SCORE	POLICIES	USABILITY	CONTENT	COMMENTS
American Airlines aa.com	○	○	○	○	Searching for and booking flights at this site is a reasonably efficient process. But browsing can be tedious and the privacy policy is unsatisfactory.
Delta Air Lines delta.com	○	○	○	○	The flight search process at this site is reasonably efficient. Information of flight status is available for wireless device customers.
Northwest Airlines nwa.com	◐	◐	◐	◐	Searching for flights is especially effective here, and there are extensive opportunities for personalization, including the ability to track fares, monitor frequent-flyer miles for all airlines, and store itineraries. This site stands out compared with others in this category.
Southwest Airlines southwest.com	○	◐	○	○	Searching for and booking flights at this site is an efficient process, but limited opportunities for personalization and the lack of an e-mail address for communication with Southwest may leave customers feeling dissatisfied.
United Airlines united.com	○	○	○	◐	Although easy to navigate, this site is a mixed bag when it comes to searching for flights. There are helpful options for selecting and sorting flights based on numerous criteria, but you won't find the cost of a roundtrip flight until you piece together the legs of departing and return flights.
US Airways usairways.com	○	○	○	○	Although you can have a generally satisfying experience here, searching for flights is an inefficient process. You won't find out the cost of a roundtrip flight until you piece together the legs of departing and return flights.

Airlines, foreign

WEB SITE	OVERALL SCORE	POLICIES	USABILITY	CONTENT	COMMENTS
AeroMexico aeromexico.com	◑	●	◑	○	There is no privacy policy information in the booking section of this site. Booking is somewhat tedious for U.S. customers. Some brief information on destinations is provided, but very little to recommend this site overall.
Air Canada aircanada.ca	○	●	○	◐	The privacy policy is confusing, and booking a flight is a somewhat lengthy process. The site offers detailed information on destinations, weather, travel tips, and more.
Air France airfrance.com/us	○	◐	◑	○	Although policies are very good at this site, the flight-search process can be inefficient. You must register and enter a personal profile before you can book a flight.
Air Jamaica airjamaica.com	◑	●	◐	○	This site provides only brief traveller information and site destination guides. However, the flight searching and booking process takes place through Expedia.com, and is basically a smooth, hassle-free experience.
British Airways britishairways.com	○	○	◑	○	This site offers extensive information on the terms and conditions for booking online. But the flight-search process is limited, and browsing can be somewhat inefficient.
Japan Airlines japanair.com	◑	◐	●	◑	Browsing the site can be confusing, and actual booking takes place through Travelocity.com. Few special features or helpful tools were found.
KLM nwa.com	◐	◐	◐	◐	KLM's partner in the United States is Northwest Airlines. All online activity for U.S.-based users of KLM's site is conducted via the Northwest Airlines site.
Lufthansa lufthansa-usa.com	○	○	○	○	Policy information is very difficult to find here, although the site does have a very good privacy policy. This site is fairly easy to navigate, but you must register before you can book a flight.

SPECIAL SECTION E-RATINGS

TRAVEL SITES *continued*

Airlines, low-fare

WEB SITE	OVERALL SCORE	POLICIES	USABILITY	CONTENT	COMMENTS
AirTran Airways airtran.com	◐ red	○	◐ red	◐ red	A very good privacy policy. Browsing is easy, and booking a flight is a fairly straightforward process. The special deals and programs offered are a plus.
Frontier Airlines frontierairlines.com	◐	◐	◐	○	This site has a confusing privacy policy and a cluttered design. Also, there are few extras offered here compared to other sites in this category.
JetBlue Airways jetblue.com	◐ red	◐ red	◐ red	⊙ red	Easy-to-find policy information, a user-friendly design, and an easy-to-use booking process make this site stand out among others in this category. There are also many fun and useful extras, including virtual aircraft tours, in-depth destination information, and special discounts.
Spirit Airlines spiritair.com	○	◐	○	○	Policies are a mixed bag. In general, the site is fairly easy to use, but some category headings are unclear, and the lack of a Help or FAQ page can make navigating this site a frustrating experience.

Car rentals

WEB SITE	OVERALL SCORE	POLICIES	USABILITY	CONTENT	COMMENTS
Alamo alamo.com	◐ red	◐ red	◐ red	⊙ red	This site stands out with its easy navigation and booking, thorough vehicle descriptions, detailed information on insurance and rental contracts, and very good policies. You don't need a credit card to book online; just print the confirmation statement and bring it to the rental counter.
Avis avis.com	○	○	○	◐ red	This site has a very good privacy policy and a thorough FAQ section, along with easy browsing and flexible booking. Useful customer service features include a mechanism for tracking awards and researching Avis travel partners.
Budget budget.com	○	◐	○	◐ red	Browsing and booking are easy here. There's an interesting Tips & Guidance section and online booking discounts are offered, but the privacy policy is poor.
Hertz hertz.com	○	◐	○	◐ red	Browsing is efficient at this site, and there are some useful customer-service features. But the booking process could use some improvement, the privacy and rental policies are poor, and "special offers" have numerous restrictions tied to them.
National nationalcar.com	◐	◐	●	○	Inefficient, convoluted browsing and booking can make for a frustrating experience at this site. Information on cancellations is buried, and the privacy policy is poor; there is no way for a customer to opt out of having personal information shared with third parties.

Cruise lines

Better ◐ ◑ ○ ◒ ● Worse

WEB SITE	OVERALL SCORE	POLICIES	USABILITY	CONTENT	COMMENTS
Carnival carnival.com	○	○	○	○	This site has a very good privacy policy. Although browsing and navigation are efficient, the booking process is limited in its usefulness.
Cruise411.com cruise411.com	○	○	○	○	Browsing this site is fairly easy, and a comparison tool lets you view cruise features side-by-side. There is a lack of specific information on the destinations and ports of call.
i-cruise.com i-cruise.com	◑	○	◑	◑	A very good privacy policy. This site provides detailed information on cabins and cruise itineraries. But customer service is hard to find, which can make for a frustrating experience
mytravelco.com mytravelco.com	○	◑	○	○	A very good privacy policy. Booking is available for most major cruise lines, but the search feature needs improvement and requesting information about cruises can be tedious
Norwegian Cruise Lines ncl.com	◑	○	○	◑	This site has a very good privacy policy, a detailed cancellation policy, easy browsing, and a thorough booking process. The wealth of detailed, useful, and well-linked information on boats, cruises and destinations, along with some special interactive features, really make this site stand out.
Princess Cruises princesscruises.com	◒	◒	◒	○	Navigation and browsing are easy. You cannot book cruises on this site, but you can get ideas. There are some interactive features that may make it worth a visit.
Royal Caribbean International royalcaribbean.com	◑	○	◑	◑	Navigation and booking are fairly easy. There is a lot of useful information about boats, destinations and more on this site.

Hotels, moderate

WEB SITE	OVERALL SCORE	POLICIES	USABILITY	CONTENT	COMMENTS
Choice Hotels choicehotels.com	○	○	◑	○	Efficient browsing, searching, and booking, plus extensive hotel information and a discount for booking online, really make this site stand out.
Hilton hilton.com	◒	◒	◒	◒	Inefficient browsing and booking and limited location-specific descriptions, especially about pricing, make it difficult to select a particular hotel for further investigation.
Hyatt hyatt.com	◒	◒	◒	◒	This site contains the basics—but little more. Superficial hotel and room descriptions plus inefficient browsing and booking can make for a frustrating experience.
Marriott International marriott.com	○	○	◒	◑	The tedious navigation here can be frustrating, but there is a wide range of hotel-room choices, plus maps, driving instructions, city facts and more. The personal profile feature is useful for repeat bookings.

CONSUMER REPORTS DIGITAL BUYING GUIDE • 95

SPECIAL SECTION E-RATINGS

TRAVEL SITES *continued*

Hotels, upscale

WEB SITE	OVERALL SCORE	POLICIES	USABILITY	CONTENT	COMMENTS
Four Seasons fourseasons.com	○	○	◐	⊖	Browsing can be fairly tedious here, but efficient booking and extensive information on spa programs, golf courses, and dining make this site worth the visit.
Renaissance Hotels, Resorts, and Suites renaissancehotels.com	○	○	◐	⊖	Limited navigational menus can be annoying, but this site offers useful, descriptive information for each of the hotel properties.
Ritz-Carton ritzcarlton.com	○	○	○	○	Although the privacy policy is less than satisfactory, this well-organized site is easy to browse via a constant main menu and a simple, neat design.
Westin westin.com	○	◐	⊖	⊖	The privacy policy is unsatisfactory, but a quick search feature and extensive hotel information (including a 360-degree virtual tour of some hotels) are a few of this site's good points.

Railways

WEB SITE	OVERALL SCORE	POLICIES	USABILITY	CONTENT	COMMENTS
Amtrak amtrack.com	○	○	○	○	A confusing privacy policy. This site is easy to browse, and the booking process is straightforward.
Rail Europe raileurope.com	◐	◐	●	⊖	There are several helpful tools at this site, but both browsing and booking a trip can be fairly tedious.
VIA Rail Canada viarailcanaca.com	○	○	○	⊖	This site offers extensive information about destinations, routes, and services. However, booking can be a lengthy process.

Theme parks

WEB SITE	OVERALL SCORE	POLICIES	USABILITY	CONTENT	COMMENTS
Anheuser-Busch Adventure Parks 4adventure.com	○	◐	○	○	This site is easy to navigate via sensible browsing categories with information on parks, including ride specs and schedules. It's easy to order tickets and merchandise, but a more straight-forward privacy policy would be a welcome addition.
Disney Vacations disney.com/vacations	○	○	○	⊖	Colorful and well organized, this site's stand-out features include live web cam shots, 360° virtual tours, and interactive travel planners. Buying park tickets through the site is easy, but the browsing categories are not always sensibly organized, making navigation a bit confusing at times.
Six Flags sixflags.com	◐	○	◐	◐	A constant menu makes browsing fairly easy, but compared with other sites in this category, information is fairly limited. Only season passes are available for purchase online.
Universal Studios universalstudios.com/themeparks	○	○	○	⊖	A very good privacy policy. Browsing can be tedious, but this site provides almost all the information you need to plan a family vacation at Universal Studios.

PART 2

Systems Analysis

CHAPTER 7
Computing

CHAPTER 8
Picture These

CHAPTER 9
Sound Investments

CHAPTER 10
Ink to Paper

CHAPTER 11
Telephones

CHAPTER 12
Working in Comfort

Computers

DESKTOP COMPUTERS

Even the least expensive desktop machines deliver impressive performance. The quality of technical support may be the deciding factor for you.

The desktop computer has reached a level of acceptance accorded the TV set or refrigerator —just another appliance you use every day. Replacement sales—as opposed to first-time purchases—now drive the computer market. Prices continue to drop. Fully loaded desktop systems selling for less than $1,000, a novelty a few years ago, are now common, even among established brands.

What's available

There are dozens of companies vying to put a new desktop in your home. Dell, Gateway, Hewlett-Packard (which merged with Compaq in 2002), IBM, and Sony all make Windows machines. Another contender, eMachines, has emerged as a player over the past few years with a series of budget-priced Windows systems. Apple is the sole maker of Macintosh models. Small mail-order and store brands cater to budget-minded buyers.

   Price range: $500 to $2,500. (The monitor is often extra.)

Key features

The **processor** houses the "brains" of a computer. Its clock speed, measured in megahertz (MHz) or gigahertz (GHz), determines how fast the chip can process information. In general, the higher the clock speed, the faster the computer. But not always. In our tests, a computer with a 1.4-GHz chip outperformed a machine driven by a 2-GHz chip. Manufacturers of Windows machines generally use 1.2- to 2.5-GHz processors with one of the following names: Intel's Pentium 4 or Celeron, or AMD's Athlon XP or Duron. Celeron

99
Desktop computers

104
Laptop computers

107
Monitors

111
PDAs

and Duron are lower-priced processors that are equal to higher-priced chips in many respects. Apple's Macintosh machines use 700-MHz to 1-GHz PowerPC G4 processors, which are manufactured by Motorola. Apple has maintained that the system architecture of G4 PowerPC chips allows them to be as fast as or faster than Pentium 4s with higher clock speeds.

All name-brand computers sold today have at least 128 megabytes (MB) of RAM, or **random access memory,** the memory that the computer uses while in operation. **Video RAM,** also measured in megabytes, is secondary RAM essential for smooth video imaging and game play.

The **hard drive** is your computer's long-term data storage system. Given the disk-space requirements of today's multimedia games and video files, bigger is better. You'll find hard drives ranging in size from 20 to 120 gigabytes (GB).

A **CD-ROM drive** has been standard on most desktops for a number of years. Fast replacing it is **CD-RW** (CD-rewritable), which lets you create backup files or make music compilations. (See Chapter 4 for more.) **DVD-ROM** brings full-length movies or action-packed multimedia games with full-motion video to the desktop. It complements the CD-RW drive on higher-end systems, allowing you to copy CDs directly between the two. A DVD drive will also play CD-ROMs. The newest in this family is the **DVD-writer,** which lets you transfer home-video footage to a DVD disk. There are three competing, incompatible formats: DVD-RW, DVD+RW, and DVD-RAM.

The **diskette drive** is where 3.5-inch diskettes are inserted, allowing you to read or store data. Apple Macintoshes don't have one built in. The traditional capacity of a 3.5-inch diskette is 1.4 MB, too small for many purposes today, so many people use a CD-RW as a large "diskette" drive to transport files.

The computer's **cathode ray tube** (CRT) or flat-panel **liquid crystal display** (LCD) monitor contains the screen and displays the images sent from the **graphics board**—internal circuitry that processes the images. **Monitors** come in sizes (measured diagonally) ranging from 15 inches to 21 inches and larger. Seventeen-inch monitors are the most common. Apple's iMac comes with a built-in monitor. For more on monitors, see page 107.

The critical components of a desktop computer are usually housed in a case called a **tower.** A **minitower** is the typical configuration. More expensive machines have a **midtower,** which has extra room for upgrades. A **microtower** is a space-saving alternative that is usually less expensive. The Apple iMac has no tower; everything but the keyboard and mouse is built into a small case that supports the monitor. Apple's Power Mac line of computers has a tower.

A **mouse,** a small device that fits in your hand and has a "tail" of wire that connects to the computer, moves the cursor (the pointer on the screen) via a rolling ball on the underside of the mouse. Alternatives include a mouse that replaces the ball with a light sensor; a trackball, which is rolled with the fingers or palm in the direction the user wants the cursor to go; a pad, which lets you move the cursor by sliding a finger; and a joystick, used to play computer games.

All computers come with a **standard keyboard,** although you can also buy one separately. Many keyboards have **CD (or DVD) controls** to pause playback, change tracks, and so on. Many also have keys to facilitate getting online, starting a search, or retrieving e-mail.

Multimedia computers for home use feature a **high-fidelity sound system** that can play music from CDs or downloaded music files, synthesized music, game sounds, and DVD-movie soundtracks. **Speaker systems** with a subwoofer have deeper, more powerful bass. Some PCs come with a **microphone** for recording, or one can be added.

You can expect a new computer to include a modem rated for 56 kilobits per second (kbps). This **speed rating** refers to how

CUSTOMIZATION AND COST

The biggest manufacturers—Compaq, Dell, Gateway, HP, and IBM—let you configure a desktop computer just the way you want. Their web sites typically present menus with step-up and step-down choices. You can also place your order over the telephone. Large retailers such as Best Buy, Circuit City, CompUSA, and Staples may have in-store kiosks that let you do a certain amount of customizing. The table below shows where you might start for a basic level of desktop computer, along with our recommendations for upgrades and downgrades.

COMPONENT	BASIC LEVEL	UPGRADE?	DOWNGRADE?
Processor	1.5 GHz	2.4 GHz. **For:** Faster speed to handle the most demanding applications. **Add:** $250	1 GHz. **For:** Basic business applications, e-mail, etc. **Save:** $100.
RAM memory	256 MB	512 MB. **For:** Editing very large files or graphics; working with many applications at once. **Add:** $100 & up.	128 MB for using basic applications one or two at a time. **Save:** $50.
Hard-drive size	80 GB	120 GB. **For:** Digital video editing, working with large applications, storing large amounts of data. **Add:** $50.	40 GB. **For:** Basic business applications, e-mail, etc. **Save:** $50.
Rewritable CD	CD-RW, 16x write	CD-RW, 24x write. **For:** Faster backup, storage, copies of music, photos, etc. **Add:** $30.	CD-ROM only. **For:** Those with no interest in burning their own disks. **Save:** $50.
DVD-ROM	Reader	DVD writer. **For:** Creating video DVDs to play on other players. **Add:** $300.	No DVD. **For:** People who aren't videophiles. **Save:** $60.
Graphics card	64 MB of video RAM	High-end card, 128 MB of video RAM. **For:** Smoothest, fastest performance on action games. **Add:** $80.	32 MB of video RAM. **For:** Word processing, Internet, many games. **Save:** $30.
Sound card	Analog	Surround. **For:** Driving back speakers for DVDs and some games. **Add:** $40	Not recommended.
Loudspeakers	Two-piece name brand	Three-piece with subwoofer. **For:** Better bass. **Add:** $30 and up.	Two-piece generic. **For:** Those with little interest in hi-fi music on computer. **Save:** $20.
Case	Minitower	Midtower. **For:** Extra room for upgrades. **Add:** $30.	Microtower or all-in-one unit. **For:** Those with limited office space. **Save:** $40.
Software	Simplified suite such Microsoft Works	Professional package, such as Microsoft Office. **For:** Advanced word-processing, financial, database, and desktop publishing. **Add:** $100.	Makes sense only if you already have good, up-to-date applications.
Monitor	17-inch CRT	19-inch CRT or 15-inch LCD display. **For:** Games, elaborate web sites. **Add:** $150 and up.	15-inch CRT. **For:** Word-processing, other basic functions. **Save:** $50.

ANATOMY OF A DESKTOP COMPUTER

The basic building blocks of a desktop computer are a CRT monitor, a keyboard, a tower that houses critical components, such as the processor and speakers. A port such as a USB port allows a printer to be attached. Digital camcorders, digital cameras, and other pieces of equipment attach to a firewire port (not shown).

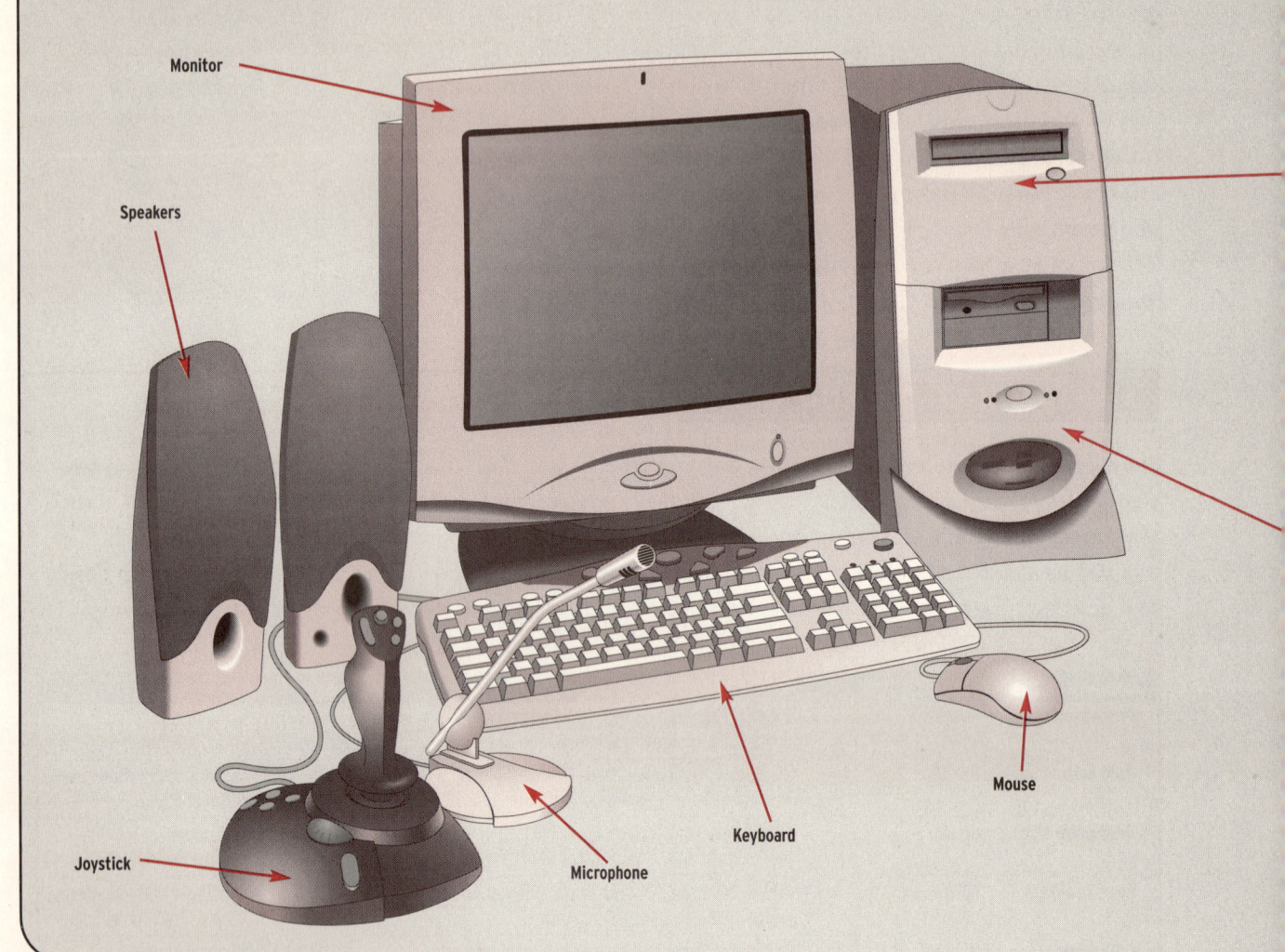

Labels: Monitor, Speakers, Joystick, Microphone, Keyboard, Mouse

quickly information travels to your modem from the Internet, although the speed is limited by federal rules to 53 kbps. In actual practice, however, the speed rarely exceeds 50 kbps. Faster ways to connect to the Internet include cable modem, DSL (digital subscriber line), and satellite. See Chapter 1 for more information.

Parallel and **serial ports** are the traditional connection sites for printers and scanners. **USB (universal serial bus) ports,** seen on all new computers, are designed to replace parallel and serial ports. **FireWire** or **IEEE 1394 ports** are used to capture video from digital camcorders and other electronic equipment. An Ethernet, Phoneline, or wireless **network** lets you link several computers in the household to share files, a printer, or an Internet connection. An **S-video output jack** lets you run video cables from the computer to a TV,

Drive bays

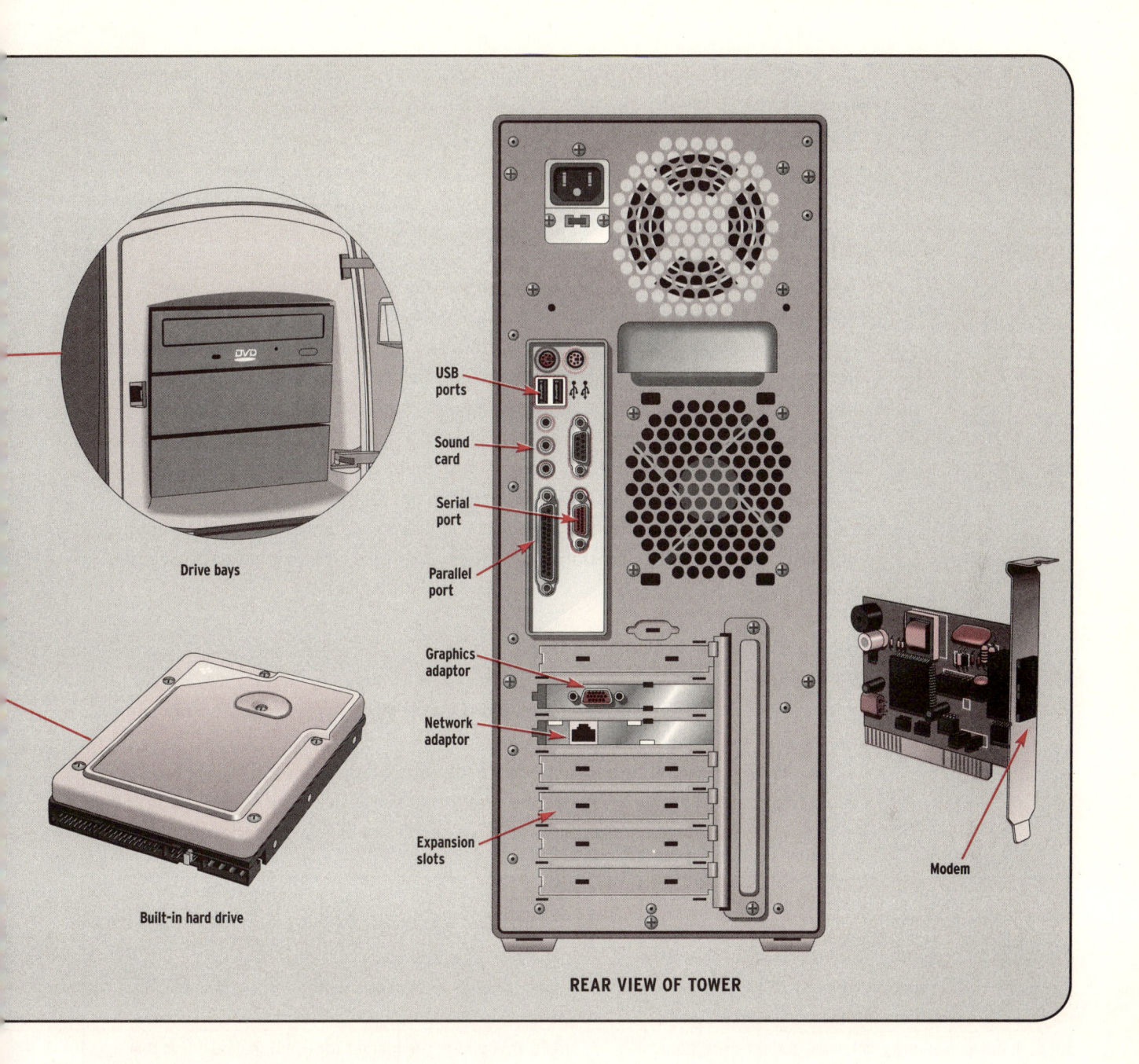

Built-in hard drive

USB ports
Sound card
Serial port
Parallel port
Graphics adaptor
Network adaptor
Expansion slots

Modem

REAR VIEW OF TOWER

which allows you to use the computer's DVD drive and view a movie on a TV instead of on the computer monitor.

How to choose

PERFORMANCE DIFFERENCES. CONSUMER REPORTS regularly tests computers. Judged on performance alone, most desktop computers are closely matched and extremely good overall. But we have found differences in reliability (frequency of repair), connectivity, expandability, the design of the keyboard and controls, and the sound of the loudspeakers. Some manufacturers are better than others at providing support to consumers with problems.

RECOMMENDATIONS. You'll have to decide between Windows and Macintosh. Windows has the advantage for its sheer number of compatible software applications and peripheral devices. Macintosh has the edge for its ease of setup and use.

◆ **Ratings:** page 163

LAPTOP COMPUTERS

A long-time companion at work, school, and on the road, the laptop is proving its mettle as a replacement or backup for a home's desktop computer.

Even as the pace of desktop computer sales slows, laptops are selling at an ever-increasing rate. It's not hard to understand why. Laptops now belong in the same league as desktop computers, thanks to brighter and larger displays, faster processors, and more efficient batteries. The thinnest laptops are only an inch or so thick and weigh only 3 to 5 pounds. To get these light, sleek models, you'll have to pay a premium and sacrifice some functionality.

A laptop makes an attractive choice as a replacement computer or the household's second machine. Laptops are already fixtures in classrooms and boardrooms. An advantage for a laptop is the growing availability of high-speed wireless Internet access at airports, schools, and hotels.

What's available

Dell, Gateway, Hewlett-Packard (which merged with Compaq in 2002), IBM, Sony, and Toshiba are the leading Windows laptop brands. Apple alone makes Macs. Laptops come in various configurations:

ALL-IN-ONE. These machines can do just about everything a desktop can. Sometimes called "three-spindle" machines because the hard drive, diskette drive, and CD-RW or DVD-ROM drive reside onboard, these models also have a full complement of jacks, connectors,

MICROPROCESSOR 101: IS INTEL INSIDE?

Critical to the operation of your computer, the micro-processor, or chip, controls how fast it crunches data and runs software. You'll see it listed first in a computer's specs in advertisements, catalogs, and on store signs.

Marketing might has made Intel as important a player as the computer manufacturers themselves. Its microprocessors are in a majority of Windows-based PCs. The Pentium 4, introduced in 2000, succeeds the Pentium III at the top of its microprocessor line. The latest generation is available in speeds of 1.2 to 2.53 GHz. Celeron, Intel's line of chips designed for the value-minded home user, debuted in 1998 and now has speeds up to 1.7 GHz.

Intel's main competitor, AMD, took a big marketing leap in 1999 with the introduction of its Athlon chip, now available in speeds from 1.4 to 1.8 GHz. Hewlett-Packard and other computer makers use them.

Chip choices in Windows laptops. The choice of chips for Windows-based laptop PCs has expanded in recent years. If you're in the market for a laptop, you'll find the following chips available: Pentium 4-M processors from 1.4 to 2 GHz, Pentium III mobile processors in speeds of 650 MHz to 1.2 GHz, and Celeron mobile processors in speeds of 500 to 1.2 GHz. AMD's mobile offerings are its Athlon 4 chip, at 1 GHz to 1.4 GHz, and its Duron chip at 900 GHz to 1.2 MHz.

Chip choices in Macs. Driving Apple's Macintosh desktop machines are 700-MHz to 1-GHz PowerPC G4 processors, made by Motorola. Apple's PowerBook laptops run on a G4 processor at speeds of 667 to 800 MHz, while its iBook laptop has a 600- to 700-MHz G3.

and expansion slots for PC cards. But they're the biggest and heaviest, measuring 1¾ inches thick and weighing 7 to 8 pounds. The keyboard is full-size, and the screen measures 14 to 15 inches diagonally. Some models can hold a second battery for increased running time, and others can shed drives to reduce size and weight. With a docking station, you can easily turn an all-in-one model into a desktop stand-in.

So-called reduced-legacy laptops from brands including Apple and IBM are similar to all-in-ones but lack a diskette drive. ("Legacy" refers to components, including the diskette drive, whose use dates back to the earliest desktop computers.) With reduced-legacy laptops, you can use a CD writer or a network for transferring files. Price range for all-in-ones: $1,000 to $2,500.

MODULAR. These "two-spindle" units come with a hard drive and space for either a diskette drive, CD-RW, combo CD-RW/DVD-ROM drive, or second battery. They're considerably slimmer than all-in-one models—about 1 to 1½ inches thick—and weigh 5 to 6 pounds. Drives can easily be swapped or left out to reduce weight, but some people find it inconvenient to swap drives regularly.

A modular model is easier to travel with than an all-in-one, provided you don't need to use all three drives at once. Other features of a modular laptop, including the keyboard and screen, are generally identical to those in an all-in-one. Some have smaller screens (12 or 13 inches). Price range: $1,200 to $2,500.

SLIM-AND-LIGHT. Especially good for traveling, these models measure about 1 inch thick and weigh 3 to 4 pounds. The case contains the hard drive and a smallish battery. The CD-ROM drive and the diskette drive are external, tethered to the laptop when need be. A port expander—a strip with jacks and connectors for printer, monitor, mouse, and the like—is also connected via cable. The screen may be only about 12 inches diagonally, and the keyboard may be small and somewhat hard to use. Price range: $1,800 to $2,500.

Key features

Laptops generally have a 1- to 1.8-gigahertz **processor** and a 20- to 40-gigabyte **hard drive.** Expect even faster processors and more capacious hard drives in the near future. Most models have 256 megabytes (MB) **of random access memory** (RAM) and can be upgraded to 512 MB or more.

Most of today's laptops use a rechargeable **lithium-ion battery.** In our tests, lithium-ion batteries provided about three hours of continuous use when running office applications. (Laptops go into sleep mode when used intermittently, extending the time between charges.) You can extend battery life somewhat by dimming the display as you work and by removing PC cards when they aren't needed. Playing a DVD movie devours battery power.

A laptop's **keyboard** can be quite different from that of a desktop computer. The keys themselves may be full-sized (generally only slim-and-light models pare them down), but they may not feel as solid. Some laptops have extra buttons to expedite your access to e-mail or a web browser.

LAPTOP CHOICES: WHAT DO YOU NEED?

The kind of laptop you need depends on how you'll use it. Here are three scenarios.

Commuter/student. *You carry a laptop to and from school or work, and on occasional trips.*

If power and comfort are most important, choose an all-in-one model or a reduced-legacy design, which is similar to an all-in-one but lacks a diskette drive. If price matters most, choose an all-in-one machine with a passive-matrix display or an active-matrix model that has been discontinued by the manufacturer but is still being sold. If you want a light but practical machine for travel, get a modular model that can accept either a drive or spare battery in one bay and that has a built-in Ethernet port that lets you connect to a network. Be sure the laptop you choose has these basics: an 800-MHz processor for Windows or a 600-MHz processor for Macintosh, 128 MB of RAM, and a 10- to 20-GB hard drive. Also consider getting a 14- to 15-inch display and a docking station or a plug for a port replicator (an attachment with connections for peripherals). Expect to pay $1,300 to $2,200.

Home user. *You use the laptop mostly at home, possibly in addition to a desktop computer. When traveling, performance and comfort are important.*

Consider an all-in-one or reduced-legacy design that has these basics: a 1-GHz processor for Windows or 700-MHz processor for Macintosh, 256 MB of RAM, and a 20- to 30-GB hard drive. Also consider a 14- to 15-inch TFT active-matrix display and a docking station, or a plug for a port replicator (an attachment with connections for peripherals). Expect to pay $1,800 to $2,200.

Road warrior. *The laptop is a standard part of your travel gear, so size and weight are important considerations for you.*

Consider a slim-and-light model weighing 3 to 5 pounds with these basics: a 900-MHz processor for Windows or 700-MHz processor for Macintosh, 128 MB of RAM, and a 10- to 20-GB hard drive. Expect a smaller display—about 12 inches. Battery life isn't likely to exceed three hours. Plan to carry spare batteries or plug in often for a recharge. Expect to pay about $2,000 to $2,500.

A 12- to 15-inch **display,** measured diagonally, should suit many people. A 15-inch display is the biggest practical size; a few larger, heavier models have 16-inch displays. With liquid crystal display (LCD) monitors, the display size represents the actual viewing area you get. (By contrast, the viewing area is smaller than the measured display with traditional cathode ray tube monitors.) A resolution of 1,280 x 1,024 pixels (picture elements) is better for fine detail than 1,024 x 768, but may shrink screen objects. A thin-film transistor (TFT) active-matrix screen provides bright, crisp images.

Most laptops use a small **touch-sensitive pad** in place of a mouse—you drag your finger across the pad to move the cursor. You can also program the pad to respond to a "tap" as a "click," or to scroll as you sweep your index finger along the pad's right edge. An alternative pointing system, less preferred by our testers, uses a pencil-eraser-sized joy stick in the middle of the keyboard.

Laptops typically include two **PC-card slots** for expansion. You might want to add a **wireless- network card** or a **digital-camera memory card reader,** for example. Many laptops offer a connection for a **docking station,** a $100 or $200 base that makes it easy to connect an external monitor, keyboard, mouse, printer, or phone line.

Most laptops let you attach these devices anyway, without the docking station. At least one **USB port,** for easy hookup of, say, a printer, digital camera, or scanner, is standard. A **wired network (Ethernet) port** is common. Some models have a **FireWire port** for digital video transfer.

Laptops typically come with far less software than desktop computers, although almost all are bundled with a basic home-office suite (such as Microsoft Works) and a personal-finance package. The small speakers built into laptops often sound tinny, with little bass. Headphones or external speakers deliver much better sound.

How to choose

PERFORMANCE DIFFERENCES. In CONSUMER REPORTS tests, most laptop computers have performed solidly in many ways. But manufacturers still have to make trade-offs. Bigger and heavier models pack almost all the computing muscle of their desktop cousins, while slimmer and lighter ones sacrifice drive space for easy portability. Aside from size and weight, a major factor distinguishing laptops is battery performance. Some models run longer on a charge and have better power management than others.

RECOMMENDATIONS. Consider buying a little more laptop than you think you need, since upgrading a notebook can be difficult or impossible. While desktop computers often use interchangeable, off-the-shelf components, a laptop's parts are typically proprietary. Adding more RAM might be relatively easy, but installing a larger hard drive or upgrading a video card might be out of the question.

MONITORS

Prices are lower for larger CRT monitors and flat-panel LCD displays, meaning that a roomier screen—or more space on your desktop—is now within reach.

Call it the incredible shrinking workspace. Over the past few years, bulky monitors have all but overrun the tops of desks. Their screens, filled nearly to overflowing with icons, web pages, and digital photos, haven't fared much better. It has become clear that computer users need more real estate—on both their screens and their desks.

If a larger screen is a must, a 19-inch cathode ray tube (CRT) may be the answer. Prices have fallen so much in the past couple of years that you can find plenty in the $250-to-$500 range. If desk space is a priority, a flat-panel monitor with a thin liquid crystal display (LCD), similar to the display that comes with a laptop, can now be had for as little as $400 for the 15-inch size. To get the best of both worlds, you can buy a 17- or 18-inch flat-panel LCD monitor in the $650-to-$1,000 range.

Desktop computers and monitors are often sold as a package, though some people decide to hold on to their old monitor and others choose to buy a new monitor for their existing PC. When buying a desktop from a direct seller such as Dell or Gateway, you choose from a selection that includes basic monitors and higher-end versions.

What's available

Apple, Dell, Gateway, Hewlett-Packard (which merged with Compaq in 2002), IBM, and Sony all market their own brands of monitors for their PCs. In addition, you'll find monitors sold separately from brands such as CTX, Mitsubishi, NEC, Philips, Samsung, ViewSonic, and eMachines. Many brands of monitor are manufactured on an outsource basis.

CRTS. Most desktop monitors sold today are CRTs, typically ranging from 17 to 21 inches. Some CRTs have flattened, squared-off screens (not to be confused with flat-panel LCD screens) that reduce glare. The nominal image size—the screen size touted in ads—is generally based on the diagonal measurement of the picture tube, usually an inch larger than the viewable image size (VIS)—the image you see. Thus a 17-inch CRT has a 16-inch VIS. As a result of a class-action suit, an ad must also display a CRT's VIS, but to find it, you may have to squint at the fine print.

The bigger a CRT, the more room it takes up on your desk, but "short-depth" models shave an inch or more off the depth, which otherwise roughly matches the nominal screen size.

A 17-inch monitor, the most popular choice these days, has almost one-third more viewable area than the 15-inch version now vanishing from the market. The larger size is especially useful when you're surfing the Internet, playing video games, watching DVD movies, editing photos, or working in several windows. Price range: $150 to $450.

If you regularly work with graphics or sprawling spreadsheets, consider a 19-inch monitor. Its viewable area is one-fourth larger than a 17-inch screen's. A short-depth 19-inch model doesn't take up much more desktop space than a standard 17-inch. Price range for 19-inch: $250 to $550.

Aimed at graphics professionals, 20- and 21-inch models provide ample viewing area but gobble up desktop space. Price range: $500 to $800.

FLAT-PANEL LCDS. These monitors, which operate with analog or digital input or both, use a liquid-crystal display instead of a TV-style picture tube and take up much less desktop space than CRTs. For desktop use, they typically measure 15 inches diagonally and just a few inches deep and weigh 10 pounds or less, compared with 40 pounds for a 17-inch CRT and 50 pounds for a 19-inch CRT. LCDs with screens 17 inches or larger are available, but they are still somewhat pricey. Unlike with a CRT, the nominal and viewable image sizes of a flat-panel LCD are the same.

Flat-panel displays deliver a very clear image, but they have some inherent quirks. Their range of color is a bit more narrow than that of CRT monitors. And you have to view a flat-panel screen straight on; the picture loses contrast as you move off-center, except those models with a wider viewing angle. Fine lines may appear grainy. In analog mode, you have to tweak the controls to get the best picture.

Price range: 15-inch, $400 to $600. 17- and 18-inch, $650 to $1,000 and up.

Key features

A monitor's **resolution** refers to the number of picture elements, or pixels, that make up an image. More pixels mean finer details. Most monitors can display several resolutions, generally ranging from 640x480 to 1,600x1,200, depending on the monitor and graphics card. Many 15-inch flat-panel displays, however, have noticeable image degradation—images look smeared and less pleasing—when set at a resolution other than 1,024x768 pixels. The higher the resolution, the smaller the text and images, so more content fits on the screen. Bigger CRT screens can handle higher resolutions and display more information.

Dot pitch, measured in millimeters, refers to the spacing between a CRT's pixels. All else being equal, a smaller dot pitch produces a more detailed image, though that's no guarantee of an excellent picture. In general, avoid models with a dot pitch higher than 0.28 mm.

A CRT requires a high **refresh rate** (the number of times per second the image is redrawn on the screen) to avoid annoying image flicker. In general, you'll be more comfortable with a 17-inch monitor set at a refresh rate of at least 75 hertz (Hz) at the resolution you want. With a 19-inch monitor, you may need an 85-Hz rate to avoid eyestrain, especially at higher resolutions. While the refresh rate of a flat panel display is 60 or 75 Hz, its native resolution is 1,024x768, unless otherwise specified. Refresh rate isn't an issue with flat-panel displays.

Monitors have controls for **brightness** and **contrast.** Most of them also have controls for **color balance** (usually called color temperature), **distortion,** and such. Buttons activate onscreen controls and menus.

Bigger CRTs use a considerable amount of juice: about 100 watts for a typical 19-inch model, more than 80 watts for a 17-incher, and about 20 watts for a 15-inch flat-panel LCD, for example. Most monitors have a **sleep mode** that uses less than 3 watts when the computer is on but not in use.

CRTs can be designed with either a **shadow mask** or an **aperture grille,** and each has a distinctive look. A shadow mask, a perforated metal sheet, directs the beam emitted by electron guns arranged in a triangle so colors are composed of little dots of red, green, and blue. An aperture grille is a shadow mask in a CRT with the electron guns arranged in a horizontal row, which results in colors that are made up of little lines. View both types to see which you prefer. **Plug-and-play** capability makes adding a new monitor to an existing computer relatively easy. Some monitors include a **microphone,** integrated or separate **speakers,** or **composite video inputs** for viewing the output of a VCR or camcorder.

FLAT PANELS VS. CRT MONITORS

Because they rely on different technologies, flat panels and CRTs produce different images. A flat panel's squarish picture elements, or pixels, line up in rows and columns, producing images with a slightly grainy texture that's especially noticeable with text. Unless viewed straight on, they lose much of their contrast.

A CRT's pixels are illuminated differently, producing a softer image viewable from virtually any angle. Its images also have somewhat less contrast than those on a flat panel.

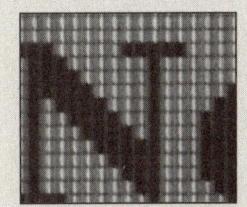

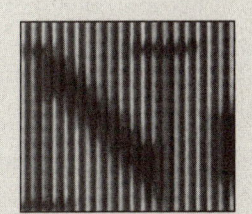

A close-up view of text produced by a flat-panel LCD monitor, left, and a CRT, right. The pixels on flat panels and CRTs are illuminated differently.

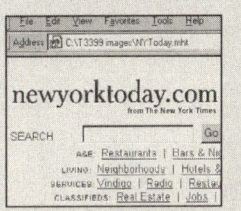

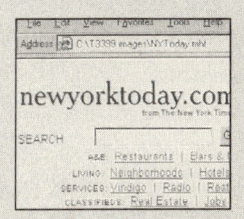

At normal viewing distance, the only obvious difference between a flat panel monitor, left, and a CRT is the flat panel's superior contrast.

NEW LIVES FOR OLD HARDWARE

The National Safety Council, an organization that promotes safety, estimates that some 300 million personal computers will become obsolete over the next five years. Only a small fraction will be recycled; the rest will add to the nation's mountain of solid waste.

Besides the bulk, there are toxic metals and compounds. Each cathode ray tube monitor contains about 4 pounds of lead, which shields users from radiation. Backup batteries contain mercury; circuit boards have cadmium; cables and casings use PVC plastics.

Several manufacturers have programs to take back used equipment. Dell either pays you for an old monitor or makes a donation to the National Cristina Foundation, a national group that matches donors of computer equipment and recipients (203-863-9100; *www.cristina.org*). Gateway pays up to $50 for proof that you've recycled a used PC at a reclamation center. For a fee, Hewlett-Packard and IBM accept computer equipment made by any manufacturer.

In 2000, Massachusetts became the first state to make the recycling of monitors and TVs (which also contain lead) mandatory and to forbid dumping them in the state's landfills. (The lead and other components are removed, reclaimed, and sometimes reused.)

Dozens of Goodwill stores and Salvation Army sites throughout Massachusetts receive equipment, which they refurbish and sell or have recycled. About a third of all Goodwill locations in the U.S. accept donations of desktop computers, but they may not take the very oldest models or nonworking machines.

In addition to those alternatives, you might also consider disposing of your old computer equipment through these other channels:

◆ Make a donation of a computer, monitor, or printer to a local school, house of worship, or charity.

◆ Contact Youth Build Boston, 617-445-8887, or Non-Profit Computing Inc., 212-759-2368. The latter organization takes donated hardware and finds new homes for it. They do not charge anything for the service.

◆ The Electronic Industries Alliance *(www.eiae.org)* lists state and local organizations that accept computer equipment, as well as 29 national programs.

You may not receive anything in return for your donations except, possibly, a tax deduction.

How to choose

PERFORMANCE DIFFERENCES. All 17-inch and 19-inch CRT monitors CONSUMER REPORTS has recently tested have at least very good display quality. Visibility differs, however. CRTs with flattened, squared-off screens may pick up fewer reflections, though not necessarily resulting in better display quality. Some CRTs have control buttons that are poorly labeled or on-screen controls that are difficult to use. Tilting is difficult with some models.

Most of the flat-panel LCDs we have tested have excellent display quality. Advantages over CRTs include compactness and lower power consumption.

RECOMMENDATIONS. Buy the right size for your task and work space. You may decide that the slim profile and power savings of a flat-panel monitor make the premium you'll pay worthwhile.

Try to view a monitor before buying it. At the store, look at a page of text to be sure both center and edges are bright and clear. Open up a picture file to see whether the colors look natural and clear. Compare monitors side-by-side, if possible, with the same image displayed on each screen.

Buying through mail order or the web won't let you see firsthand. If you aren't planning to buy from a bricks-and-mortar store, see if an acquaintance has the model you're considering or try to see it in a store. Wherever you buy, try to get a 30-day money-back guarantee.

Once you've bought a monitor, think about where you'll place it. You should sit 18 to 30 inches away, with the top line of text just below eye level. Good lighting and correct placement of the keyboard and mouse are also critical. See page 149 for more on home-office ergonomics.

◆ **Ratings:** page 167

PDAS

Besides keeping track of phone numbers, appointments, and things to do, many personal digital assistants can now deliver wireless access to the web and manage your e-mail.

The personal digital assistant, or PDA, seems to be showing up in everyone's hands. The dot-com CEO has one, naturally, but so does the dot-com gofer. The soccer mom uses one, and maybe her kids do, too. The college freshman is just as likely as the dean of students to have a PDA.

What all PDAs have in common—and why people buy them—is the ability to store and retrieve thousands of phone numbers, appointments, to-do chores, and notes. All models can exchange, or synchronize, information with a full-sized computer.

What's available

There are now nearly two dozen models on the market. Most are the now-familiar tablet with a stylus and squarish display screen, a design pioneered by Palm Inc. several years ago. Today the main choices are PDAs using the Palm operating system (Handera, Handspring, Palm, and Sony) and Pocket PC devices from Audiovox, Casio, and Hewlett-Packard that use a stripped-down version of Microsoft Windows. A few PDAs use a proprietary operating system.

Most PDAs can be made to work with both Windows and Macintosh computers, either out of the box, with an inexpensive adapter, or with third-party software. Most provide access to an abbreviated form of the Internet, most often with the addition of separately purchased accessories such as a modem. Some PDAs can record your voice, play videos, display digital photos, or hold maps, city guides, or a novel. Handspring, Kyocera, Nokia, and Samsung offer units that combine a cell phone and PDA.

PDAs allow information to be exchanged, or synchronized, with a desktop computer. To do that, you place the PDA on a cradle, or docking station, and press a button. The cradle connects directly to your desktop computer with a cable. For models that run on rechargeable batteries, the cradle doubles as the charger. Infrared technology can let you synchronize with a computer without wires or a cradle.

Many Palm OS PDAs run on AA batteries. These are the easiest to maintain. Many newer PDAs (both Palm and Pocket PC based) use rechargeable lithium-ion batteries. In

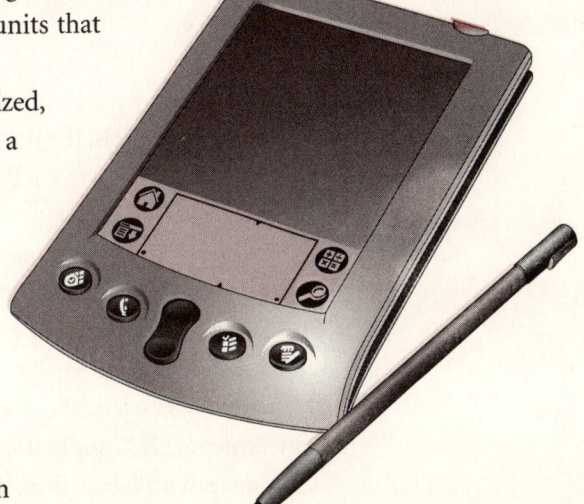

WHEN YOU HAVE A PROBLEM PC

Computers have a higher problem rate than most other products. Problems range from computers that are inoperable to missing components to mysterious error messages. CONSUMER REPORTS has put together a troubleshooting guide, available on Consumer Reports.org, that includes a set of self-help tips. Here are two common problems and strategies for solving them:

Problem: Your system is ohhhh-so-slooooow.

◆ You might need more RAM (random access memory). Take your computer owner's manual with you to a full-service computer retailer to help find and purchase the appropriate memory module(s) for your computer. Installing memory is usually easy enough to do yourself, or the retailer's service department can do it.

◆ Or your computer's hard drive may be fragmented. That's not as bad as it sounds, and it is easy to remedy in Windows; simply defrag your hard drive using the Disk Defragmenter utility that comes with Windows or use a faster one purchased separately, such as SpeedDisk, from Norton Utilities.

◆ If your Mac is operating slowly, you can rebuild your desktop, which helps the hard drive locate files. To do this, you need to have at least 5 percent of your hard drive free. First, turn off extensions through the Extensions Manager control panel. Then simultaneously hold down the Apple and Option keys while the system boots up. You will then see a dialog box that asks whether you want to rebuild the desktop. Click OK, and the system will take it from there.

◆ If none of the above solutions works, give the manufacturer a chance to fix the problem.

Problem: An important file has disappeared.

◆ If the file is a Word or Excel file, click on File. At the bottom of the pull-down menu you'll find a list of the last several files used.

◆ A feature called Windows Search can help you locate a stray file. From the Start menu, select Find or Search, then Files or Folders, then type in the name of the wayward file. Has the file name escaped you? Try Search's Advanced option, which will let you search by date, file type, or content.

◆ If you're using a Mac, click on File at the top of your screen. On the drop-down menu, click on either Find (in all older versions of the Mac OS) or Sherlock (the new advanced search engine in OS 8.5 and higher versions). This will find a lost file by name, size, date, or content.

The guide also lays out the most efficient and effective step-by-step procedures to follow to get retailers and manufacturers to fix a problem quickly. There is also information you may need to argue your case effectively, including the latest news about recalls, product reports and Ratings, and links to the text of applicable consumer-protection laws. You'll also find phone numbers and street and web addresses as well as letter templates to help you communicate with equipment manufacturers forcefully.

To access the guide, go to *www.ConsumerReports.org*, click on "Consumer Advice," then "Consumer Interest," and then "Help for problem PCs."

---

some of these models, the batteries are sealed inside the case and can only be replaced by the manufacturer. There are PDAs with removable rechargeable batteries, which are obviously more convenient.

PALM OS SYSTEMS. Equipped with software to link with Windows and Macintosh computers, Palm units and their clones are small and simple to operate. You use a stylus to enter data on these units by tapping on an onscreen keyboard or writing in a shorthand known as Graffiti. Or you can download keyed data from your computer. Most can synchronize with a variety of e-mail software and include their own basic personal information management (PIM) application.

Models with a backlit monochrome display are easy to read under normal lighting conditions and very easy on batteries. CONSUMER REPORTS tests have shown that monochrome models can operate continuously with the backlight off for at least 24 hours, equivalent to seven weeks of use at a half hour per day. Models with a color display last just a few hours in continuous use.

While Palm OS based units are easy to use, navigation between different programs is cumbersome because of the "single-tasking" nature of the operating system.

New Palm-OS models have expansion slots that let you add memory or attach separately purchased accessories. All Palm-based PDAs can be enhanced by adding third-party software applications—the more free memory in a model, the more software that can be accommodated. There is a large body of Palm OS-compatible freeware, shareware, and commercial software available for download at such sites as *www.palmgear.com*. Many Palm models come with Documents To Go, word-processing and spreadsheet software similar to that used in Pocket PCs.

Price range: $130 to $500.

POCKET PC SYSTEMS. These resemble Palm-based models, but they are more like a miniature computer. They have a processor with far more horsepower and come with familiar applications such as a word processor and a spreadsheet. Included is a scaled-down version of Internet Explorer, plus voice-recording and some financial functions. An application that plays MP3 music files, as well as Microsoft Reader, an e-book application, is also standard.

As you might expect, all the application software included in a Pocket PC integrates well into the Windows computer environment. You need to purchase third-party software to use a Mac. And you'll need Microsoft Office programs such as Word, Excel, and Outlook to exchange data with a PDA. Most have a color display that livens up the interface but also drains their rechargeable lithium-ion batteries quickly. As with some Palm-based PDAs, the battery of most Pocket PCs must be removed and replaced by a dealer when it can no longer be recharged.

For basic functions, CONSUMER REPORTS tests have shown that Pocket PCs are generally easier to use than Palm OS models. Navigation between programs is easier than with the Palms because you can run several programs simultaneously. Onscreen keyboards leave most of the display visible.

Price range: $200 to $550.

Key features

Whichever operating system your PDA uses, you'll need to install programs in your main computer to enable the PDA to synchronize with it. Most such software lets you swap data with leading personal-information-manager programs such as Lotus Organizer or Microsoft Outlook; some do not.

Most PDAs have the tools for basic tasks: a **calendar** to keep track of your appointments, **contact software** for addresses and phone numbers, **notes/tasks** for reminders and to-do lists, and a **calculator**. A **memo function** allows you to make quick notes to yourself. Other capabilities include **word-processing, spreadsheet, database,** and **money-management functions. A voice recorder,** which includes a built-in microphone and speaker, works like a tape recorder.

A PDA's **processor** is the system's brain. In general, the higher the processing speed of this chip, the faster the unit will execute tasks—and the more expensive the unit will be. But higher-speed processors require more battery power and may deplete batteries quickly. Processing speeds are 16 to 200 megahertz.

Models typically have 8 to 64 megabytes of user memory. Even the smallest amount in that range should be more than enough for most people.

A **backlight** for the display, which illuminates the characters, is standard. With monochrome screens, you need the backlight when using the PDA in the dark. The backlight is always used with color screens.

In general, the degree of web accessibility for PDAs is not yet equal to what you can get from your desktop or laptop computer. Some applications can browse specially designed pages known as "clipped web pages." Other applications (such as Avant-go) allow you to download text-based information from a desktop computer.

How to choose

PERFORMANCE DIFFERENCES. Palm-based units, which tend to be the least expensive, offer simple operation, compact size, an easy-to-use interface, a wide range of features, and expandability. All can work with Macintosh computers. Pocket PCs are easier to use for basic functions, and have built in multimedia capability. Their biggest drawback is price and short battery life. They also work only with Microsoft applications, such as Word, Excel, and Outlook.

RECOMMENDATIONS. The PDA hasn't completely replaced the handwritten shopping list or the printed address book. That's all the organizing some people need. But if you need to keep tabs on a great deal of data, a PDA makes sense.

If you expect to put fairly basic demands on a PDA, choose one of the low-priced Palm-based units with 8 MB of memory. On the other hand, if you already have a Palm-based PDA and find it needs more memory, choose a unit with 16 MB of memory. And if you need a PDA for wireless e-mail access, choose the Palm i705.

If you want a computer (a Windows computer, that is) in your pocket and regularly run Microsoft applications or want multimedia capability, choose a Pocket PC.

◆ **Ratings:** page 171

8

Picture These

CAMCORDERS

Fine picture quality and easy editing have improved the functionality of these movie makers. That's especially true for digital models, which are replacing analog.

Home movies—those grainy, jumpy productions of yesteryear—have been replaced by home movies shot on digital or analog camcorders that you can edit and embellish with music using your PC and play back on your VCR, or even turn into video shorts to e-mail.

Digital camcorders generally offer very good to excellent picture quality, along with very good sound capability, compactness, and ease of handling. Making copies of a digital recording won't result in a loss of picture or sound quality.

Analog camcorders generally have good picture and sound quality and are less expensive. Some analog units are about as compact and easy to handle as digital models, while others are a bit bigger and bulkier.

What's available

Sony dominates the camcorder market, with multiple models in a number of formats. Other top brands include Canon, JVC, Panasonic, and Sharp.

Most digital models come in one of two formats: MiniDV or Digital 8. New formats such as the disc-based DVD-RAM and DVD-R and tape-based MicroMV have also appeared. Some digital models weigh as little as one pound.

MINIDV. Don't let the size deceive you. Although some models can be slipped into a large pocket, MiniDV camcorders can record very high-quality images. They use a unique tape cassette, and the typical recording time is 60 minutes at SP (standard play) speed. Expect to pay $9 for a 60-minute tape. You'll need to use the camcorder for playback—it converts its recording to an analog signal, so it can be played directly into a TV or VCR. If

115
Camcorders

118
Digital cameras

121
Scanners

the TV or VCR has an S-video input jack, you can use it to get the best possible picture. Price range: $600 to more than $2,000.

DIGITAL 8. Also known as D8, this format gives you digital quality on Hi8 or 8mm cassettes, which cost $6.50 or $3.50 respectively, less than MiniDV cassettes. The Digital 8 format records with a faster tape speed, so a "120-minute" cassette lasts only 60 minutes at SP. Most models can also play your old analog Hi8 or 8mm tapes. Price range: $500 to $900.

DISC-BASED. Capitalizing on the explosive growth and capabilities of DVD movie disks, these formats offer benefits tape can't offer: long-term durability, a compact medium, and random access to scenes as with a DVD. The 3¼-inch discs record standard MPEG-2 video, the same format used in commercial DVD videos. The amount of recording time varies according to the quality level you select: from 20 minutes per side at the highest-quality setting for DVD-RAM up to about 60 minutes per side at the lowest setting. DVD-RAM disks are not compatible with many DVD players, but the discs can be reused. DVD-R is supposed to be compatible with most DVD players and computer DVD drives, but the discs are write-once. Expect to pay $25 to $30 for a blank disc.

Most analog camcorders come in one of three formats: VHS-C, Super VHS-C, and Hi8. They usually weigh around 2 pounds. Picture quality is generally good, though a notch below that of digital.

VHS-C. This format uses an adapter to play in any VHS VCR. Cassettes most commonly hold 30 minutes on SP and cost $3.50. Price range: $300 to $500.

SUPER VHS-C. S-VHS-C is the high-band variation of VHS-C and uses special S-VHS-C tapes. (A slightly different format, S-VHS/ET-C, can use standard VHS-C tapes.) The typical S-VHS-C tape yields 30 minutes at SP and costs $6.50. JVC is the only brand that offers models in this format. Price range: $350 to $500.

HI8. This premium, "high-band" variant of 8mm (an analog format that is virtually extinct) promises a sharper picture. For full benefits, you need to use Hi8 tape and watch on a TV set that has an S-video input. A 120-minute cassette tape costs about $6.50. Price range: $200 to $400.

Key features

A flip-out **LCD viewer** is becoming commonplace on all but the lowest-priced camcorders. You'll find it useful for reviewing footage you've shot and easier to use than the eyepiece viewfinder for certain shooting poses. Some LCD viewers are hard to use in sunlight, a drawback on models that have only a viewer and no eyepiece.

Screens vary from 2½ to 4 inches measured diagonally, with a larger screen offered as a step-up feature on higher-priced models. Because an LCD viewer drains the battery pack faster than an eyepiece manifold does, you don't have as much recording time with an LCD viewer.

An **image stabilizer** automatically reduces most of the shakes from a scene you're capturing. Most stabilizers are electronic; a few are optical. Either type can be effective, though mounting the camcorder on a tripod is the surest way to get steady images. If you're not using a tripod, you can try holding the camcorder with both hands and propping both elbows against your chest. Designing a camcorder means trying to strike the proper balance between picture quality, low-light performance, and image stabilization; we've seldom seen a camcorder that excels in all three areas. If you need a camcorder with very good low-light capability, check the specs.

Full auto switch essentially lets you point and shoot. The camcorder automatically adjusts the color balance, shutter speed, focus, and aperture (also called the "iris" or f-stop with camcorders).

Autofocus adjusts for maximum sharpness; manual focus override may be needed for problem situations, such as low light. (With some camcorders, you may have to tap buttons repeatedly to get the focus just right.) With many camcorders, you can also control exposure, shutter speed, and white balance.

> ### CAMERA AND CAMCORDER BATTERIES
>
> **Digital cameras and camcorders all consume giant gulps** of power. That can pose a problem when you have a golden photo or video opportunity and you're running low on juice.
>
> Digital cameras often come with rechargeable batteries—lithium ion, nickel metal hydride (NiMH), or, rarely now, nickel cadmium (NiCD)—but many also take AA alkaline cells. Rechargeable lithium-ion, NiMH, or, rarely, NiCD battery packs are used in camcorders.
>
> Consumer Reports' tests have found that NiMH cells are a fine choice for devices with a high power drain. In a test mimicking the high power drain of a film or digital camera with a flash, the best NiMH battery significantly outperformed the best alkaline cell. Use of NiMH has a relatively high initial cost—about $30 to $50 for a system comprising a charger and four AA batteries—but the reusability of NiMH cells makes them less expensive long-term than standard alkalines. NiMH cells are also an environmentally safe choice. Unlike the NiCD cells they're replacing, they can be disposed of with ordinary refuse.
>
> The newer lithium-ion rechargeables also work well and can be disposed with ordinary refuse, but they don't come in AA configurations.

The **zoom** is typically a finger control—press one way to zoom in, the other way to widen the view. (The rate at which the zoom changes will depend on how hard you press the switch.) Typical optical zoom ratios range from 10:1 to 26:1. The zoom relies on optical lenses, just like a film camera (hence the term "optical zoom"). Many camcorders offer a digital zoom to extend the range to 400:1 or more, but at a lower picture quality.

Regardless of format, analog or digital, every camcorder displays **tape speeds** the same way as a VCR. Every model, for example, includes an SP (standard play) speed. MiniDV and Digital 8 types have a slower, LP (long play) speed, which adds 50 percent to the recording time. A few 8mm and Hi8 models have an LP speed that doubles the recording time.

All VHS-C and S-VHS-C camcorders have an even slower, EP (extended play) speed that triples the recording time. With analog camcorders, slower speeds can worsen picture quality. Slow-speed picture quality doesn't suffer on digital camcorders. Using slow speed, however, means sacrificing some seldom-used editing options and may restrict playback on other camcorders.

Quick review lets you view the last few seconds of a scene without having to press a lot of buttons. For special lighting situations, preset **auto-exposure settings** can be helpful. A "snow & sand" setting, for example, adjusts shutter speed or aperture to accommodate the high reflectivity of snow and sand.

A **light** provides some illumination for close-ups when the image would otherwise be too dark. **Backlight** compensation increases the exposure slightly when your subject is lit from behind and silhouetted. An **infrared-sensitive recording mode** (also known as "night vision," "zero lux," or "MagicVu") allows shooting in very dim or dark situations, using infrared emitters. You may use it for nighttime shots, although colors won't register at all in this mode.

Audio/video inputs let you record material from another camcorder or from a VCR, useful for copying part of another video onto your own. (A digital camcorder must have such an input jack if you want to record analog material digitally.) Unlike a built-in microphone, an external microphone that is plugged into a **microphone jack** won't pick up noises from the camcorder itself, and it typically improves audio performance.

Features that may aid editing include a **built-in title generator,** a **time and date stamp,** and a **time code,** which is a frame reference of exactly where you are on a tape—the hour, second, and frame. A **remote control** helps when you're using the camcorder as a playback device or when using a tripod. **Programmed recording** ("self-timer") starts the camcorder recording at a preset time.

How to choose

PERFORMANCE DIFFERENCES. Digital camcorders get high marks in CONSUMER REPORTS picture-quality tests. The top-performing models yield pictures that are sharp and free of streaks and other visual "noise" and have accurate color. Audio quality is not quite as impressive, at least using the built-in microphone. Still, digitals record pleasing sound that's devoid of audio flutter (a wavering in pitch that can make sounds seem thin and watery), if not exactly CD-like, as some models claim.

Typically, the best analog models we've tested are good—on a par with the lowest-scoring digitals. The lowest-scoring analog models delivered soft images that contained noticeable video noise and jitter, and they reproduced colors less accurately than any digital model. And while sound for 8mm and Hi8 analog camcorders is practically free of audio flutter, all the VHS-C analog camcorders suffered from some degree of that audio-signal problem.

RECOMMENDATIONS. If you don't want to spend a lot, an analog camcorder is a good value—many are now priced at about $300. Analog models may also appeal to you if you have little interest in video editing. If you want to upgrade, however, consider a digital model. Prices are as low as $500 and are continuing to fall.

Try before you buy. Make sure a camcorder fits comfortably in your hand and has controls that are easy to reach.

◆ **Ratings:** page 156

DIGITAL CAMERAS

Compared with images captured on film, digital images allow you to be more involved in the creation of the print.

Digital cameras, which employ reusable memory cards instead of film, give you far more creative control than film cameras can. With a digital camera, you can transfer shots to your computer, then crop, adjust color and contrast, and add textures and other special effects. Final results can be made into cards or even T-shirts, or sent via e-mail, all using the software that usually comes with the camera. You can make prints on a color inkjet printer, drop off the memory card at one of a growing number of photofinishers, or upload the file to a photo-sharing web site for storage, viewing, or reprinting.

Digital cameras share many features with digital camcorders, such as an electronic image sensor, LCD viewer, and zoom functions. They also share some features with film cameras, such as focus and flash options. Some camcorders can be used to take still pictures, but a typical camcorder's resolution is no match for a good still camera's.

What's available

The leading brands are Kodak, Nikon, Olympus, and Sony; other brands come from consumer-electronics, computer-imaging, and traditional camera and film companies.

Digital cameras are typically categorized by how many pixels, or picture elements, the image sensor contains. A 1-megapixel camera has 1 million such elements. The more pixels, the sharper the image can be. A 1-megapixel model makes sharp 5x7-inch prints and very good 8x10s; 2- and 3-megapixel models can make excellent 8x10s and pleasing 11x14s. There are also 4-, 5-, and 6-megapixel models, which are well suited for making larger prints or for maintaining sharpness if you want to use only a portion of the original image.

Price range: 1-megapixel models, $150 to $250; 2-megapixel, $200 to $600; 3-megapixel, $350 to $800; 4-megapixel and up, $400 to $1,000 or more.

Key features

Most digital cameras are highly automated, with features such as **automatic exposure control** (which manages the shutter speed, aperture, or both according to available light) and **autofocus.**

Instead of film, digital cameras typically record their shots onto **flash-memory cards.** CompactFlash and SmartMedia, which come in capacities of 8 to 512 megabytes, are the most widely used. Once quite expensive, such cards have tumbled in price—a 64-megabyte card can now cost less than $50. A few cameras store shots on a MemoryStick or an SD card. A few newer cameras use 3¼-inch CD-R or CD-RW discs.

To save images, you transfer them to a computer, typically by connecting the camera to the computer's USB or serial port or inserting the memory card into a special reader. Some printers can take memory cards and make prints without putting the images on a computer first. **Image-handling software** such as Adobe PhotoDeluxe, MGI PhotoSuite, Microsoft PictureIt!, and Ulead PhotoImpact lets you size, touch up, and crop digital images using your computer. Most digital cameras work with Windows or Macintosh machines.

The **file format** commonly used for photos is the highly compressed JPEG. (It's also used for

> **PRINTING PHOTOS ON AN INKJET**
>
> **Most inkjet printers can turn out high-quality color photos. Here are some tips on getting the best results:**
>
> ◆ Use the Print Preview feature, found in most image-handling programs, to avoid false starts. If you want to try out your print during the editing process, use standard-bond instead of pricey photo paper. Or print in a smaller size.
>
> ◆ Handle with care. Inkjet ink can smear if touched before it dries. Color inks in general are less water-resistant than black inks, especially on photo paper. Some ink is vulnerable to light, meaning exhibited photos may eventually show fading and color shifts.
>
> ◆ Shop for cartridges. Comparison-shopping sites such as www.computershopper.com can yield savings of 25 percent or more (not including shipping). With prices in hand, try bricks-and-mortar office-supply chains or warehouse clubs. Don't overbuy—an ink cartridge's shelf life is about 18 months unopened, six months once installed. Be wary of off-brand refills or refilling cartridges yourself with ink-and-syringe kits. Printer warranties often exclude coverage for damage attributable to third-party refills.

photos on the Internet.) Some cameras can save photos in uncompressed TIFF format, but this setting yields enormous files.

Digital cameras typically have both an **optical viewfinder** and a small color **LCD viewer.** LCD viewers are very accurate in framing what you get—better than most of the optical viewfinders, but they gobble up battery power and can be hard to see in bright sunlight. You can also view shots you've already taken on the LCD. Many digital cameras provide a video output, so you can view your pictures on a TV set.

Certain cameras let you record an **audio clip** with a picture. But these clips devour storage space. Some allow you to record limited video, but the frame rate is slow and the resolution poor.

A **zoom lens** provides flexibility in framing shots and closes the distance between you and your subject—ideal if you want to quickly switch to a close shot. A 3x zoom is comparable to a 35-to-105-mm lens on a film camera; a 2x zoom, to a 35-to-70-mm lens. **Optical zooms** are superior to **digital zooms,** which magnify the center of the frame without actually increasing picture detail, resulting in a somewhat coarser view.

Sensors in digital cameras are typically about as light-sensitive as ISO 100 film, though some let you increase that setting. (At ISO 100, you'll likely need to use a flash indoors and in low outdoor light.) A camera's **flash range** tells you how far from the camera the flash will provide proper exposure: If the subject is out of range, you'll know to close the distance. But digital cameras tolerate some underexposure before the image suffers noticeably.

Red-eye reduction shines a light toward your subject just before the main flash. (A camera whose flash unit is farther from the lens reduces the risk of red eye. Computer editing may also correct red eye.) With **automatic flash** mode, the camera fires the flash whenever the light entering the camera registers as insufficient.

How to choose

PERFORMANCE DIFFERENCES. In CONSUMER REPORTS most recent tests, image colors looked fine. Digital cameras did much better with fluorescent lighting than regular film processing labs have done. (Fluorescent lighting can give film photos a greenish cast.) Our tests have also shown that a higher pixel count alone doesn't necessarily produce better picture quality.

The image-handling software provided with a digital camera is generally easy to use. The results are usually pleasing—or readily altered further if you are not satisfied. The software does have its limits, though. It can't fix an out-of-focus image, for example.

RECOMMENDATIONS. A 2-megapixel model is likely to offer you the best overall value:

good quality at a relatively moderate price. Look for a camera with a 3x optical zoom lens and good image-handling software.

A 1-megapixel camera is fine for small snapshots or photos you e-mail to friends and family, but it's not the best choice if you want to make 8x10 enlargements.

A 3-megapixel camera provides some breathing room: files large enough for enlargements, yet not so gargantuan that you'll have difficulty saving, storing, or e-mailing them.

The current high-end cameras—those in the 4- to 6-megapixel range—are for people with plenty of cash and who need a camera verging on professional-grade for special uses.

When comparing cameras, be sure you compare the so-called native pixel count. Some cameras employ software that lets them share pixels and raise the apparent pixel count.

Try before you buy. Quite a few digital cameras offer a shallow grip or no grip. Some LCD viewers are awkwardly situated and could easily be soiled with nose or thumbprints. If you wear glasses, you might look for a camera viewfinder with a diopter adjustment that may allow you to see the image without your glasses while using the camera.

◆ **Ratings:** page 165

SCANNERS

A scanner is a simple, cheap way to digitize images for editing on your computer. Paying more for a scanner with a higher maximum optical resolution probably isn't worth it.

You don't have to have a digital camera to take advantage of the computer's ability to edit photos. Images captured on film can be digitized by the photo processor and delivered on a CD or via the web. But if you do more than a modest amount of film photography, having a processor digitize your photos, at $5 to $10 per roll, can become expensive quickly, and means you pay for digitizing outtakes as well as winners. A more cost-effective way to digitize select photographs is with a flatbed scanner, which can capture the image of nearly anything placed on its glass surface—even those old photos you've tucked away in a family album or a shoebox.

But flatbeds aren't the only type of scanner you may see in stores. Sheet-fed models can automatically scan a stack of loose pages, but they sometimes damage pages that pass through their innards. And they can't scan anything much thicker than a sheet of paper. There are also multifunction devices, which save space by combining a scanner, printer, and a fax modem (see "Multifunction Devices" in Chapter 10). Serious photographers may want a film-only scanner that scans directly from an original slide or negative. But for most home needs, flatbed models offer the best combination of versatility, performance, and price.

Most scanners basically work the same way. As with photocopiers, a bar housing a light source and an array of sensors pass beneath a plate of glass on which the document lies facedown (or, in the case of a sheet-fed model, is passed over). The scanner transmits data from the sensor to the host computer, which runs driver software that works in coordination with the hardware to scan at certain settings. Once the image is in the computer, software bundled with the scanner (or purchased separately) lets you crop, resize, or otherwise edit it to suit your needs. From there, you can print the image, attach it to e-mail, or post it on the web.

What's available

A number of scanners come from companies that made their names in scanning technology, including Microtek and Visioneer. Other brands include computer makers and photo specialists such as Canon, Epson, Hewlett-Packard, and Nikon.

What type of scanner you should consider—flatbed, sheet-fed, or film—depends largely on how you will use it.

FLATBED SCANNERS. More than 90 percent of the scanners on the market are flatbeds. For most home needs, these offer the best combination of versatility, performance, and price. They work well for text, graphics, photos, and anything else that is flat, including a kindergartner's latest drawing. Flatbeds include optical character recognition (OCR) software, which can convert words on a printed page into a word-processing file in your computer. Some stores may throw in a flatbed scanner for free, or for a few dollars extra, when you buy a desktop computer.

Most flatbeds fall into two main categories based on maximum optical resolution, measured in dots per inch (dpi): 1,200 dpi and the generally more expensive 1,600 or 2,400 dpi. Price ranges: 600 x 1,200 dpi, under $100; 1,200 x 1,200 dpi and 1,200 x 2,400 dpi, $100 to $200; 1,600 x 3,200 and 2,400 x 2,400 through 2,400 x 4,800, $180 to $500.

SHEET-FED MODELS. This is the type often used in multifunction devices, which can also print, send, and receive faxes. Sheet-fed scanners also use OCR software. Price range for multifunction devices: $200 to $600.

FILM SCANNERS. These offer a higher maximum resolution than you get from an ordinary flatbed or sheet-fed model. Some can accept small prints as well. Price range: $400 to $800.

Key features

While the quality of images a scanner produces depends in part on the software included with the scanner, there are several hardware features to consider.

GUIDE TO PICTURE FILE FORMATS

Ready to hook up your scanner and begin playing with photos and other graphics? First you'll need to understand the differences between the various file formats available for storing your scanned images. Here's a look at four major formats, which are indicated in a document name by the extension, a three- or four-letter suffix such as .tif or .gif:

TIFF. This stands for Tagged Image File Format (represented by the .tif extension), a format that works well for the storage and exchange of images between high-end desktop-publishing and graphic-arts applications.

JPEG. Short for Joint Photographic Experts Group, this is a common method of compressing photographic images. It has surprisingly little effect on image quality when used at moderate levels of compression. Compression can save space and speed up communications, such as when an image is downloaded from the web. These files have the .jpg extension.

GIF. This is short for Graphics Interchange Format. GIF files (extension .gif) are a compressed file format commonly used for graphics on the web.

Bitmap. Represented by the suffix .bmp, bitmap files are also commonly used to display and store photos and graphic images.

You start scanning by running **driver software** that comes with the scanner or by pressing a **preprogrammed button** on the scanner itself. Models with buttons automate routine tasks to let you operate your scanner as you would other office equipment; on some models, you can customize their functions. Any of these tasks can also be performed through the scanner's software without using buttons. A copy/print button initiates a scan and sends a command to print the results on your printer, effectively making the two devices substitute as a copier. Other button functions found on some models include scan to a file, scan to a fax modem, scan to e-mail, scan to web, scan to OCR, cancel scan, power save, start scanner software, and power on/off.

You can also start the driver software from within an application, such as a word processor, that adheres to an industry standard known as TWAIN. A scanner's driver software allows you to preview a scan onscreen and crop it or adjust contrast and brightness. Once you're satisfied with the edited image, you can perform a final scan and pass the image to a running program or save it on your computer. You can make more extensive changes to an image with specialized image-editing software. And to scan text from a book or letter into a word-processing file in your computer, you run OCR software.

Many documents combine text with graphic elements, such as photographs and drawings. A handy software feature called **multiple-scan mode,** found on many scanners, lets you break such hybrids down into different sections that can be processed separately in a single scan. You can designate, for example, that the sections of a magazine article that are pure text go to the OCR software independently of the article's graphic elements. Other scanners would require a separate scan for each section of the document.

How to choose

PERFORMANCE DIFFERENCES. In recent tests of flatbed scanners, CONSUMER REPORTS used the scanner software provided by the manufacturer to print scanned photos on a high-resolution inkjet printer at 150, 300, 600, and (when possible) 1,200 dpi. There was little improvement in the quality of scanned color and black-and-white photographs above 300 dpi. For the flatbed scanners tested, the manufacturer-recommended scan ranges were 150 to 300 dpi for photos, text, and line art, and 72 to 96 dpi for e-mail, web sites, and onscreen viewing. Taking the time and trouble to do high-resolution scans is worse than unnecessary. It results in scans that take two to four times longer and creates files that are much larger.

Another specification is color depth, a measure of the number of colors the scanner is able to recognize. This is expressed as the number of data bits (ones or zeroes) that are associated with each pixel of a scanned image. Recently tested models scanned with at least 36-bit depth (some have a 42-bit depth), but their software usually reduced the output images to 24-bit depth. Even 24-bit equates to more colors than the human eye can distinguish, so there's certainly no point in paying extra for 42-bit depth.

The OCR software that came with our test models did a nearly error-free job of converting a typewritten memo. The scanners made more errors processing a page from CONSUMER REPORTS magazine, but few enough that our testers were able to fix them with minimal effort.

Images produced with film-scanning adapters that come with some flatbed scanners aren't really worth the effort, according to our tests. The adapters weren't very effective at flattening the film and had no focus adjustment to control the distance between the scan head and the film. The resulting images were usually slightly fuzzy. Worse, the images were off in color or contrast. Some even looked grainy. If you need to scan film or slides frequently, it's generally worth buying a dedicated film scanner. Matching the original version of a color photo is the most demanding of a scanner's functions. You'll sometimes need to use image-editing software to get a printed version that's faithful to the original.

RECOMMENDATIONS. Most consumers don't need a high-resolution scanner with considerably more than 300 dpi. Look instead for features and conveniences you can use, such as photo-editing software or one-button functions. If your older Windows PC does not have a USB port, make sure the scanner you're buying can be connected to a parallel port.

Sound Investments

CD PLAYER/RECORDERS

For years, cassette tapes were the only means to make your own recordings. Now you can "burn" the music you want onto CDs.

Audio CD player/recorders are relatively new devices that finally let you do with compact discs what tape decks have long allowed with tape: Make your own recordings and play back prerecorded material. Player/recorders still cost more than CD changers without recording capability, but prices are dropping. These products sell as stand-alone units and as components of some minisystems.

There's another way to make your own music CDs: Record them using a computer. You'll find that CD drives that record, or burn, CDs are now standard on many computers. These drives, originally intended for archiving data, can be as adept as component CD player/recorders.

Both CD player/recorders and computer CD burners let you copy entire discs or dub selected tracks to create your own CD compilations, with no quality loss in high-speed CD-to-CD dubbing. Recording speeds usually are real-time or 4x, which records in one-quarter of that time. Computer CD burners can be as fast as 16x. CD player/recorders and computer CD burners will record to either CD-Rs (discs you can record on only once) or to CD-RWs (discs that can be erased and rerecorded repeatedly). CD-Rs play on almost any CD player, whereas CD-RWs generally play only on new disc players that are configured

125
CD player/recorders

127
MP3 players

to accept them. Note that some older DVD players have problems reading CD-R and CD-RW discs.

What's available

Audio CD player/recorders come from audio-component companies such as Denon, Harmon-Kardon, JVC, Philips, and Pioneer.

DUAL-TRAY AND CHANGER MODELS. In a dual-tray model, one tray is for play/record, another for play. Most multidisc changer models on the market hold four discs, three for play and the fourth for play/record. Price range for dual-tray and changer models: $300 to $800.

THE COMPUTER ALTERNATIVE. If your computer doesn't have a CD burner drive, you can buy an internal or external drive at prices starting at about $160. Manufacturers include Adaptec, Hewlett-Packard, Iomega, and Sony. Software, such as Adaptec's Easy CD Creator and just!audio from Adaptec-owned CeQuadrat, costs $80 to $150 if you buy it separately, but it's often bundled with the drive. A computer's Internet link also makes it easier to record electronically stored music such as MP3 files.

Of the software products mentioned above, Easy CD Creator is the better choice if you're familiar with the Windows operating system. (Its Macintosh sister product is DirectCD.) It also has a superior help-menu system. For the computer neophyte running Windows, just!audio may be less daunting; its hipper design also helps make it more fun to use than Easy CD Creator.

Key features

The computer approach makes compiling "mix" discs pretty easy. Once a blank CD is inserted into a computer CD drive, the accompanying software displays a track list and allows you to "drag" the desired tracks into the lower panel. As you insert successive CDs, you can see the playlist for your CD-to-be and even change the order of the tracks, combine two or more tracks or files into one, or split a track or file into two or more. With CD recorders, you program your selections from up to three discs installed in the changer; the steps will be familiar to anyone who has programmed a CD changer. Most units give you a running total of the accumulated time of the tracks as you are programming them. With both the computer option and a CD player/recorder, you must program selections from each disc in succession.

Defining tracks on the CD onto which you're recording is accomplished with varying degrees of flexibility. How many **track numbers** a given player/recorder can add per disc, for example, differs from one model to another; additionally, assigning track numbers when you're recording from cassettes may be automatic or manual. (Such tracks are inserted automatically when recording from CDs.) **Text labeling** lets you type in short text passages such as artist and song names, a much easier procedure with a computer keyboard than with a console's remote control.

The number of **delete-track modes** grants you flexibility, whether you need to delete one track or the entire disc. One-track, multitrack, and all-disc are three common modes.

For playback, an audio CD player/recorder typically has three modes: **Program** is used to play tracks in a specific order, **Repeat** plays a track again, and **Random Play** (or Shuffle) plays tracks randomly.

Connection types can affect what external sources you're able to use to make a CD. A **digital input jack** may be optical or coaxial; the latter is for connecting older digital devices. An **analog input jack** lets you record your tapes and LPs. A **microphone input** offers a low-cost way for home musicians to make digital recordings of their performances. A **record-level control** helps you control loudness while recording digitally from analog sources—a problem you don't face when recording from digital sources. An **input selector,** included on some models, makes for faster connections than when going through a menu process.

How to choose

PERFORMANCE DIFFERENCES. By burning a CD, using either an audio CD player/recorder or a computer, you can make a recording that's audibly (even electronically) indistinguishable from the original CD.

Audio CD player/recorders excel in versatility; you can record from CDs, LPs, cassettes, and even TV or radio sound (anything, in fact, that you can connect to a sound system's receiver). This method is the clear standout for recording LPs, since connecting a turntable to a computer requires additional equipment.

The computer method has its own strengths. Because it affords a connection to the Internet, the computer option lets you burn downloaded MP3-encoded files onto CDs. A computer offers more setup choices when you're assembling your own CD from several prerecorded discs. And when you're recording from analog sources, the computer's burning software often includes sound processing that will reduce the snap and crackle of a vinyl LP or the tape hiss of a cassette tape.

RECOMMENDATIONS. The relatively low cost of making high-quality CDs makes CD recording a good alternative to making cassette tapes. If you're buying a CD player/recorder, first consider a changer model; its multidisc magazine or carousel will make it easy to record compilation CDs or to play uninterrupted music.

The computer-based CD-recording option allows you to record music from both CDs and the Internet. If you don't already have a CD-burning drive in your computer, you can buy it and the necessary software for about $160 to $250. If you're buying a new computer, you'll find that a CD-RW drive is standard equipment on many models. We'd expect any CD-burner drive to perform competently.

MP3 PLAYERS

They usually store at least a CD's worth of music files. But they take work to load, and legal controversy surrounds some usage.

Music fans already have downloaded millions of copies of software programs that play computer files using MP3 encoding—currently the predominant means of compressing music files online. Many of those files are transferred from computers to handheld MP3 players.

Despite copyright-infringement lawsuits by the music and movie industries, free music-sharing web sites carry on. The sites let users download music files for transfer to MP3 players or recording ("burning") onto CDs. The music industry has responded with subscription-based services that allow you to stream or download music and play it on your computer. (For a rundown of some of the leading subscription services, see Chapter 4.) Even without an outlet for free music, you can load these small devices with music "ripped" from CDs, creating your own custom play lists.

Many MP3 players look like portable radios—headphones and all. Others resemble large pens or even watches. A player with 64 megabytes (MB) of memory holds about an hour of music recorded at CD-quality setting. A player with 128 MB holds twice that. The MP3 standard also lets you save music at lower sampling rates; this may diminish quality but increases the amount of music you can store. High-capacity versions (sometimes called "jukeboxes") are similar in size to a portable CD player and store the music on a hard drive. These currently store as much as 20 gigabytes (GB), equivalent to more than 300 hours of music.

Compressed digital-audio files can be stored in internal memory, external memory, or a combination of both, depending on the player. Music can be encoded digitally in a number of formats, of which MP3 is the best known. The abbreviation stands for Moving Pictures Expert Group 1 Layer 3, a file format that compresses music to one-tenth to one-twelfth the space it would ordinarily take. Other encoding schemes include Windows Media Audio (WMA) and Adaptive Transform Acoustic Coding (ATRAC), a proprietary format used by Sony products.

The recording industry has largely been successful in using litigation to limit the free offerings by Napster, whose web site, Napster.com, facilitated the downloading of "swapped" music files. In its defense, Napster contended that swapping music files is protected under the "fair use" provision of copyright law, which allows people to make a small number of copies of a recording for their personal use.

Several web sites now offer free downloadable programs that let you connect to other people's computers to share files. In theory, a network of servers that has been downloaded on individual computers can't be shut down. Nevertheless, a Dutch court has ordered the closure of Kazaa, a Netherlands-based peer-to-peer file-sharing service. (At this writing, it's unclear how Kazaa would implement the order.) Groups representing songwriters and moviemakers have sued U.S.–based peer-to-peer networks Grokster, FastTrack, and MusicCity for copyright infringement. They maintain that while these networks don't offer a Napster-like centralized server, they essentially behave like Napster.

What's available

More than 30 brands of MP3 players are on the market. Most models cost between $90 and $300. High-capacity players, including the Apple iPod, may cost $400 or more. Some hybrid models incorporate CD-player functionality and PDA-like features. MP3 playback has been incorporated into some digital cameras and even cell phones, as well as some CD players and Sony's MiniDisc player. Sony and SonicBlue, which makes the Rio line, are the biggest brands, followed by RCA, Samsung, Creative Labs, and other smaller brands.

Many devices offer the option to add more memory via card slots or "backpacks" on the unit. Players typically come with some combination of internal and/or external memory such as CompactFlash, MultiMedia Card, or Smart Media. Some models use MagicGate (an encrypted-audio version of Sony's existing MemoryStick media) or SecureDigital. Additional memory can cost anywhere from $10 to more than $150, depending on what's compatible with your player.

All players are battery-powered and have headphone outputs, along with a means of connecting to a computer for file transfer.

Key features

MP3 players come with **software** for interfacing with a computer, using a universal serial bus (USB) or less often, the faster FireWire connection. Most support Windows and many support Macs; more manufacturers are working toward Mac compatibility. Apple's iPod is compatible only with Macs. The computer-to-player interface consists of software drivers that let the computer and player communicate, along with a software application for transferring files to the player's memory. Some players appear as hard drives on your computer for easy drag-and-drop transfer of files. Many players are bundled with a more fully featured software application, such as MusicMatch or Real Jukebox, that helps you keep track of your MP3 files, manage playlists, and record songs from audio CDs.

On many players, the **firmware**—the player's built-in operating instructions—can be upgraded so the player does not become obsolete. Upgrades can add or enhance features, fix bugs, and add support for other formats and operating systems. (Check the manufacturer's web site for such upgrades.) Most upgrades these days are to eliminate bugs.

LCD screens on most players show such information as track number, song title, and memory used. Volume, track forward/reverse, and pause-play controls are standard. Most have play modes such as Repeat All and Random. A **customizable equalizer (EQ) setting** gives you the most control over the sound, but some units have just a simple bass boost control. Many also have presets for various music types (rock, classical, and so forth), along with viewable song lists.

Standard players generally use one or two AA or AAA batteries, either alkaline or rechargeable. Most high-capacity models use four AA rechargeable batteries. Either alkaline or rechargeable batteries are preferable to nonremovable batteries; when the latter no longer hold a charge, the player must be professionally serviced. A **battery-life indicator** on most models helps keep track of how much power is left.

A number of players incorporate an **FM radio tuner.** Some MP3 players have features more commonly found on a PDA, such as **voice recording** and **data file storage capability.** (PDAs that run the newest version of the Pocket PC operating system from Microsoft, and some Sony PDA models, can play MP3-encoded files. Handspring's Visor clones of Palm PDAs have an expansion slot to which you can attach an MP3 player.) Certain models can be used to transfer data files between computers, sometimes via the external memory card.

How to choose

PERFORMANCE DIFFERENCES. In recent CONSUMER REPORTS tests, the processing necessary to turn music into an MP3 file led to very slight degradation of the audio signal on most models, evidenced by noise or a muffling in some frequency ranges. Poor sound quality was more likely to be caused by mediocre or poor headphones bundled with the player.

SOUND QUALITY
Figure on roughly one minute of music per megabyte to save MP3 files at the CD-quality level.

These can be replaced, so the problem can be remedied easily and cheaply.

The CONSUMER REPORTS tests found that the players will run between five and 24 hours before their batteries give out—a wide range. Most play eight hours or more. Manufacturers' specifications are useful guides to battery life.

Getting started can be tricky with some devices. When CONSUMER REPORTS engineers connected some tested models to a computer, it often didn't recognize the player; it took some trial and error to make everything work as it should. Upgrading firmware also proved time-consuming. MP3 players use one of two methods for upgrading; one method, which executes the upgrade file on the PC while the player is still attached, can cause permanent damage to the player if there's even a slight interruption during execution.

RECOMMENDATIONS. As with computers, memory size counts. For people who like to have lots of music in a small package, choose a standard MP3 player that has some memory built in (often 64 MB, but some range from 32 to 128) yet allows expansion via external memory cards. A 64-MB card usually costs $35 to $70. If capacity is more important than the smallest size, a high-capacity model would be a better choice. The 20 GB of storage on the most capacious models provides enough space to archive and organize a sizable library of music. Some let you record from an audio system onto the player without a computer. If you want to minimize the odds that your player will fall behind the technology curve, look for a player with upgradable firmware that can accommodate newer encoding schemes or variations of MP3 compression. The more additional formats a model can play—such as WMA or ATRAC—the more flexibility you have in downloading and transferring music files now and in the future.

Before you buy, be sure the player is compatible with your Windows or Mac computer (including the version of the operating system your computer uses) and that your computer has the USB or FireWire connection the player requires. (Apple's iPod supports FireWire.) Also, look for LCD displays and controls that are easy to read and controls that can be worked with one hand, as you would with other handheld devices.

To avoid problems:

◆ Follow installation steps precisely. For instance, note if the player should or shouldn't be connected during software installation.

◆ Test out the ripping (recording) process by setting the bit rate at which to encode. The application software default settings on the computer may not be at the CD-quality setting.

◆ Read the message boards at the manufacturer's web site to determine what's bugging consumers about the product.

◆ Surf the manufacturer's web site for upgrades of firmware and software.

◆ Don't interrupt a firmware upgrade to the player. You risk causing it permanent damage.

◆ **Ratings:** page 169

Ink to Paper

PRINTERS

**New, inexpensive inkjets print color superbly and faster than ever.
An alternative is a laser printer, which excels at printing black-and-white text.**

Inkjet printers are now the standard computer accompaniment. They do an excellent job with color—turning out color photos nearly indistinguishable from photographic prints, along with banners, stickers, transparencies, T-shirt transfers, and greeting cards. Some even turn out excellent black-and-white text. With some very good models selling for less than $200, the vast majority of printers sold for home use are inkjets.

Laser printers still have their place in home offices. If you print reams of black-and-white text documents, you probably need the speed, quality, and low per-copy cost of a laser printer.

Printers use a computer's microprocessor and memory to process data. The latest models are so fast partly because computers themselves have become more powerful and contain much more memory than before.

Unlike the computers they serve, most home printers can't be upgraded except for adding memory to laser printers. Most people usually get faster or more detailed output by buying a new printer.

What's available

The printer market is dominated by a handful of well-established brands. Hewlett-Packard is the market leader. Other brands are Brother, Canon, Epson, Lexmark, and Samsung.

The type of computer a printer can serve depends on its ports. A universal serial bus (USB) port lets a printer connect to Windows or Macintosh computers. Some models have a parallel port, which lets the printer work with older Windows computers. Many printers

131 Printers

134 Multifunction devices

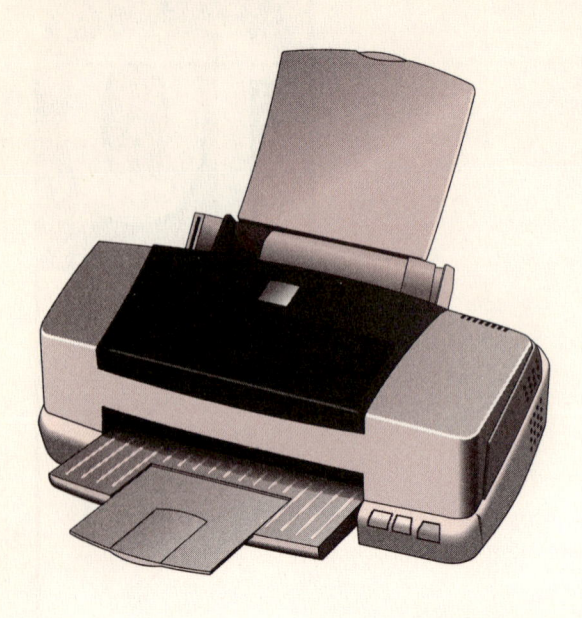

lack a serial port, which means they won't work with older Macintosh computers.

INKJET PRINTERS. Inkjets use droplets of ink to form letters and graphics. Most inkjet printers use two cartridges to supply the droplets. One holds cyan (greenish-blue), magenta, and yellow inks, the other black. Both cartridges are used for full-color work, the black one alone for plain text. Some low-priced inkjets take either a black or a color cartridge, but not both at the same time; they're usually sold without the black cartridge and use all three colors to print–expensively– "black." For photos, some inkjets also have additional cartridges that contain lighter shades of some inks. But CONSUMER REPORTS tests have shown that the three basic colors can produce excellent photos. Most inkjets print at two to four pages per minute (ppm) for black-and-white text, but are much slower for color photos, taking four to 18 minutes to print a single 8x10. The cost of printing a black-and-white page with an inkjet varies considerably from model to model–3 to 11 cents. The cost of printing a color photo can range from 70 cents to $1.40. Inkjet printer prices range from $50 to $400.

LASER PRINTERS. These work much like plain-paper copiers, forming images by transferring toner (powdered ink) to paper passing over an electrically charged drum. The process yields sharp black-and-white text and graphics. Color laser printers used to be beyond the range of most home users' budgets. Laser printers usually outrun inkjets, cranking out black-and-white text at a rate of five to eight ppm. Black-and-white laser printers generally cost about as much as high-end inkjets, but they're cheaper to operate. Laser cartridges, about $100, often contain both the toner and the drum and can print thousands of black-and-white pages, for a per-page cost of 2 to 3 cents. Price range: black-and-white, $200 to $500; color, $1,200 and up.

Key features

Printers differ in the fineness of detail they can produce. **Resolution,** expressed in dots per inch (dpi), is often touted as the main measure of print quality. But other factors count too, such as the way dot patterns are formed by software instructions from the printer driver. Maximum printer resolution is often touted as a selling point. But a high maximum printer resolution is not necessarily synonymous with quality. At their default settings— where they're usually expected to run—inkjets currently on the market typically have a resolution between 600x600 dpi and 4,800x1,200 dpi. Lasers for home use typically offer 600 or 1,200 dpi. Printing photos on special paper at a higher dpi setting can produce smoother shading of colors.

Most inkjet printers include an **ink monitor** to warn you when you're running low. Generic ink cartridges and refill kits can cut costs, but think twice before using them. Usually a printer's warranty won't cover repairs if an off-brand cartridge damages the printer.

For **double-sided printing,** you can have printers print the odd-numbered pages of a document first, then flip those pages over to print the even-numbered pages on a second

THE SUPPLY CLOSET

The eventual cost of printing supplies can easily top the cost of your printer. Here's a look at what you'll need.

Ink and toner

The cost of ink and toner depends on how much you put on a page. In general, for a page of black-and-white text, ink or toner costs 3 to 14 cents per page. Color printing runs 50 to 75 cents per page for color graphics and from 90 cents to $1.50 for color photos, including about 60 cents or more per sheet for glossy photo paper. Inkjet cartridges cost $20 to $40 for black-and-white and $50 to $70 for color. Black-and-white laser cartridges, usually including the drum and toner, cost about $100 but aren't changed as frequently as inkjet cartridges. You can get cartridges through the web sites of printer manufacturers, as well as office-supply stores, web sites, and warehouse clubs. To compare prices, check out price-comparison sites such as www.shopper.com.

Basic paper

Keep boxes of paper in a cool, dry place. Humidity can adversely affect how the paper feeds through the printer. For the most part, good quality copier paper or midweight (20-pound) paper designed for use in either inkjet or laser printers will be a staple. You can buy either in reams of 500 sheets or boxes of 5,000 sheets at most computer stores, office-supply stores, or warehouse clubs for less than a penny per sheet. Paper specially designed for use in laser printers costs a bit more, but doesn't provide much improvement.

For most text jobs, printing on anything other than plain paper is probably a waste of money; CONSUMER REPORTS tests have found that a printer's black-and-white text looked much the same on one grade of paper as another.

Specialty paper

When you need good-quality color printouts, for graphics and photos, it's worthwhile to invest in more expensive paper. Most printers produce only so-so color images on copier paper. Papers designed to enhance colors and avoid smudging fall into four common types:

Coated. Coated paper is designed to work with inkjets to minimize drying time. It's about 5 to 10 cents per sheet. Quality falls between that of copier paper and glossy or high-resolution stock. All printers accept paper of this type.

High-resolution. Some printer models accept high-resolution stock, which is quick to dry and less expensive than glossy stock but produces similar results. Expect to pay 11 to 15 cents per sheet.

Glossy. Glossy paper gives crisp color and resolution but is very expensive–typically 60 cents to $2 per sheet. Images printed on glossy stock take about an hour to dry. Tests, however, showed that using glossy paper improved the color performance of nearly every printer.

Photo. There's a wide array of photo-quality papers, costing from 60 cents to about $1.50 a sheet. Some of these heavy papers are perforated, allowing you to print out two 5x7 prints from one sheet.

Greeting cards, decals, etc.

There are dozens of ways to get creative with your home computer–banners, greeting cards, decals and temporary tattoos, iron-on transfers–and there are all sorts of new papers designed to enhance the look of these projects.

Greeting cards. These make it relatively easy to turn out a personalized greeting card, whether it's something unique to cheer up a friend or an entire batch of holiday greetings featuring a family photo. They come complete with envelopes, 35 to 75 cents per card.

Decals. Decal paper lets you create signs or decorations with your computer and inkjet printer. Each sheet, sold in packs of five or 10, costs from $1.50 to $2.

Iron-on transfers. To create personalized T-shirts, pillows, cloth banners, and other projects, iron-on transfer sheets let you take an image from your computer's screen, print it in water-resistant inks, and iron it onto any smooth cloth surface. Check manufacturer information for washability. Each transfer sheet costs about $1.50.

Business cards. You'll find specialized paper that can turn out professional-looking cards for a fraction of the cost of having them done for you. Each sheet of perforated paper gives you 10 cards and costs $12 to $15 for 25 sheets. Such paper works in both inkjets and laser printers.

Labels. You can find a broad array of labels, including mailing labels, packing labels, and filing labels. Prices start at about $6 for a package of 180 mailing labels.

> **PUT YOUR PRINTER ON A BUDGET**
>
> **While it's true that printer prices are lower than ever, the cost of necessities such as ink, toner, and paper quickly adds up. You can save ink and paper by following these tips:**
>
> ◆ For not-yet-final versions of letters or photos, use draft mode, which saves ink or toner (and often speeds printing as well). You may find that you're satisfied with less than the highest-resolution mode even for final copies.
>
> ◆ Print out photos still being edited onto standard bond paper and save the pricey photo paper for the finished product. You can also print works in progress in a smaller size, or several to a page, to save ink and paper.
>
> ◆ Print a multipage document as smaller "thumbnails," with four or more pages to a sheet, if your printer can do so. This helps if you need a pre-final view of printed pages.
>
> And, of course, there are times you need not use up any consumables:
>
> ◆ Preview before printing. The Print Preview feature of most software programs lets you see how a printout will look so you can avoid false starts.
>
> ◆ Print selectively. Instead of printing web pages, bookmark them or do a "Save As" to a default folder. If you do print them, use black-and-white, not color, if your printer allows it.

pass through the printer. A few printers can automatically print on both sides, but doing so slows down printing considerably.

How to choose

PERFORMANCE DIFFERENCES. When it comes to producing graphics and photos, many inkjets do an excellent job. The best in CONSUMER REPORTS tests print graphics that are crisp, clean, and vibrant-looking. Photos rival the output of a photofinishing lab, with smooth gradations and deep blacks. The worst inkjets turn out graphics that are dull, grainy, or banded. Photos may suffer from overinked dark areas, textures that make skin seem pebbled and grainy, or dull colors.

In recent tests, laser printers generally had the advantage when it came to producing excellent-quality black-and-white text. But more than half of the dual-cartridge inkjets we tested rivaled them. Page for page, laser models are cheaper to operate.

In tests, printing results were sometimes better for one side of the paper than the other. Some brands of paper indicate on the package which side to use.

RECOMMENDATIONS. An inkjet printer is the more versatile choice, and the only inexpensive one for both color and black-and-white output. If you plan on printing color graphics and photos, then a dual-cartridge inkjet printer is the way to go. A single-cartridge inkjet might be inexpensive to purchase, but it will be more costly to use and usually delivers inferior results. Buy a laser printer if you need to turn out a large amount of high-quality black-and-white text.

If the printer and the computer allow it, connect the printer to a USB port for easy setup. If you have to use the parallel port, use an IEEE 1284-compliant printer cable.

◆ **Ratings:** page 174

MULTIFUNCTION DEVICES

With a multifunction device, you get a printer, scanner, copier, and sometimes a fax machine in a single small unit, often for less than $500.

A multifunction device offers compactness, versatility, and affordability. You get a printer, scanner, copier, and fax machine all in one. That's great if you need all that compatibility and you're pressed for space. But a basic printer and a separate fax machine may be all you need, for about $400. Multifunction devices have improved greatly over the past few years, so even a workhorse home office that produces a substantial amount of printed material will be satisfied with their print quality.

What's available

The main types are inkjet and laser. Inkjet models can print and copy in color. Laser units print and copy in black-and-white only, but some can scan in color. Most multifunction devices support both Windows and Macintosh computers, but models usually don't have a serial port, which means that not all work with Macintosh computers manufactured before mid-1998. Most major printer manufacturers are also in the multifunction business. The key brands in this category are Brother, Canon, Hewlett-Packard, and Lexmark. Price range: $200 to $600.

Key features

The **resolution** at the default setting is usually 2,400 x 1,200 dots per inch (dpi) and all are TWAIN-compliant (TWAIN refers to an interface between image-processing software and a scanner or digital camera). As with printers, maximum printer resolution, or maximum dpi, is often used as a selling point. But a model with a high maximum printer resolution does not necessarily produce the highest quality output. Note that not all multifunction devices can reduce or enlarge images.

All multifunction devices (with fax capabilities) can fax in black-and-white, but some can also **fax in color** to other color-capable devices. Multifunction devices with **sheet-fed scanners** can't scan or copy material such as books. Most current models have **flatbed scanners**. After scanning, text must be "read" by an optical-character-recognition (OCR) program before it's edited on the computer. Images can be used immediately by a graphics program that either comes with the scanner or that you can buy separately.

How to choose

PERFORMANCE DIFFERENCES. CONSUMER REPORTS tests have shown that the print quality of multifunction devices usually matches that of a printer-only model that uses the same ink cartridges or toner and that has the same resolution options.

RECOMMENDATIONS. If you're outfitting a home office from scratch and space is scarce, a multifunction device can be a good choice. If you do choose to count on one machine to do everything, you will sacrifice some future flexibility. You can't upgrade just one function in a multifunction device. And if a major part breaks down, the entire machine will be out of service. A separate fax machine and printer may make more sense. Also consider how the machine will be used. If you scan and print mostly color photos or graphics, look for an inkjet model. But if you only plan to print or copy black-and-white text or graphics, a laser multifunction device is the more appropriate choice.

◆ **Ratings:** page 174

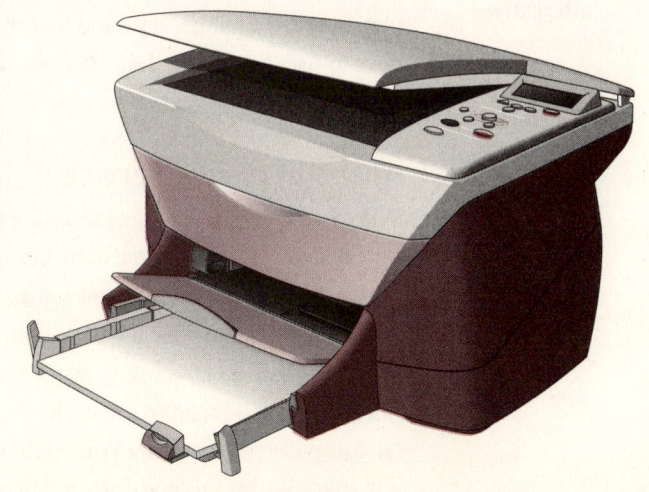

# Telephones

136 Cell phones

139 Cordless phones

142 Corded phones

143 Cell-phone alternatives

CELL PHONES

Complex pricing schemes and incompatible technologies can make it hard to find the right calling plan and handset. Fortunately, with a little research it doesn't have to be difficult.

More than 150 million people now own a cell phone. If current trends hold, one in five cell-phone users will switch carriers this year, seeking better service or lower rates or both. A cell phone is undeniably convenient, often essential, and has forever changed the way people keep in touch with one another. Because a cell phone offers so many clear benefits, people appear to be willing to forgive a lot. But you need not make sacrifices. If you choose wisely you can get reliable service that's easy to understand.

To use cellular service, you'll need both a phone and a service provider. But all cell phones won't work with all service providers. It's best to select a service provider and calling plan first, then choose a phone that the provider offers. If you buy the phone first, you may have to use a provider that offers mediocre service where you live or that doesn't offer the best rates for your calling pattern.

What's available: Service

With a cell phone, you pay for all the time you're connected—both for calls you make and for calls you receive. With a conventional wired phone ("landline" service, to cellular devotees), you pay only for calls you make. Landline service is fairly straightforward, divided into local (or, sometimes, local and regional) and long-distance charges. Cellular service is more complex. If you're making a call from outside your home calling area, you may pay a roaming charge in addition to the basic per-minute cost of the call, to compensate another cellular company for handling your call. And whether in the home area or across the country, you may also pay a long-distance charge. Most big service providers offer plans with hundreds, even thousands, of airtime minutes each month for a flat fee. However, not all cellular minutes are created equal. In many plans, the big bucket of minutes touted in the headline is divided into minutes you can use anytime and minutes good only on nights and weekends; when you exceed your allotment, you pay 30 to 60 cents per minute for additional calling time. Most calling plans also entail a one- or two-year commitment to the carrier, with cancellation fees of $100 or more if you want to switch before the time is up.

The basic types of calling plans are:

LOCAL. These cover the smallest geographic area—as the name implies—just the central metropolitan area where you live. As a rule, calls outside the local area are subject to roaming or long-distance charges. Local plans tend to offer the smallest bucket of minutes. As such, they are best suited for people who rarely leave town.

REGIONAL. These cover a larger area, typically, all or part of several states. There's no roaming or long-distance for calls within the region. Some plans treat every call as a local call, so you never pay long-distance charges; roaming fees could still apply, however. Minutes offered range from medium- to large-sized buckets. These plans are best suited for people who do some traveling, but in a well-defined area.

NATIONAL. These plans treat all 50 states as a local calling area. There are no roaming or long-distance fees. However, the basic per-month charge tends to be highest for national plans. Most national plans offer large buckets of minutes, but with fairly high per-minute charges if you exceed the basic allotment. These plans may be well suited for people with a far-flung network of friends and family, and for those who do lots of traveling across the U.S.

FAMILY. These plans let you put as many as four separate phones on one plan, whether local, regional, or national, for a combined monthly fee that may be far lower than you'd pay for separate service for each phone. In some family plans, calls among family members are always free. Otherwise, roaming and long-distance charges apply.

PREPAID. The antithesis of the big-bucket plans, prepaid service means you buy only the calling time you think you'll need. Once you select a phone and opt for a prepaid plan, you pay for a certain number of minutes, which you generally must use within two months. When you need more minutes, you buy more. There's no long-term commitment. A prepaid plan is well suited for people who truly want a cell phone only for emergencies and occasional use, not as a virtual substitute for the regular phone. But you must keep renewing the minutes—whether you use them or not—or your phone will be disconnected.

The leading national service providers include AT&T Wireless, Cingular, Nextel, Sprint PCS, Verizon, and VoiceStream. In addition to those big six, there are dozens of smaller regional and local providers. Each provider uses one of four distinct digital formats—none of which are compatible with one another.

Digital phones operate in the cellular band, the personal communications services (PCS) band, or the enhanced specialized mobile radio (ESMR) band. There are four incompatible digital formats: Code Division Multiple Access (CDMA), Global System for Mobile Communications (GSM), Integrated Digital Enhanced Network (iDEN), and Time Division Multiple Access (TDMA). CDMA and TDMA are the dominant digital formats in the U.S.

GSM, the de facto standard around the world, is used in the U.S. by VoiceStream and some regional carriers. Cingular and AT&T plan to migrate to GSM service as well. The iDEN format, developed by Motorola, is used by Nextel and a few others. All carriers operating in the cellular band are also required to support the other analog format, AMPS. It's the closest thing to a standard in the U.S.

What's available: Hardware

The leading cell-phone brands include Audiovox, Kyocera, Motorola, Nokia, Samsung, and Sony Ericsson. LG, Panasonic, and Sharp also offer cell phones. Newer handsets are thinner and lighter than older models, with a large array of features on even the least expensive models. Voice-activated dialing, one-key redial, and a large memory for storing names and numbers are just a few of the common features. Prices range from $0 (with rebates equaling the initial price of the phone) to $300 or more. Handspring, Nokia, and Samsung are among the companies selling a phone/PDA combination. Price: $150 and up.

There are several types of digital phones:

TRI-MODE. The most versatile, these can handle calls in the CDMA or TDMA formats in both the cellular and PCS bands. They can default to analog in the cellular band.

DUAL-MODE. These use either the CDMA or TDMA digital format and default to analog if the phone can't detect a digital signal.

DUAL-MODE, DUAL-BAND. These operate in the PCS band and use the CDMA format. If they can't detect a compatible PCS signal, they default to cellular analog.

SINGLE-MODE, SINGLE-BAND. These use the CDMA, TDMA, or GSM format in the PCS band, or the iDEN format in the ESMR band. If they can't detect the home carrier, they don't work.

Key features

Cell-phone makers and service providers are beginning to offer so-called **3G service.** At this point, 3G is the frosting, not the cake. Its main benefit at present: providing business users with a higher data-transfer rate for retrieving e-mail. It's still more important to find the right service and calling plan.

Among basic cell-phone features, look for an **LCD screen** that is readable in both low- and direct-light conditions. The **keypad** should be clearly marked and easy to use. **Programmable speed dial** allows you to store the names and numbers of the people you most frequently call. **Single-key last-number redial** is useful for dropped calls or when you're having trouble connecting. Some providers offer **caller ID, voice mail,** and **messaging,** often for an extra charge.

Some handsets let you switch to a **vibrating alert** or a flashing light to let you know about an incoming call, useful when you're in a meeting or at the movies. An **any-key answer** feature lets you answer the phone by pressing any key rather than the Talk or Send key. Many folding phones answer the call when you open the mouthpiece flap.

The **battery** offered with the phone you buy won't necessarily give you the best service —and it's not your only option. There are usually several choices of battery size, each offering different amounts of talk time and standby time. Some phones come with a base that has an extra battery that can be kept charged while the handset is in use; that way you don't lose any time waiting for a recharge, which can take 6 to 24 hours in some "trickle" chargers. An

automobile adapter lets you power the phone by plugging it into your car's cigarette lighter.

Some models include a **hands-free kit,** which works like a speakerphone, or a headset. Such capability is increasingly demanded by law by more and more states for drivers using cell phones. Phones vary widely in terms of keypad design, readability of screen displays, the ease of using the function menu, and how simple it is to perform such basic tasks as one-button redial and storing frequently called numbers. It's important to handle a phone in the store before you buy to be sure its design and your fingers are well-matched.

How to choose

PERFORMANCE DIFFERENCES. Today's cellular phones use digital technology. Carriers have long touted digital as offering high-quality sound and longer battery life. CONSUMER REPORTS tests have found essentially no difference in the quality of the voice between older analog phones and digital technology. Digital does deliver improved battery life. All phones in the digital mode that we've seen are able to remain in standby mode for at least 24 hours without recharging.

To assess service differences, study the carriers' service-area maps closely. Also ask friends and business associates who travel in the same areas that you do which provider offers the best service. Dead zones and fringe areas, where coverage isn't available, can make a plan worthless if that's where you want to use your phone.

RECOMMENDATIONS. Choose a service provider and calling plan first. What you pay to use the phone will cost far more than the phone itself. If you're switching providers, check two to three months' bills to gauge not only how many minutes of calling time you actually use per month, but how many of those minutes are at night and on weekends. Select a new plan accordingly. If you're buying a cell phone for the first time, make your best guess about usage, but be prepared to switch to a different bucket of minutes after a month or two, once you know your cellular habits. You can efficiently gather wireless prices by visiting web sites such as *www.getconnected.com* and *www.telebright.com*. Telebright makes both a cellular and long-distance selector available to subscribers of ConsumerReports.org.

Before you commit to a plan, make sure you have a trial period that lets you test the network and cancel the service without penalty if it doesn't deliver reliable signals in places where you make calls. All cell phones must be able to dial 911 for emergencies, even older cell phones for which the service contract has lapsed. But the more sophisticated E911 service that the federal government has mandated for cell phones, which allows emergency-service workers to pinpoint the location of a cellular caller, won't be fully operational until 2005 at the earliest. So it's important to be able to give officials an exact location when calling for emergency aid from a cell phone.

◆ **Ratings:** page 159

CORDLESS PHONES

If you have a cordless phone and it's several years old, it's probably a 49-megahertz (MHz) analog model. Newer phones use higher frequencies, either 900-MHz or 2.4 gigahertz (GHz), in analog or digital versions. Poised to enter the market are 5.8-GHz phones. The higher-frequency phones we've seen aren't inherently better at sending or receiving calls, nor do they offer better voice quality or appreciably longer range. Yet manufacturers persist in introducing higher-frequency phones, selling their capabilities in rather the same way Detroit once sold horsepower in new cars.

Digital technology offers less interference and improved security from eavesdroppers. Step-up features include two lines (good for home businesses), multiple handsets, built-in answering machines, caller ID, and hands-free speakerphones. At 5 to 10 ounces, cordless handsets are generally heavier than corded-phone handsets.

What's available

A few brands—Bell South, General Electric, Panasonic, Uniden, and VTech—account for more than 70 percent of the market. VTech owns the AT&T Consumer Products Division and now makes phones under the AT&T brand as well as its own name.

A main distinction between cordless phones is how they transmit their signals. The major types are:

900-MHz ANALOG. These phones offer enough range to let you chat anywhere in your house and yard, or even a little beyond. But they're not very secure if there is no voice-scrambling capability; anyone with a scanner can listen in. They're also more likely than digital models to suffer occasional static and interference from other devices. Price range: $20 to $100.

900-MHz DIGITAL. These models offer about the same range as 900-MHz analog phones, but with better security. Price range: $50 to $150.

900-MHz DIGITAL SPREAD SPECTRUM (DSS). With these models, a call is distributed across several frequencies, providing still tighter security. The range is slightly better than that of other 900-MHz models. Price range: $60 to $200.

2.4-GHz ANALOG OR DSS. The analog phones have pros and cons similar to those of 900-MHz analog phones. Some digitals claim better voice quality, longer range, or less interference; CONSUMER REPORTS tests haven't supported those claims. Indeed, some DSS phones, both 2.4-GHz and 900-MHz, use such a wide swath of the spectrum—even in standby mode—that they may interfere with baby monitors and other devices operating in the same frequency band. It's not a good idea to have a 2.4-GHz analog phone in the kitchen, where the microwave oven could create interference.

Some 2.4-GHz DSS phones support multiple handsets, so you can have several handsets around the house, each charging in a base, without the need for extra phone jacks. Price range: $30 to $230 (the higher prices for multiple-handset systems).

Key features

Most cordless phones have a **jack** for a headset, plus a **belt clip**, allowing hands-free conversation. About a third of the cordless phones sold include an **answering machine,** nearly always a digital unit that works without tape. Useful answerer features include message recording time of 15 to 20 minutes; **separate mailboxes** where callers can direct messages for different family members; and **advanced playback controls** for fast playback, rewind, and skip forward or back.

Caller ID displays the name and number of a caller and the date and time of the call if you use your phone company's caller ID service. If you have caller ID with call waiting, the phone will display data on a second caller when you're already on the phone.

Some models include a **speakerphone,** which lets you make hands-free calls from the base. **Two-way intercom** allows for conversation between the handset and the speakerphone. For multi-handset models, **handset-to-handset talk,** also called handset-to-handset intercom, allows conversation between handsets. **Conferencing** allows multiple-party conversation that can include outside callers.

A **secondary keypad** on the base can be handy for navigating menu-driven systems because you don't have to take the handset away from your ear to punch the keys.

A phone with **two lines** is useful for subscribing to online services or separating a business and home number. Some phones have **two ringers,** each with a distinctive pitch, to let you know which line is ringing. A two-line phone can receive calls for two numbers. Some have an **auxiliary jack data port** to plug in a fax, modem, or other phone device.

On most models, the handset rings, and many phones have a second ringer in the base. An **LCD screen** on the handset or base can provide useful information such as the phone number dialed, battery strength, or how long you've been connected.

All cordless phones have a **handset-locator button** to help you find the handset when it is hiding under a sofa cushion or somewhere else besides on the base.

Cordless-phone **batteries** may be rechargeable nickel-cadmium or nickel-metal hydride. Some models may provide a compartment in the base for charging a spare handset battery and, on some, can be used as the base power backup in the event of a power outage. Keep a corded phone somewhere in your home; it will work in a power outage because it draws its power from the phone system, not the household wiring.

How to choose

PERFORMANCE DIFFERENCES. Most new cordless phones have very good voice quality, CONSUMER REPORTS tests show. Some are excellent, approaching the voice quality of the best corded phones. Size and shape vary considerably, as do features.

In our latest tests, fully charged nickel-cadmium or nickel-metal hydride batteries handled anywhere from 4 to about 13 hours of continuous conversation before they needed recharging. Most manufacturers claim that a new battery will last at least a week in standby mode.

Some phones offer better surge protection than others against damage from lightning or faulty wiring.

RECOMMENDATIONS. A 900-MHz phone should suit most users. Analog models, apt to be less expensive than digital, are fine for many people. However, these phones may soon disappear from the market, replaced by higher-frequency hardware. We don't think 2.4-GHz phones offer enough added functionality to be worth their higher cost. But it won't be long before these phones are considered entry-level.

To ensure voice transmission security, look for wording in ads and packaging such as "digital phone," "digital spread spectrum," or "phone with voice scrambling." Just because the word "digital" is used, however, doesn't mean the company is promising a secure transmission. Phones that aren't secure might have packaging with wording such as "phone with digital security code," "phone with all-digital answerer," or "spread-spectrum technology."

Before you buy, hold the handset to your head to see if it feels comfortable. The handset of a cordless phone should fit the contours of your face. The earpiece should have rounded edges and a recessed center that fits nicely over the middle of your ear. Also, check the buttons and controls to make sure they're reasonably sized and readable.

If possible, see what the LCD display looks like as well. You might also want to determine how easy it is to use the functions, especially for models with an answering machine.

CORDED PHONES

Today's basic phone is sleeker and more versatile than its boxy predecessor. For $10, you can now buy a phone with such features as volume control and speed-dialing for 10 or more numbers. For $50 or more, you get a console with speakerphone or two-line capability, sometimes both. Every home should have at least one corded phone, if only for emergencies. You can't always rely on a cell phone because circuits fill up quickly in emergencies or the signal may not reach your house. A cordless phone may not work if you lose electrical power. But because a corded phone draws its power from the phone network, it will operate even in a blackout.

What's available

AT&T (currently made by VTech) and GE are the dominant brands. When shopping, you'll find these types:

CONSOLE MODELS. These are updated versions of the traditional Bell desk phone. Price range: $15 to more than $100.

TRIM-STYLE MODELS. These spacesavers have push-buttons on the handset, and the base is about half as wide as a console model's. Price range: $10 to $30.

PHONES WITH ANSWERERS. Combo units can sometimes be less expensive than buying a phone and an answerer separately. Price range: $50 to $150.

Key features

Corded phones tend to be less feature-laden than cordless ones. Even some less expensive phones have a **volume control** on the receiver, handy if the voice at the other end of the line starts to fade.

It's practically standard for any phone to have **last-number redial** and **speed dialing.** Features such as a **speakerphone, two-line capability,** or **caller ID** add to the price.

Trim-style phones, with a keypad on the handset, can be hard to use if you need to listen and punch buttons at the same time, which you might have to do when navigating an unfamiliar voice-mail or automated-banking menu.

How to choose

PERFORMANCE DIFFERENCES. Most corded phones perform quite capably, conveying voices intelligibly under normal conditions, according to CONSUMER REPORTS tests. The variations in sound quality that we have found are likely to matter only in very noisy environments.

RECOMMENDATIONS. Since good quality is pretty much a given, your main considerations should be features and price. Before you buy, make sure the handset is comfortable to hold in your hand and to your ear. Look for a good-sized, clearly labeled keypad, especially if your eyesight isn't good.

CELL-PHONE ALTERNATIVES

A cell phone isn't the only way to stay in touch with people who are nearby. Here's a rundown of widely used, economical alternatives.

Even though cell-phone sales remain strong, and cell phones are one of the best ways to reach people when you or they traveling, there are alternatives that work at shorter range—and, more important, without needing an often-expensive monthly service plan.

What's available

Two-way radios are the leading cell-phone alternatives. There are two types: family radio service (FRS) models, which transmit with enough power to cover about two miles in an open field, and general mobile radio service (GMRS) models, which transmit at higher power and can cover five miles under ideal conditions. Neither type carries activation or service fees, but GMRS radios require a $75, five-year license from the Federal Communications Commission. Two-way radios don't rely on transmission towers, so they can operate in remote locations. Leading brands include Motorola, Cobra, Uniden, and Audiovox. Price range: $40 to $200 for a pair of radios.

Pagers also make a good alternative to a cell phone, although they are less widely used than they were a few years ago. The newest pagers let a caller send full-text messages—not just a phone number or a few numbers of code (1-4-3 equals "I love you" in "pagerspeak"). Pagers can be one-way (receive only) or two-way (send and receive via a tiny keyboard). Price range: $50 to $150 for the pager; $10 to $60 for monthly service, depending on the volume of messages you exchange.

Text-messaging services provide pagerlike functions through a cell phone. Many new phones and some older ones can perform this function. Text messaging lets you exchange messages of up to 160 characters with other cell phones or e-mail addresses. Some phones receive only these messages, called Short Message Service, or SMS. Others let you enter messages via the phone's keypad, which is tedious. Typical SMS charges are 10 cents per message sent or a few dollars a month for 100 messages. You get the service through your cellular provider.

Key features

With two-way radios, look for **22 channels with subcodes.** This effectively expands the number of channels you can communicate on to more than 500. Any two-way radio can communicate with any other brand as long as both are tuned to the same channel and subcode. A **side-mounted talk button** is easier to use than one on the front. **Button lock** prevents important controls from accidentally being pressed when you carry the radio. **Vibrate alert** signals an incoming call without disturbing those around you. **Transmitter cutoff** stops transmissions when you've held the talk button for longer than a minute, to

FREE DIRECTORY ASSISTANCE

Americans spend billions on directory assistance. These six web-based services give you listings for free:
- www.anywho.com
- www.infospace.com
- www.infousa.com
- www.switchboard.com
- www.whowhere.com
- www.555-1212.com

conserve battery power. **Auto squelch** automatically quiets background noise when no signal is present. **Batteries** that can recharge in the radio are also handy (however, some radios use only disposable batteries). A **low-battery indicator** helps you monitor battery usage. Pagers have no important features to speak of.

How to choose

PERFORMANCE DIFFERENCES. You can expect a two-way radio to perform as expected in the open or in a vast interior space such as a shopping mall. But reception may suffer downtown or in the suburbs. Pagers also communicate reliably, although those with minuscule keyboards tend to be hard to use, and service may be hard to get. With SMS messaging, most providers now let you send messages to—and receive messages from—phones connected to other providers. But SMS may only work when you are in your home area.

RECOMMENDATIONS. All the cell-phone alternatives have their uses. The type you choose will depend on how you need to stay in touch. If a brief text message will suffice, then a pager or SMS service is what you want. If messages must arrive reliably, look into pager service. SMS is best when time isn't critical and you're in your home area. If you need to have a conversation, then choose a two-way radio.

◆ **Ratings:** page 161

Working in Comfort

ERGONOMIC CHAIRS

Of course the chair you sit in should be comfortable. But the right chair can also help you adapt to a less-than-perfect office setup, and can be adjusted for different users.

Although you can find office-type chairs sold for as little as $25, you'll have to spend more to get what is considered a basic ergonomic chair—one with a lever to adjust seat height pneumatically, a contoured backrest, armrests, and a five-wheel base that swivels. First impressions of a chair's comfort seem to correspond well with long-term impressions. So if you sit in a chair at a store or dealer showroom and like it after adjusting it, you will probably find it comfortable after you get it home.

What's available

The major brands are EckAdams, Global, Herman Miller, HON, Knoll, and Steelcase. You'll find them at mass merchandisers or office superstores. Furniture retailers such as IKEA and Workbench also sell office chairs. Price range: $60 to $1,000.

Key features

Being able to adjust the **seat height** is critical. If your feet aren't flat on the floor at the seat's lowest setting, the chair doesn't go low enough; if your knees angle up at the highest setting, it doesn't go high enough.

Generally, a chair with **five wheels** is more stable than one with four, a rule that's important for larger and heavier users and for people who are accustomed to scooting around their work area. Even with five wheels, some chairs still wobble noticeably. Try sitting far forward and back in a chair when trying it out; reject any chairs that seem prone to tipping.

145
Ergonomic chairs

148
Workstations

151
Surge suppressors

ERGONOMICS

Ergonomics is the study of what makes things easy, comfortable, and safe to use. Ergonomic principles were first explored in this country during World War II in research showing that fighter pilots needed cockpits with controls placed logically and within easy reach.

A **forward-tilt lever** on some chairs angles the seat and backrest forward. Designed for typing, this adjustment lets you lean into your work without losing the support of the backrest. The **backrest angle** is an adjustment on some chairs. The models that are easiest to adjust let you lean back while keeping your feet flat on the floor. Others require you to press a lever.

How to choose

PERFORMANCE DIFFERENCES. In panel tests, CONSUMER REPORTS found that no chair pleases everybody. Judgments were often connected with body size: Some taller panelists complained of seats that were too shallow; some shorter panelists complained that they couldn't adjust a backrest contour low enough for them to be comfortable. The lowest-priced chairs weren't great, but the most expensive ones weren't necessarily the best for each panelist.

RECOMMENDATIONS. Before you choose an ergonomic chair, decide how adjustable you'll need it to be. If you plan to share the chair with someone who has a different height and build, you'll want a chair whose seat height and backrest easily adjust up and down. If you spend long hours at the computer, it's worth spending more to buy a well-designed chair. Adjustable armrests are important, too.

Comfort is personal, so sit in a chair before you buy it. We suggest that you "try on" at least several chairs before you choose one. Sit before a workstation if the store has one on display to get a feel for positioning your arms. If, after you make a few adjustments, you still find that some contour hits you in the wrong place, or that the whole chair feels too big or small, then you're never likely to be very comfortable sitting in it.

Don't be oversold on adjustability. More adjustable parts don't necessarily make a better chair. Labels on the levers and knobs are nice, but they aren't much help on chairs whose controls are cluttered or otherwise confusingly designed. Look for effective and easy-to-use adjustments—a seat-height control that is simple and responsive, or armrests that notch into place on the first try. You should be able to easily make important adjustments while seated. Less important are controls such as tilt-tension knobs, which often don't seem to make a difference and are sometimes hard to reach.

Catalog pictures and manufacturers' specs won't give you the information you need. Don't buy a chair through a catalog or from a web site unless you've "sit-tested" the exact model in a store and are getting a better price through the mail or the Internet. Some chairs come in a variety of sizes, so make sure you try the size you intend to buy.

Tips on fitting a chair. Cushioning should be soft enough that you don't feel pressure at points where your body hits the chair, but not so soft that you sink into the chair and can't move around freely.

Match the contours in the back of the chair to the natural curve of your spine by adjusting the backrest height or moving the lumbar support. If you have a chair with too little curve, attach a special lumbar pillow or rolled-up towel to its back. A regular pillow might help if the chair curves more than your back does, but it won't offer much support.

Armrests should support your arms naturally. If you have to drop your shoulders to use them, the armrests are too far apart or too low. If you have

HOME-OFFICE SCENARIOS

Design your home office to meet your specific needs.
Someone planning to do occasional work at home might need only a computer, phone, phone line, and web access. The entrepreneur planning to build a business from scratch might need all of the above, plus fax capabilities, teleconferencing, postage metering, remote access, and more. Here are three scenarios and how much they cost.

Scenario 1: The all-in-the-family home office
You want a setup that will accommodate regular family use of the computer and occasional at-home work. Your needs are not sophisticated, and you'd like to keep the budget modest. You'll need:

◆ An 800-MHz Windows PC and 17-inch cathode ray tube (CRT) monitor or a 400-MHz Apple iMac with 128 megabytes (MB) of RAM and a hard drive of 20 to 40 gigabytes (GB)–$800 to $1,100.

◆ A basic desk–$100 to $400.

◆ A basic ergonomic chair–$60 to $90.

◆ A midpriced inkjet printer–$100 to $150.

◆ A basic, single-line corded phone with answering machine–$40 to $60.

◆ Basic monthly Internet service (using 56-kbps modem)–$20 per month.

Total: $1,100 to $1,800 (plus $20 per month for Internet access).

Scenario 2: The compact and efficient home office
You do a lot of work from home, and your needs are intermediate. You have little space, and you want technology that will grow with you as your business and personal needs evolve. You'll need:

◆ A 1-GHz Windows PC with a 15-inch flat-panel liquid crystal display (LCD) monitor, a 900-MHz full-sized laptop with 128 MB of RAM and a 20- to 40-GB hard drive–$1,600 to $2,000–or a 600-MHz iMac–$800 to $2,000.

◆ A quality computer desk with an adjustable keyboard shelf that fits your space–$300 to $700.

◆ A higher-end ergonomic chair–$90 to $400.

◆ An inkjet or laser multifunction device (including printer, scanner, fax, and auto document feed)–$200 to $600.

◆ A dual-line phone with answering machine–$100.

◆ A high-speed cable-modem or DSL Internet connection–$100 to $150 for connection, about $50 per month for access.

Total: $1,590 to $3,950 (plus $50 per month for cable-modem or DSL access).

Scenario 3: The state-of-the-art home office
You want every angle covered: computer, communications, teleconferencing, postage, and fast Internet access. You look at this home-office setup as an investment in your future. You want technology that will show the world you mean business. You'll need:

◆ A powerful, state-of-the-art 1.5- to 1.8-GHz Windows PC or 733-MHz PowerPC G4 Macintosh with plenty of RAM (256 MB), a huge hard drive (60 to 80 GB), a DVD-ROM drive, and a backup drive such as a CD-RW drive–$1,800 to $2,500.

◆ A 17- or 19-inch CRT monitor–$200 to $500–or a 15- to 18-inch flat-panel LCD monitor–$450 to $4,500.

◆ A full-sized executive desk with plenty of work, drawer, and filing space–$600 to $2,000.

◆ A high-back, well-padded, ergonomic chair–$200 to $1,000.

◆ Two or more extra chairs or a small sofa for visitors–$200 to $600.

◆ An inkjet or laser multifunction device (including printer, scanner, fax, and auto document feed)–$200 to $600.

◆ A speakerphone with answering machine–$140 to $200.

◆ A cellular phone with a monthly plan–$500 to $1,000 per year.

◆ High-speed cable-modem or DSL Internet access–$100 to $150 for installation and $50 per month for access.

◆ A slim-and-light laptop or a personal digital assistant with wireless Internet access for mobile e-mail and web surfing–$400 to $3,000.

◆ At-home postal metering–$25 and up per month.

Total: $3,840 to $15,550 (plus $120 to $160 per month or more for Internet access, cell-phone service, and postage).

WORKSTATION TYPES

Desk with hutch

Corner unit

Armoire

Cart

to hunch your shoulders, they're too high. Make sure the armrests are adjustable and feel OK against your skin—a concern for warm-weather months when you might not be wearing long sleeves.

Consider the seat depth, as well. When you sit back, there should be a few fingers' to a fist's worth of space between the edge of the chair and the back of your knees, so that the seat doesn't press into your calves. With too much space, the chair won't support your thighs properly. In a chair that's too deep, you could consider using a pelvic cushion that could push you forward sufficiently. There's no way to fix a chair that's too shallow unless its back has a depth adjustment.

WORKSTATIONS

A workstation holds all the components of a desktop computer and often a printer. There are hundreds of workstation options currently on the market.

Traditional writing desks aren't good for computer use for several reasons. Most have a surface that's too high for a keyboard—and those low enough for a keyboard are probably too low for a monitor. Also, unless a desk is large, it's unlikely to have enough depth to place the monitor back far enough, especially if you have a big monitor. An ergonomically correct workstation puts you in a comfortable and safe working position.

If you're willing to do some investigating, you can combine a regular desk or table with a few accessories to create a workstation that costs a few hundred dollars or less. But it's often more convenient and just as economical to buy furniture designed specifically for computer use. A workstation you put together yourself—often called ready-to-assemble (RTA) and sometimes called flat-packed—is what most people buy for their home offices. Most RTA workstations are made of laminated particleboard and sell for $65 to $300 or so. Those made with wood and wood veneer are more expensive—$300 or considerably more for a desk with hutch. You can also tuck your computer equipment into a fully assembled workstation made of finely finished solid wood, which costs several thousand dollars at the high end.

What's available

Most of the computer furniture you'll see comes from about a dozen manufacturers. The major brands are Bush, IKEA, O'Sullivan, and Sauder. Computer furniture you assemble yourself can be found at office-supply stores, home centers, home-furniture stores, and catalogs. You can find some higher-end furniture at specialty retailers such as Levenger and Crate & Barrel. Computer furniture comes in a range of styles, from contemporary to country to mission.

You'll find several types:

DESKS WITH HUTCH. The most popular type of workstation is a desk with a hutch, a cupboardlike attachment that sits atop the desk and provides extra storage space. Most such units consist of two pedestals that support a desktop with 300 to 500 square inches of usable work space. There's often a shelf for a printer and room for files and such. Assembly time for our engineer: 2 to 4 hours. Price range: $100 to $350.

CORNER UNITS. If you need room to spread out papers, choose a corner-unit desk. The trade-off is that these pieces need a lot of floor space. Some have a desktop with more than 1,000 square inches of usable work space. Some have a printer shelf. Assembly time for our engineer: 1½ to 4 hours. Price range: $150 to $400.

ARMOIRES. These units can pretend to be a china cabinet in a dining room or a free-standing closet in the bedroom. They are a great way to hide computer paraphernalia, but you'll need room alongside the unit to fully open the doors. The desktop is usually smaller than that of traditional desks. Most units have a printer shelf. Assembly time for our engineer: 2 to 4 hours. Price range: $300 to $500.

CARTS. If space is tight or you'll need to move your workstation on occasion, a cart may be the best option. The trade-off for compact portability: limited legroom. Some have a printer shelf or hutch, providing racks for CDs and a bit of storage for paperwork, but desktop space is typically meager. Assembly time for our engineer: 45 minutes to 2 hours. Price range: $65 to $180.

SETTING UP AN ERGONOMIC WORK SPACE

Unless you want to experience discomfort or even risk physical problems while using your computer, don't just clear a little space on any old flat surface, especially if you're immersing yourself in computer work. Typing in an improper position for a long time may lead to problems as serious as carpal tunnel syndrome, a condition caused by repetitive motion that leaves a person's hands, wrists, and forearms aching and weak—and, over time, barely usable. Treatment is rest, special braces, and sometimes surgery.

Staring for hours on end at a computer screen can cause headaches, eyestrain, and blurred vision. Craning to view a too-high monitor can hurt your neck and back.

You can reduce your risk of injury by adopting good computer work habits. Consider how your body matches your furniture and computer equipment—and how the pieces of equipment work together.

Lighting. Avoid glare and keep the light in the room balanced. You can minimize glare by controlling light sources in the room or by placing your monitor at a 90-degree angle to a window or other bright light. To balance the light (so your eyes don't get tired from constantly adjusting to different light levels), keep overall "ambient" lighting lower when you're working with a computer than you would if you were reading from paper. Use a focused task light to illuminate documents you're reading.

Seeing the screen. Position the top of the screen at eye level or slightly below so you don't have to tilt your head back or forward. Bifocal and trifocal wearers may need to lower the monitor, too, or get special glasses for computer use. Raise a too-low monitor with a support arm or stand (or a couple of thick books). You can also adjust your chair, keeping your feet flat on the floor or using a footrest. Place the monitor at about arm's length. Keep it clean and, if necessary, use a glare screen to improve screen contrast. If you look at documents while you type, attach a document holder ($5 to $10) to the side of the monitor.

Typing. Position the keyboard and mouse together on a surface in front of you, low enough so that you can type and move the mouse while holding your forearms comfortably at a right angle. The goal is to neither slump nor lift your shoulders. A desktop is often too high for a keyboard and mouse—you may need to use a keyboard shelf, which you bolt to the underside of the desk. Many such shelves have an extension for the mouse, necessary to keep the mouse on the same level as the keyboard.

Type with your wrists flat. Don't bend them up or down, and let them float over the keyboard. Don't rely on a wrist rest to anchor your wrists while you type. That's for resting your wrists when you're not typing. Armrests can help support the elbows. Above all, relax, and don't pound the keys. If you find it awkward moving a mouse around, try a trackball.

POSITIVE POSTURE
Relax, but don't slouch. Get into the habit of changing positions from time to time. Vary your tasks if you can and take frequent, short breaks. You can install software programs to periodically remind you–or simply set a kitchen timer.

How to choose

PERFORMANCE DIFFERENCES. Many workstations that CONSUMER REPORTS recently tested were serviceable. None of them, however, were top-notch in terms of ergonomics. The main reason was that most of the tested models lacked a keyboard shelf that could be raised or lowered to suit the user. A height-adjustable chair can help solve the problem by putting you in the correct position. On some of the units we tested, the keyboard shelf was too small for both the keyboard and mouse. If the mouse has to sit on the desktop, you have to reach up and over to maneuver it, which can strain your wrist and shoulders. Some units had a monitor shelf set too high, forcing you to tilt your head back; on others the shelf was too far from the user. On a few models, the monitor was too close because the desktop was too shallow or a hutch's back wall got in the way.

Overall, the assembly of our test units went fairly smoothly. Problems arose when pieces didn't fit tightly or line up correctly. Generally, the major panels of the tested models fit well, but we did see problems with some shelves and doors. Screws and cam-bolt systems—a type of fastener used by many manufacturers—gave the tightest fit. We found Sauder's proprietary TwistLocks harder to align, which may cause gaps.

The need to piece together a jigsaw puzzle of parts underscores the importance of clear instructions. Most units we tested did fine in that regard. Sauder's were consistently among the best. But we found other instructions, especially from IKEA, to be unclear, incomplete, or incorrect.

Most of the furniture tested was fine in terms of fit and finish. A couple of units had many defects, though.

RECOMMENDATIONS. Your top priority should be to get a unit that's ergonomically sound. You also need to consider how much room you have and how much work space you need. Measure your monitor, computer tower, and printer to make sure the furniture can hold all of them.

Many consumers find that a desk with a hutch provides adequate room to work without hogging floor space. If you have ample floor space and crave elbow room, a spacious corner or L-shaped unit should be just right. Keep in mind that their size and shape can make these units difficult to move once assembled. You may want a cart if space or money is tight or if you want to move your computer around. But you will have to put up with limited work space and mediocre ergonomics—be prepared to hit your shins or your feet on the lower shelves. If you want to hide the computer when it's not being used, consider an armoire.

If you're the do-it-yourself type, you can build an ergonomically sound workstation by combining a large, plain table or desk with an adjustable keyboard shelf and, if needed, a stand that puts the monitor at the correct height. Keep in mind, however, that the result may not be a perfect match stylistically and aesthetically.

WORKSTATIONS THAT WORK

Here are some key points to consider when choosing computer furniture:

◆ The keyboard and monitor should be placed directly in front of you, not at an angle, so that you don't have to twist or turn either your head or your body.

◆ The keyboard shelf should be large enough to hold both the keyboard and mouse, at a height enabling you to keep your shoulders relaxed and your wrists straight and flat.

◆ The monitor should be about an arm's length away, at a height that puts the top line of text at or just below eye level. If you'll be consulting paperwork, use a copyholder to position it at the same height as the screen.

Getting it together. Assembling a workstation takes two to nine hours depending on your skill level. Before you begin, lay out and inspect all the parts to see if anything is missing or damaged. If you need a replacement part, call the manufacturer; then be prepared to wait a week to 10 days to receive it.

Set the unit up in the location where it will be used—it may be very hard to move once assembled. To put most units together, you'll need a hammer, a screwdriver, an Allen-head wrench (included with the unit), and possibly a partner to help lift or position components. Some manufacturers warn that you can strip out a screw hole if you use a power screwdriver or drill. We used a cordless drill with an adjustable clutch and had no problems. If you're handy with tools, you shouldn't have difficulty either. Otherwise, we wouldn't advise experimenting with a project such as this.

If you lack the mechanical aptitude or time to assemble the workstation yourself, you can hire a pro to do it for you. The retailer may offer setup service or refer you to a company that will do the job. Assembly may cost $35 to $100 or so.

Packaged furniture often comes in large, heavy boxes. You'll need a big vehicle and a strong friend to help you move them—or consider having the furniture delivered. Many office-supply chain stores offer free delivery.

◆ **Ratings:** page 176

SURGE SUPPRESSORS

A surge suppressor can help protect computers and other pieces of home-office equipment from electrical slings and arrows.

A voltage spike caused by lightning, faulty wiring, or a return to service after a power outage can cause an array of computer problems, from keyboard lockup to damaged internal components. A surge suppressor can help minimize the risk of electrical damage by redirecting the energy surge away from your vulnerable equipment. It's also a handy way to plug in multiple equipment.

What's available

Most surge suppressors come with six to eight outlets and various indicators. Major brands are APC, Belkin, Monster Cable, Power Sentry, and Tripp Lite. Price range: $15 to $70.

Key features

Although most computers draw a maximum of 500 watts, surge suppressors are typically rated to carry 1,875 watts. Look for models with a **circuit breaker** that trips (and can be reset) when more than 15 amps are drawn. Better surge suppressors have rugged circuitry and use a variety of components that include capacitors, inductors, and **multiple metal-oxide varistors** (MOVs) to absorb or divert voltage spikes. Simpler models have MOVs and little else. Packaging can help you to spot better-quality suppressors by listing or showing cutaways of their internal parts.

Most surge suppressors come with **indicator lights** that show if previous spikes have compromised protection. A ground-indicator light tells you if the ground or wiring in your home is sound, though we've found that these lights aren't always accurate. Most models also provide at least one **telephone jack** to shield the phone line from surges—a feature we didn't test.

How to choose

PERFORMANCE DIFFERENCES. Most surge suppressors meet the Underwriters Laboratories' UL 1449 electrical-safety standard. CONSUMER REPORTS tested models for their ability to protect computers. All could protect a test computer from lower-energy surges. The best withstood hundreds of surges up to 6,000 volts, however, while some no longer provided protection when jolts reached 4,000 volts.

RECOMMENDATIONS. Every computer should be plugged into a surge suppressor. At the store, look for the words "inductors," "capacitors," "MOVs," "glass discharge tubes," "fuses," and "transorbs" on a surge suppressor's packaging. Also look for a UL rating, as well as enough space between outlets so that the transformer at the end of some accessory power cords won't cover adjacent outlets.

Still another consideration is the location of the on/off switch. Some models have it at the end opposite from the cord, making the unit convenient for use on a desk, with the switch near you and the cord leading back to a wall outlet. And if you live in an area with frequent lightning storms or power-line problems, consider replacing the surge suppressor every few years or so.

You can also help protect what you're working on by unplugging your computer and the modem's phone line when lightning storms are expected. For added peace of mind, consider buying an uninterruptible power supply (UPS). These begin at about $100 and contain a battery pack that provides a temporary energy source, giving you time to save your work and shut down the computer during a power outage. Some UPS devices also provide some surge protection.

PART 3

Reference

Ratings of the Equipment

Guide to the Brands

Glossary

Index

Ratings of the Equipment

156
Camcorders

159
Cell phones

161
Cell-phones alternatives

163
Desktop computers

165
Digital cameras

167
Monitors

169
MP3 players

171
PDAs

174
Printers

176
Work stations

HOW TO USE THE RATINGS

Read the report on the product you're interested in. The page number is noted for each Ratings category. The Overall Ratings gives the big picture in performance. Notes on features and performance for individual models are listed under Recommendations & Notes. Key numbers let you easily track between the Ratings and paragraphs. "Features at a Glance" sums up key aspects for some products.

We verify availability for most products especially for this book. Some tested models may no longer be available. Models similar to the tested models, when they exist, are listed in Recommendations & Notes. Such models differ in features, not essential performance, according to manufacturers.

Camcorders

Digital camcorders generally capture high-quality images and very good sound. They're easy to use and come with lots of features. If you want to try video editing or downloading to the web, invest in a digital model. The Sony DCR-PC120BT, $2000, is a very good though expensive choice. The Panasonic PV-DV402 and PV-DC152, both $800, and the Sony DCR-TRV240, $600, are worthy alternatives. Analog models are generally good and cost hundreds of dollars less than digital models. Picture quality, though generally a notch below digital, is still perfectly fine. Consider the moderately priced Sony CCD-TRV608, $400, or the Sony CCD-TRV308, $350.

Overall Ratings — In performance order

Ratings key: ● Excellent ◓ Very good ○ Good ◐ Fair ● Poor

KEY NO.	BRAND AND MODEL	PRICE	FORMAT	OVERALL SCORE	PICTURE QUALITY SP	EASE OF USE	IMAGE STABILIZER	WEIGHT (LBS)
DIGITAL MODELS								
1	Sony DCR-PC120BT	$2,000	MiniDV		◓	○	●	1.5
2	Panasonic PV-DV402	800	MiniDV		●	◓	●	1.4
3	Panasonic PV-DC152	800	MiniDV		●	○	◐	1.2
4	Sony DCR-TRV240	600	D8		◓	○	○	2.1
5	JVC GR-DVL920	900	MiniDV		●	○	◐	1.5
6	Sony DCR-TRV140	500	D8		◓	◓	●	2.2
7	Canon ZR45MC	700	MiniDV		◓	◓	○	1.4
8	Panasonic PV-DV102	600	MiniDV		◓	○	●	1.4
9	Canon Optura 100MC	1,500	MiniDV		◓	○	○	1.7
10	Panasonic PV-DV52	500	MiniDV		◓	○	●	1.4
11	Sony DCR-IP7BT	1,700	MicroMV		◓	◐	●	0.8
12	Sharp VL-NZ50U	500	MiniDV		◓	○	●	1.2
ANALOG MODELS								
13	Sony CCD-TRV608	400	Hi8		○	◓	○	2.2
14	Sony CCD-TRV308	350	Hi8		◓	◓	●	2.2
15	JVC GR-SXM240	300	SVHS-C		○	◐	○	2.4
16	Sony CCD-TRV108	300	Hi8		○	◓	NA	2.1
17	Samsung SC-L700	270	Hi8		○	◓	NA	2.0
18	Panasonic PV-L352	280	VHS-C		○	○	◐	2.6
19	Panasonic PV-L652	400	VHS-C		◐	○	◐	2.9
20	Sharp VL-AH131U	280	Hi8		◐	○	NA	1.9

See report, page 115. Based on tests posted on ConsumerReports.org in July 2002.

CONSUMER REPORTS DIGITAL BUYING GUIDE ● 157

The tests behind the Ratings

Format lists the recording format used. **Overall score** mainly reflects SP picture quality and ease of use. **Picture quality** is based on the judgments of trained panelists, who viewed still images shot at standard (SP) tape speed. **Ease of use** takes into account ergonomics, weight, how accurately the viewfinders framed the scene being shot, and measurements of the LCD's contrast. **Image stabilizer** scores reflect how well the circuitry worked. "NA" in a column means the camcorder lacks it. **Weight** is our measurement. **Price** is the approximate retail.

Recommendations and notes

Models listed as similar should offer performance comparable to the tested model's, although features may differ.

Most of these camcorders have: Rechargeable battery pack. AC adapter/battery charger. A/V cable. Playpack adapter (VHS-C and S-VHS-C models only). Ability to load tape, plug in power, or change battery when mounted on tripod. Selection of built-in autoexposure programs. Audio and video fade. Backlight compensation. High-speed manual shutter. Image stabilizer. LCD panel brightness control. Manual aperture control, focus, and white balance. Quick review. Soft eyecup. S-video out (not on 8mm and VHS-C). Tape counter. **Most digital camcorders also have:** FireWire or iLink connection, digital still function.

Optical zoom is as stated by the manufacturer. Audio frequency response, when recording with the built in microphone, was very good and relatively noise-free for most camcorders. Most camcorders with LP/EP mode yielded same picture quality as in SP mode. In dim lighting, most camcorders yielded a tolerable picture quality.

DIGITAL MODELS

1> **SONY** DCR-PC120BT **Excellent image stabilization in a feature-laden model, but sacrifices performance in low light.** Includes Bluetooth wireless interface and advanced communications capability to send video clips, stills, or e-mail over the Internet without a computer. Includes medium-resolution digital-camera capability via its memory card.

2> **PANASONIC** PV-DV402 **Excellent in performance in good lighting, but poor image stabilization and zoom is noisy.** Barely adequate in low light, but using built-in light and manual controls help. Includes a very large LCD viewer (3.5 in.) and medium-resolution digital-camera capability via its memory card. CCD and battery warranties on the short side (6 mos. and 10 days, respectively). Similar to the PV-DV102, which has a smaller viewer.

3> **PANASONIC** PV-DC152 **Very good overall, but LCD viewer hard to see in bright light.** CCD and battery warranties on the short side (6 mos. and 10 days, respectively). Poor picture quality in low light but using manual controls helps.

4> **SONY** DCR-TRV240 **Moderately priced and very good overall, with a zoom that's among the longest.** But LCD viewer hard to see in bright light and not as accurate as most at framing scenes. Can play back analog tapes in Hi8 and 8mm formats. Related to the less expensive DCR-TRV140.

5> **JVC** GR-DVL920 **Very good overall, and good in low light (but only if manual settings are used).** Includes a very large LCD viewer (3.5 in.), but hard to see viewer in bright light. Has medium-resolution digital-camera capability via its memory card. Battery life is under one hour. CCD and battery warranties on the short side (3 mos.).

6> **SONY** DCR-TRV140 **A lower-priced, more basic variant of the DCR-TRV240, but cannot play back analog tapes.** Good in low light, and easy to use overall, but poor image stabilization and noisy audio.

7> **CANON** ZR45MC **Very good and easy to use, with large controls, good low-light performance (on manual setting), and flutter-free audio.** Has low-resolution digital-camera capability via its memory card. Tape-head warranty on the short side (3 mos.).

8> **PANASONIC** PV-DV102 **Very good overall, and good in low light if built-in light and manual settings used.** Includes medium-resolution digital-camera capability via its memory card. But image stabilizer is poor, and its zoom is noisy. CCD and battery warranties on the short side (6 mos. and 10 days, respectively). Similar to the PV-DV402, but with a smaller LCD viewer (2.5 in.).

9> **CANON** Optura 100MC **Very good overall, with medium-resolution digital-camera capability via its memory card.** Includes features advanced users might want (microphone jack, hot shoe, A/V input), which bring up the price. Tape-head warranty on the short side (3 mos.). Poor low-light picture quality, but using its low-light program helps.

10> **PANASONIC** PV-DV52 **Good overall with very good picture quality in low light if built-in light and manual settings used.** But image stabilizer was poor and zoom is noisy; LCD hard to view in bright light. CCD and battery warranties on the short side (6 mos. and 10 days, respectively). Similar to the PV-DV102 but without the digital still camera.

11> **SONY** DCR-IP7BT **Good overall and very compact, but with cumbersome menu system and uses new recording format (MicroMV tape).** Includes Bluetooth wireless interface and advanced communications capability to send video clips, stills, or e-mail over the Internet without a computer. Has low-resolution digital-camera capability via its memory card. Poor low-light performance and image stabilizer.

12▷ **SHARP** VL-NZ50U **Like other Sharps, this one lacks an eyepiece, high-speed manual shutter, and S-video jack.** Good overall, with a larger LCD viewer but otherwise few frills. Poor image stabilizer. Zoom is noisy. Battery warranty on the short side (1 mo.).

ANALOG MODELS

13▷ **SONY** CCD-TRV608 **The more full-featured sibling of Sony's CCD-TRV308, with a larger LCD viewer.** Both are good in low light. Its image stabilization is better, though picture quality is a notch below the 308. Picture quality drops a notch at LP speed.

14▷ **SONY** CCD-TRV308 **Its LCD viewer is the smaller, more typical size, than its sibling, the CCD-TRV608.** Both are good in low light. This model offers poorer image stabilization, and its audio quality is only adequate. Surprisingly, the picture at SP speed is better than on the higher-priced CCD-TRV608.

15▷ **JVC** GR-SXM240 **A good, basic unit with good low-light performance.** VHS playback on a VCR is a plus, but the system brings inferior audio. LCD viewer hard to see in bright light, and camcorder not as easy to use as many. Battery and CCD warranties are on the short side (3 mos.).

16▷ **SONY** CCD-TRV108 **A good and basic camcorder.** Lack of image stabilizer and video light help hold the price. Performance in low light is only fair. Picuture quality drops a notch at LP speed.

17▷ **SAMSUNG** SC-L700 **Good, basic, easy to use, and very inexpensive as camcorders go, with a zoom that's among the longest.** No image stabilizer or slow recording speed.

18▷ **PANASONIC** PV-L352 **Good overall, with picture quality a notch better than its pricier sibling, the PV-L652.** It includes video time-lapse recording mode. VHS playback on a VCR is a plus, but background noise and flutter mar audio quality, and battery life is under one hour. Eyepiece not too accurate at framing scenes. CCD and battery warranties on the short side (6 mos. and 10 days, respectively).

19▷ **PANASONIC** PV-L652 **Higher-priced sibling of the PV-L352, this model includes low-resolution digital-camera capability via its memory card and video time-lapse recording mode.** VHS playback on a VCR is a plus, but it shares its sibling's audio problems, and it's among the heaviest camcorders. CCD and battery warranties on the short side (6 mos. and 10 days, respectively).

20▷ **SHARP** VL-AH131U **Like other Sharps, it lacks an eyepiece, high-speed manual shutter, and S-video jack.** Has a hard-to-use menu and no image stabilizer or slow recording speed. Fair performance overall, and battery warranty on the short side (1 mo.).

Cell phones

First, choose the service plan that best fits your calling patterns. Then choose a phone. To ensure that your cell phone can send and receive calls in the widest geographical area possible, buy a handset that uses both digital and analog technology. Get a dual-mode or tri-mode handset that can operate in analog mode when you travel outside the more limited digital cellular and PCS Networks. Most carriers use one of two incompatible digital formats called TDMA and CDMA. We've not found that either has an edge in conveying voice quality. The format your carrier uses will determine which handset you can use. Key features for these models are listed in the table on page 160. See product report for explanation of features.

Overall Ratings — In performance order

Ratings key: Excellent ● / Very good ◓ / Good ○ / Fair ◐ / Poor ●

KEY NO.	BRAND & MODEL (MAJOR PROVIDERS)	PRICE	OVERALL SCORE	VOICE QUALITY NOISY	VOICE QUALITY QUIET	EASE OF USE	BATTERY LIFE	DIGITAL-MODE TALK TIME (HR.)	BATTERY CAPACITY (MAH)
CDMA PHONES									
1	**Samsung** SPH-N200 (Sprint)	$200		◓	◓	○	●	4½	800
2	**Kyocera** Smart Phone QCP-6035 (Sprint, Verizon)	450		◓	◓	◓	○	2	1,550
3	**Nokia** 5180 (Alltel, US Cellular)	20		◓	◓	○	◓	2¾	900
4	**LG** TM510 (Verizon)	130		◓	◓	◓	◐	1¾	875
5	**Motorola** V120c (Verizon)	100		○	◓	○	○	2¼	1,100
6	**Motorola** V60c (Alltel, Verizon)	400		◓	◓	◓	◐	1½	450
7	**Motorola** Timeport P8767 (Sprint, Verizon)	150		○	◓	○	◐	2¼	900
TDMA PHONES									
8	**Nokia** 8260 (AT&T, Cellular One, Cingular, US Cellular)	200		○	◓	○	◓	3¼	900
9	**Motorola** V2397 (AT&T)	50		◓	◓	○	○	2¼	700
10	**Ericsson** R278d (Cingular)	100		◓	◓	○	○	2¼	800

See report, page 136. Based on tests published in Consumer Reports in February 2002, with updated prices and availability.

The tests behind the Ratings

Overall score combines voice quality; ease of use based on a phone's features, controls, display, and design; and battery life. **Voice quality** scores cover listening and speaking; they are derived from high-quality recordings of conversations, taped through the phone's earpiece and microphone, made by the side of a busy highway and in a quiet room; a computer analyzed the recordings, scoring for what listeners would respond to as the difference between clear, high-quality speech and speech mixed with noise. **Battery life** reflects how efficiently the phone uses the battery it came with. **Talk time** is for digital calls, rounded to the nearest quarter hour; analog talk time is always less. **Battery capacity** shows the power available, in milliampere-hours. **Price** is the average of prices charged by carriers offering the phones, as determined by TeleBright, a company that provides data for the interactive plan selector at ConsumerReports.org, and our own research.

Recommendations and notes

CDMA PHONES

1. **SAMSUNG** SPH-N200 (Sprint) **Very good overall.** 4.8 oz. Folding-case design. Very good performance in a small package.

2. **KYOCERA** Smart Phone QCP-6035 (Sprint, Verizon) **Very good overall.** 7.3 oz. Folding-case design. Speakerphone. Voice memo. Infrared link. Combines PalmOS PDA with phone. You can't dial 911 with keyguard on. Larger case than most. Less than 24 hours analog standby time.

3. **NOKIA** 5180 (Alltel, US Cellular) **Very good overall.** 6 oz. Less than 24 hours analog standby time. Discontinued, but similar 5185i is available.

4. **LG** TM510nn (Verizon) **Very good overall.** 4.4 oz. Folding-case design. Voice memo. Lots of features in a small package. Less than 24 hours analog standby time.

5. **MOTOROLA** V120c (Verizon) **Very good overall.** 4.5 oz. Voice memo. Worse than most in noisy background.

6. **MOTOROLA** V60c (Alltel, Verizon) **Good overall.** 3.9 oz. Folding-case design. Voice memo. Smaller case than most. Expensive for what you get. Less than 24 hours analog standby time.

7. **MOTOROLA** Timeport P8767 (Sprint, Verizon) **Good overall.** 4.6 oz. Folding-case design. There are better choices. Worse than most in noisy background. Less than 24 hours analog standby time.

TDMA PHONES

8. **NOKIA** 8260 (AT&T, Cellular One, Cingular, US Cellular) **Very good overall.** 3.5 oz. Very good battery life for a small phone. Headset connector incompatible with any other phone. Worse than most in noisy background. Discontinued, but may still be available.

9. **MOTOROLA** V2397 (AT&T) **Very good overall.** 5.3 oz.

10. **ERICSSON** R278d (Cingular) **Very good overall.** 6 oz. Less than 24 hours analog standby time.

Features at a glance — Cell phones

Tested products (keyed to the Ratings) Key no.	Brand & model	Tri-mode	Vibrating call alert	Roaming lock	One-touch redial	Voice-activated dialing	Web browser	Volume control on side	Can send SMS
CDMA PHONES									
1	Samsung		•	•		•	•	•	•
2	Kyocera	•	•		•		•	•	
3	Nokia								
4	LG	•		•				•	
5	Motorola		•			•	•	•	
6	Motorola		•	•		•	•	•	
7	Motorola		•					•	
TDMA PHONES									
8	Nokia	•	•				•	•	
9	Motorola			•				•	•
10	Ericsson		•			•	•		

Cell-phone alternatives

Two-way radios, cell phones, and pagers all have their uses. For conversations among a small group in a well-defined area, two-way radios are a good choice. Among FRS models, the Cobra FRS 225-2 is **A CR Best Buy**, at $70 per pair. Among GMRS models, the Cobra PR900-2DX, $100 a pair, is the better value. For brief text messages that must arrive reliably, a pager is a good alternative. Cell-phone short-messaging is best when time isn't critical and you're close enough to home to avoid roaming charges.

Overall Ratings — In performance order

Ratings key: Excellent ●, Very good ◖, Good ○, Fair ◐, Poor ●

KEY NO.	BRAND & MODEL	PRICE	OVERALL SCORE	VOICE QUALITY	EASE OF USE	FEATURES	BATTERY LIFE
FRS RADIOS These cover distances up to two miles.
1	RadioShack 21-1860	$200		◐	◐	○	◐
2	Motorola T-6200	110		◐	○	◖	◐
3	Audiovox FR1500XTM	180		◐	◐	◐	○
4	Cobra FRS 225-2 **A CR Best Buy**	70		◐	○	○	◐
5	Midland F12	60		○	◖	◐	○
6	Motorola T-5200	50		◓	○	◐	◖
7	BellSouth 1050 BK	40		●	◖	◐	○
8	Uniden FRS 440	100		◓	○	○	◖
GMRS RADIOS These cover distances up to five miles.
9	Cobra PR900-2DX	100		○	◖	○	○
10	Motorola T-6400	200		○	○	◖	○

See report, page 143. Based on tests published in Consumer Reports in July 2002.

The tests behind the Ratings

Overall score combines voice quality, ease of use, features, and battery life. **Voice quality** is our assessment of how natural voices sound and how easy they are to understand. **Ease of use** includes the display's clarity, how well buttons are labeled, and how easy it was to replace batteries. **Features** includes a variety of amenities, such as a battery gauge and display backlight. **Battery life,** a combination of transmitting and receiving times, measures how long fresh batteries will last. When continuously transmitting, the best lasted 10 hours and the worst, 3. When receiving, the best lasted 61 hours and the worst, 9. **Price** is approximate retail for a pair of units.

Recommendations and notes

All radios have: Subcodes for each channel to provide more frequency combinations. Low-battery indicator. Nonretractable antenna. Call function to page other units. Headset jack. Button to fully open squelch. **Most radios have:** A one-year parts-and-labor warranty. A weight of between 6 and 8 ounces, including batteries.

FRS RADIOS

1. **RADIOSHACK** 21-1860 **Very good performer, but expensive.** Charges batteries without removing them. Monitors two channels. Scans channels for activity. Factory-reset button. Backlight. Belt clip. Four AA batteries. Heavier than the others. 90-day warranty.

2. **MOTOROLA** T-6200 **Very good and feature laden.** Stops transmitter after 1 minute. Charges batteries without removing them. Battery gauge. Scans channels for activity. Button lock. Factory-reset button. Backlight. Belt clip. Three AA batteries. But talk button is on front. Similar: T-6220.

3. **AUDIOVOX** FR1500XTM **Very good performer geared for outdoor enthusiasts, but expensive.** Battery gauge. Scans channels for activity. Vibrate alert. Button lock. Backlight. Belt clip. Compass. Weather radio. Thermometer. Clock. Stopwatch. FM radio. Four AAA batteries. 90-day warranty.

4. **COBRA** FRS 225-2 **A CR Best Buy Good price for a very good performer.** Charges batteries without removing them. Button lock. Backlight. Hand strap. Belt clip. Three AA batteries. Units sold in pairs only. 2-yr. warranty.

5. **MIDLAND** F12 **Good price for a good performer.** Lighter than the others. Charges batteries without removing them. Automatic standby mode. Monitors two channels. Scans channels for activity. Button lock. Factory-reset button. Hand strap. Three AAA batteries. Units sold individually or in pairs.

6. **MOTOROLA** T-5200 **Good price, but voice quality is only fair.** Stops transmitter after 1 minute. Battery gauge. Button lock. Backlight. Belt clip. Three AA batteries. But talk button is on front. Units sold in pairs only. Discontinued, but similar T-5400, T-5420 are available. Similar models are slimmer and lighter than the T-5200 and have talk button on the side. Their voice quality is comparable with that of the T-5200.

7. **BELLSOUTH** 1050 BK **Good price, but voice quality is only fair.** Lighter than the others. Charges batteries without removing them. Battery gauge. Automatic standby mode. Scans channels for activity. Button lock. Backlight. Belt clip. Four AAA batteries.

8. **UNIDEN** FRS 440 **Geared to outdoor enthusiasts, but other models performed better.** Battery gauge. Automatic standby mode. Scans channels for activity. Vibrate alert. Backlight. Belt clip. Weather radio. Thermometer. FM radio. Microphone and headset. Three AA batteries. But no end-of-transmission beep. Similar: FRS 420.

GMRS RADIOS

9. **COBRA** PR900-2DX **Good price and very easy to use.** 15 channels. Charges batteries without removing them. Battery gauge. Scans channels for activity. Button lock. Backlight. Belt clip. 2-yr. warranty. Four AAA batteries. But no end-of-transmission beep. Units sold individually or in pairs.

10. **MOTOROLA** T-6400 **Good, with lots of features, but expensive.** 22 channels. Stops transmitter after 1 minute. Charges batteries without removing them. Battery gauge. Scans channels for activity. Vibrate alert. Button lock. Factory-reset button. Backlight. Belt clip. Clock. Stopwatch. Three AA batteries. But talk button is on front.

Desktop computers

Prices for new computers are as low as they've ever been for the amount of features and speed you receive. Your first consideration is whether you want a Windows-based or a Macintosh computer. Among the Windows computers we tested, the Dell Dimension 4400, $1,380, offers the best overall combination of performance, customer support, and reliability. The Gateway 500X, $1,480, performed well, but it's been among the more repair-prone brands. The Apple New iMac, $1,600, a fine machine, continues Apple's tradition of design innovation.

Overall Ratings   In performance order

Ratings key: Excellent ● | Very good ◕ | Good ○ | Fair ◐ | Poor ●

KEY NO	BRAND & MODEL	PRICE	OVERALL SCORE	APPLICATION SPEED	GRAPHICS SPEED	FEATURES	POWER USE	WARRANTY, SUPPORT
	WINDOWS COMPUTERS							
1	**Gateway** 500X	$1,480*		◕	◕	●	◕	○
2	**Dell** Dimension 4400	1,380*		◕	◕	●	◕	●
3	**Compaq** Presario 6000	1,430		◕	◕	◕	◕	◕
4	**HP** Pavilion 701	1,625		◕	●	◕	◕	○
5	**Sony** Vaio PCV-RX600N	1,110		◕	●	◕	◕	◐
6	**IBM** NetVista 2292 CJU	1,510*		◕	◕	◕	●	○
7	**eMachines** T4170	1,035*		◕	◕	◕	●	○
	MACINTOSH COMPUTER							
8	**Apple** New iMac	1,600		●	●	●	●	◕

See report, page 99. Based on tests published in Consumer Reports in September 2002.

The tests behind the Ratings

Overall score includes speed, features, and power efficiency. **Application speed** tracks how the computer compared with an 866-megahertz (MHz) Pentium III computer for Windows machines and a 333-MHz iMac for the iMac doing typical office work. The iMac is measured on a scale that's different from the others, so its scores aren't directly comparable. **Graphics speed** measures the ability to render smooth motion in game-style graphics. **Features** includes myriad conveniences, such as well-marked and easily accessible connectors, comprehensive manuals, audio capabilities, expandability, and upgradability. **Power use** measures the computer's electricity consumption and power-saving features. **Warranty, support** reflects our judgment of service and support. **Price** is approximate retail with manufacturer's 17-inch flat-screen CRT monitor (or the closest equivalent). An asterisk (*) denotes a model usually sold by mail or at an in-store kiosk.

Recommendations and notes

Most tested computers have: 2-GHz Pentium 4 processor. 256 megabytes (MB) of RAM with room for more. 60- to 80-gigabyte (GB) hard drive. CD-RW and DVD drives. Standard floppy drive. 32 to 64 MB of video RAM. AGP graphics port. Brand-name speakers without a separate woofer. Keyboard with multifunction control panel. Separate standby button. Mechanical mouse with scrolling control. "Works"-level application package. V.90 modem and Ethernet network connection. 3 to 4 free USB ports, at least 2 on front. 2 free PCI slots for internal expansion cards. 1 or 2 free internal bays for additional hard drive. 1 free front-drive bay. Microtower case that opens without tools.

WINDOWS COMPUTERS

1. **GATEWAY** 500X **Excellent overall, but among the more trouble-prone brands.** 5 free USB ports. S-video output. Optical mouse. Includes microphone. Drives install without screws. Keyboard has CD/DVD function keys. Sound with standard speakers better than most. No standby button. Only 1 free PCI slot. No hard-drive access light. Current version has 2.4-GHz processor.

2. **DELL** Dimension 4400 **Excellent overall.** S-video output. Includes microphone. Fast graphics, good for gamers. Drives install without screws. Quieter than most. Case opens easily, but must first be placed on its side. Replaced by similar 4500 series.

3. **COMPAQ** Presario 6000 **Very good overall.** 1.4-GHz Athlon XP processor. 5 free USB ports. More-compact tower case than previous models. Optical mouse. Drives install without screws. No free drive bays on front. No sleep button. Desktop crammed with promotional items such as Internet links to Disney. Current version has 1.5-GHz processor.

4. **HP** Pavilion 701 **Very good overall.** 1.7-GHz Athlon XP processor. 3 FireWire ports, 2 on front. S-video output. Very fast graphics, good for avid gamers. Well-designed keyboard. No free drive bays on front. Only 1 free PCI slot. Lacks power indicator on case. Desktop crammed with promotional items such as HP shopping toolbar. System-restore CD not supplied; available only on request. Replaced by similar 525 Series.

5. **SONY** Vaio PCV-RX600N **Very good overall.** 2 FireWire ports, 1 on rear. Quieter than most. Comes with a good selection of multimedia content-creation software, including Sound Forge, ACID, and DV Gate. No free drive bays on front. Compact keyboard may feel cramped. Replaced by similar PCV-RX750.

6. **IBM** NetVista 2292 CJU **Very good overall.** Combo DVD/CD-RW drive. Angular, black case may appeal to some. Only 1 free PCI slot. No free internal-drive bay. Compact keyboard may feel cramped. No keyboard control panel or standby button.

7. **EMACHINES** T4170 **Very good overall.** Basic and inexpensive, but reliability may be a problem. 1.6-GHz Pentium 4 processor. CD-RW drive; no DVD drive available. Small, unbranded speakers are poor for music. No keyboard control panel or standby button. Noisier than most while running.

MACINTOSH COMPUTER

8. **APPLE** New iMac **Very good overall, unique design.** 700-MHz PowerPC G4 processor. Both OS 9.2 and OS X installed. Combo DVD/CD-RW drive. 40-GB hard drive. Slot for AirPort wireless networking card ($90). 2 FireWire ports on rear. Connector for VGA monitor. Built-in microphone. Optical mouse. Excellent built-in 15-inch liquid crystal display, easy to adjust position. Compact design with sleek styling. Only one CD-type drive, so copying data or files becomes a two-step process. No floppy drive, hard-drive access light, internal expansion, or sleep button. Power switch in awkward location.

Digital cameras

Paying more gets you more pixels, but not always improved results. The 2-megapixel Nikon Coolpix 2500, $380, produced excellent images. Consider a 3- to 5-megapixel camera for greater latitude in cropping and enlarging. The Sony DSC-F707, $1,000, topped the Ratings. The Olympus Camedia D-40 Zoom, $650, is a high-scoring model for less money.

Overall Ratings — In performance order

Excellent ● · Very good ◔ · Good ○ · Fair ◐ · Poor ●

KEY NO.	BRAND & MODEL	PRICE PAID	OVERALL SCORE	PRINT QUALITY	MEGA-PIXELS	WEIGHT (OZ.)	FLASH RANGE (FT.)	NEXT-SHOT DELAY (SEC.)	BATTERY LIFE (SHOTS)
2 MEGAPIXELS									
1	Nikon Coolpix2500	$380		●	2	7	10	2	140
2	Olympus Camedia C-700 Ultra Zoom	500		◐	2.1	14	18	2	70
3	Minolta Dimage X	400		◐	2	6	10	3	240
3 TO 5 MEGAPIXELS									
4	Sony DSC-F707	1,000		●	5	25	15	1	240
5	Canon PowerShot G2	800		●	4	18	15	2	600
6	Olympus Camedia D-40 Zoom	650		●	4.1	8	10	3	700
7	Sony Cyber-shot DSC-S75	500		●	3.3	16	10	3	300
8	Kodak DX-4900	400		●	4	10	10	2	95
9	Olympus E-10	1200		●	4.1	40	21	2	50
10	Casio QV-4000	700		◐	4.1	17	11	3	460
11	Panasonic Lumix DMC-LC5	800		◐	3.9	16	15	4	240
12	Minolta Dimage 7	900		◐	5.24	22	12	9	45
13	Minolta Dimage S404	500		◐	4.1	16	7	4	70
14	Toshiba PDR-M81	500		◐	4.2	12	10	4	110
15	Kyocera Finecam S3	500		◐	3.34	7	8	11	80

See report, page 118. Based on tests posted on ConsumerReports.org in July 2002.

The tests behind the Ratings

Overall score is based mainly on print quality and convenience. **Print quality** reflects the judgments of trained viewers who compared glossy 5x7-inch test photos made on a high-quality inkjet printer, using glossy photo paper. **Megapixels** shows how many million elements the image sensor has. **Weight** includes battery and memory card or disk. **Flash range** is the maximum claimed range for a well-lighted photo. **Next-shot delay** is the time a camera needed to ready itself for the next photo. **Battery life** reflects our tests to measure the number of high-resolution photos taken on a fresh set of alkaline batteries (or, if included, with rechargeables fully charged); half the shots used flash, and the zoom lens was racked in and out. **Price** is approximate retail.

Recommendations and notes

Most cameras have: Optical viewfinder and LCD viewer, autofocus and autoexposure, built-in automatic flash that can be switched off, multiple flash modes, exposure-compensation settings, self-timer, tripod socket, software for Windows and Macintosh, ability to connect to a computer through a USB port, and a one-year warranty on parts and labor.

2 MEGAPIXELS

1. **NIKON** Coolpix 2500 **Very good overall with good battery life.** Lacks viewfinder, swivel lens. Software: Nikon View 5.

2. **OLYMPUS** Camedia C-700 Ultra Zoom **Very good overall.** Excellent battery life using lithium batteries; fair with AA batteries. 10x optical zoom, electronic viewfinder. Software: Olympus Camedia Master 2.5.

3. **MINOLTA** Dimage X **Very good overall with very good battery life.** No grip for holding camera. Very small shape, lens shoots though prism. Software: ArcSoft PhotoImpression.

3 TO 5 MEGAPIXELS

4. **SONY** DSC-F707 **Very good overall with good battery life.** Night shot IR photography. Well-shaped grip for holding camera, heavier and bulkier than most. Has electronic viewfinder, tilt body. Software: MGI PhotoSuite.

5. **CANON** PowerShot G2 **Very good overall with excellent battery life.** Has direct printing without computer, swing out LCD display, histogram on preview. Well-shaped grip for holding camera. Has hot shoe. Software: Photoshop 5.0 LE.

6. **OLYMPUS** Camedia D-40 Zoom **Very good overall with very good battery life.** No grip for holding a camera. Very small shape, Software: Photoshop Elements.

7. **SONY** Cyber-shot DSC-S75 **Very good overall.** Uses camcorder-type battery (included). Well shaped grip for holding camera. USB connection only. Can record audio and movie clips. Software: MGI PhotoSuite 8.1 (no instant fix).

8. **KODAK** DX-4900 **Very good overall.** Supplied AA batteries gave poor results. Optional Camera Docking for easy picture transfer. Software: Kodak picture software.

9. **OLYMPUS** E-10 **Very good overall.** Battery life: 540 shots using Olympus lithium batteries. SLR viewfinder very accurate. Bulky and heavy. Well-shaped grip for holding. LCD image relatively bright. USB connection only. Software: Camedia Master 2.5, Adobe Photoshop 5.0 LE.

10. **CASIO** QV-4000 **Very good overall with very good battery life.** Displays histogram in record mode. Has external flash socket. Well-shaped grip for holding camera. Software: Photohands.

11. **PANASONIC** Lumix DMC-LC5 **Very good overall with good battery life.** Large LCD screen, well shaped grip for holding camera. Has hot shoe. Software: ArcSoft.

12. **MINOLTA** Dimage 7 **Very good overall.** SLR viewfinder accurate. LCD image relatively bright. Bulky, heavy. Well shaped grip for holding camera. USB connection only. Can record movie clips. Can take IBM Microdrive. Hard to change flash mode. Software: Dimage Image Viewer (lacks cropping, printing).

13. **MINOLTA** Dimage S404 **Very good overall with fair battery life.** Displays histogram in playback mode. Well-shaped grip for holding camera. Has 4X optical zoom. Software: ArcSoft PhotoImpression.

14. **TOSHIBA** PDR-M81 **Very good overall with fair battery life.** Displays histogram window in real time and playback mode. Software: ImageExpert. Discontinued, but may still be available.

15. **KYOCERA** Finecam S3 **Good overall.** Tiny camera. No grip for holding camera. No port for connecting camera to computer; user must transfer memory card to card reader. Uses camcorder-type battery (included). Can record movie clips. Software: ArcSoft PhotoImpression 3.0.

Monitors

If you spend hours staring at a computer screen, it may be wise to pay more for a flat-panel LCD screen. In our tests, LCDs provided the clearest, sharpest images. Still, the best CRTs are very good and cost significantly less. LCD monitors deliver crisp pictures and text while saving desk space. The top 15-inch models—the Philips 150P2E and the NEC MultiSync LCD 1550X, each $550—offer flexible adjustments and easy-to-use controls. CRT monitors are an excellent value and can show a wider range of colors than an LCD; they also display videos especially well. But they're big and use a lot of power. The Dell P992, $430, like many big-screen CRTs, costs less than smaller LCD models.

Overall Ratings — In performance order

Ratings key: Excellent ● Very good ◖ Good ○ Fair ◐ Poor ●

KEY NO.	BRAND & MODEL	PRICE	OVERALL SCORE	VIEWABLE IMAGE	DISPLAY	EASE OF USE
LCD MONITORS *These have a space-saving flat display like that on notebook computers.*
1	Apple Studio Display	$1,000		17 in.	●	◖
2	Philips 150P2E	550		15	◖	◖
3	IBM T750	875		17	◖	●
4	NEC MultiSync LCD 1550X	550		15	◖	●
5	Sony SDM-S51	500		15	◖	◖
6	Gateway FPD1810	980		18	◖	◖
7	Apple New iMac	1,500		15	◖	◖
8	ViewSonic VX500	500		15	◖	◖
9	HP Pavilion f50	600		15	○	◖
CRT MONITORS *These use a bulky TV-style cathode-ray tube.*
10	Dell P992	430		19	◖	○
11	Sony HMD-A440	400		19	○	●
12	NEC MultiSync FE700+	220		17	◖	◖
13	Dell M782	200		17	○	◖
14	Sony CPD-E240	250		17	○	◖
15	IBM G78	230		17	○	◖
16	Gateway EV700	230		17	○	◖
17	IBM P97	550		19	○	○
18	Compaq FS7550	400		17	○	◖
19	HP Pavilion mx75	500		17	○	◖
20	Philips 107B30	200		17	○	○
21	ViewSonic A90f	300		19	○	◖
22	eMachines MF 17c	260		17	○	○
23	HP Pavilion mx90	550		19	○	○

See report, page 107. Based on tests published in Consumer Reports in September 2002.

The tests behind the Ratings

Overall score is based mainly on image clarity. Image gives a monitor's nominal image size, measured diagonally; the **viewable image** size is the same as the nominal size for LCD monitors; an inch less than the nominal size for CRTs. Our viewing panelists gauged **display** quality for text and photo. Ease of use covers the front-panel controls, onscreen menus, tilt adjustment, and the like. **Price** is approximate retail.

Recommendations and notes

Most monitors have: A control to restore factory settings; a three-year warranty on parts, labor, tube or backlight; multilingual menus; nondetachable video cable; setup guide; no adapter for Macintosh. **These LCD monitors have:** Factory-set resolution of 1,024x768 pixels (15-inch), 1,280x1,024 (17- and 18-inch); depth of 6½ to 9½ inches and weight of 8 to 16 pounds. **These CRT monitors have:** Maximum resolution of 1,280x1,024 pixels (17-inch), 1,600x1,200 (19-inch); depth that's roughly equal to nominal screen size; weight of 35 to 57 pounds.

LCD MONITORS

1> **APPLE** Studio Display **Excellent overall, with wide viewing angle.** But harder to tilt, and control buttons are harder to use than most. Warranty of only 90 days on parts, 1 year on labor.

2> **PHILIPS** 150P2E **Very good overall, but control buttons harder to use than most.** Detachable video cable. Display rotates from landscape to portrait. Mac adapter supplied. Similar: 150B2B, 150P2M.

3> **IBM** T750 **Very good overall, with wide viewing angle.** But control buttons harder to use than most. Detachable video cable.

4> **NEC** MultiSync LCD 1550X **Very good overall, with wide viewing angle.** Detachable video cable. Display rotates from landscape to portrait, but monitor is harder to tilt than most. 3-year warranty.

5> **SONY** SDM-S51 **Very good overall.** Detachable video cable.

6> **GATEWAY** FPD1810 **Very good overall.** Detachable video cable. Warranty of only 1 year on parts and labor.

7> **APPLE** New iMac **Very good overall, but control buttons harder to use than most.** Sold only as integral part of Apple iMac computer. Has microphone, speakers. Warranty of only 90 days on parts, 1 year on labor. Monitor supplied with computer rated on page 163.

8> **VIEWSONIC** VX500 **Very good overall, with wide viewing angle.** Has microphone, speakers, detachable video cable.

9> **HP** Pavilion f50 **Good overall.** Detachable video cable. Only 1 year warranty on parts and labor.

CRT MONITORS

10> **DELL** P992 **Very good overall, but harder to tilt than most.** Menu and controls harder to use than most.

11> **SONY** HMD-A440 **Very good overall, but control buttons harder to use than most.** Only 1-year warranty on parts and labor. Monitor supplied with computer rated on page 163.

12> **NEC** MultiSync FE700+ **Very good overall, but harder to tilt than most.** 3-year warranty. Similar: FE700M+.

13> **DELL** M782 **Good overall, but harder to tilt than most.** Monitor supplied with computer rated on page 163.

14> **SONY** CPD-E240 **Good overall.** Similar: HMD-A240.

15> **IBM** G78 **Good overall, but control buttons harder to use than most.** Monitor supplied with computer rated on page 163.

16> **GATEWAY** EV700 **Good overall, but control buttons harder to use than most.** Curved screen. Only 1-year warranty on parts and labor. Monitor supplied with computer rated on page 163.

17> **IBM** P97 **Good overall, but menu and control buttons hard to use.**

18> **COMPAQ** FS7550 **Good overall.** Has speakers.

19> **HP** Pavilion mx75 **Good overall, but harder to tilt than most.** Has microphone. Only 1-year warranty.

20> **PHILIPS** 107B30 **Good.**

21> **VIEWSONIC** A90f **Good.**

22> **EMACHINES** MF 17c **Good overall, but harder to tilt than most.** Only 1-year warranty. Monitor supplied with computer rated on page 163. Discontinued, but similar eView 17f is available.

23> **HP** Pavilion mx90 **Good overall, but harder to tilt than most.** Has microphone. Only 1-year warranty.

CONSUMER REPORTS DIGITAL BUYING GUIDE ❖ 169

MP3 players

Which MP3 player you choose depends on how much music you want to tote around and what you're willing to pay for more storage. Capacity, cost, and size vary widely. For PC owners, the feature-laden Creative Labs Nomad IIc 64MB, $130, is **A CR Best Buy.** Among high-capacity players, the Creative Labs Nomad Jukebox 6GB, $250, is a very good choice, though its battery life is short—five hours. Like the Archos Jukebox Recorder, $300, it lets you record from an audio system onto the player without a computer. Mac users: Consider the feature-rich SONICblue Rio 800 128MB, $250 (it's also PC compatible). The compact Apple iPod, also $300, now works with both Mac and Windows.

Overall Ratings In performance order

Ratings key: Excellent ● | Very good ◓ | Good ○ | Fair ◑ | Poor ●

Key No.	Brand & Model	Price	Overall Score	Capacity Provided	Storage Format	Signal Quality	Headphones	Ease of Use	Battery Life
STANDARD MODELS — These players must receive music files from a computer.
1	**Creative Labs** Nomad IIc 64MB **A CR Best Buy**	$130		64 MB	SmartM	●	◓	●	13 hr.
2	**Panasonic** SV-SD80	280		64 MB	SD	●	◓	●	24
3	**SONICblue** Rio 800 128MB	250		128 MB	Proprietary	●	◓	●	9
4	**Bantam Interactive** BA350	200		128 MB	MMC	●	○	●	11
5	**SONICblue** Rio One	90		32 MB	VFlash	○	◓	●	15
6	**Nike** psa play 120	250		64 MB	MMC	●	◑	●	10*
7	**SONICblue** Rio 600 32MB	130		32 MB	Proprietary	●	●	●	12
HIGH-CAPACITY MODELS — These players can receive music files from a computer.
8	**Creative Labs** Nomad Jukebox 6GB	250		6 GB	None	●	○	●	5
9	**D-Link** Roq-it DMP-HD610 10GB	230		10 GB	None	●	○	●	6
10	**Apple** iPod	300		5 GB	None	●	◓	●	15
11	**Archos** Jukebox Recorder	300		6 GB	None	●	◑	●	9

See report, page 127. Based on tests published in Consumer Reports in May 2002, with updated prices and availability.

The tests behind the Ratings

Overall score is based primarily on signal quality, with headphone quality and ease of use also considered. **Capacity provided** combines built-in and external memory supplied with the unit. External **storage format** types include SmartMedia (SmartM), Secure Digital (SD), MultimediaCard (MMC), and 3.3V FlashMemory (VFlash). "None" means memory not expandable. **Signal quality** reflects frequency response and any noise or distortion, and judgments of testers using high-fidelity headphones. **Headphones** indicates their accuracy in reproducing sound. **Ease of use** reflects player controls and selected features. It also reflects **battery life,** a measure of playing time when display is backlit at minimum. An asterisk (*) indicates manufacturer's specification. (All uncompressed music and test sources were ripped to manufacturer's recommended CD-quality setting using provided PC software. MusicMatch was used when no ripping software was provided with the player.) **Price** is approximate retail. In recommendations & notes, data storage means you can transfer files other than MP3, such as text or video, without reformatting. Line out or output enables connection to an audio system. Digital or line input allows recording from an audio system to the player.

Recommendations and notes

Models listed as similar should offer performance comparable to the tested model's, although capacity or features may differ.

All players: Include software, headphones, batteries, and at least three months' parts and labor warranty. **Most:** Support USB. Play back in MP3 and other formats. Have upgradable firmware. Have play modes such as Repeat All and Random. Have backlit display. Show song titles. Have equalizer controls, custom and/or presets. **Most standard players:** Are sized like a deck of cards. Use one or two AA or AAA batteries. **Most high-capacity players:** Resemble portable CD players in size and weight. Use four AA rechargeable batteries. Have no expandable memory.

STANDARD MODELS

1. **CREATIVE LABS** Nomad IIc 64MB **A CR Best Buy Has easy-to-use song list, voice recording, line output.**

2. **PANASONIC** SV-SD80 **Tiniest.** Data storage. But no firmware upgrades. Nonstandard battery. No equalizer or backlit display.

3. **SONICBLUE** Rio 800 128MB **Stylish, feature-rich.** Voice recording. But battery is not removable. Discontinued, but may still be available.

4. **BANTAM INTERACTIVE** BA350 **Palm-sized.** But recharge battery through USB.

5. **SONICBLUE** Rio One **Inexpensive, but audible background hum during play.** No song titles or backlit display. Discontinued, but may still be available.

6. **NIKE** psa play 120 **Computer-mouse-shaped.** But no play modes. Remote display not backlit. Didn't work with some PCs.

7. **SONICBLUE** Rio 600 32MB **Stylish, but there are better choices.** Discontinued, but may still be available.

HIGH-CAPACITY MODELS

8. **CREATIVE LABS** Nomad Jukebox 6GB **Very good.** Has line in for recording, two line outputs. Similar: Nomad Jukebox 20GB, $350.

9. **D-LINK** Roq-it DMP-HD610 10GB **Inexpensive.** Data storage. But nonstandard battery. Line output. No playback in other formats. Discontinued, but may still be available.

10. **APPLE** iPod **Compact.** Easy-to-use song list. FireWire. Data storage. But Mac only. No equalizer. Nonremovable battery. Similar: iPod 10GB, $400; iPod 20GB, $500.

11. **ARCHOS** Jukebox Recorder **Voice recording, line and digital input for recording.** Data storage. Displays text files. But no playback in other formats. Similar: Jukebox Recorder 10GB, $240; Jukebox Recorder 20GB, $350; Jukebox 6000 6GB, $250; Jukebox Studio 10GB, $230; Jukebox Studio 20GB, $350.

PDAs

First decide which of the two leading PDA styles you prefer: a Palm-based unit or a Pocket PC. Palm-based models offer easy access to an address book, memo pad, appointment calendar, and to-do list. The Palm m105, $150, is an economical option that can be used with either a PC or a Mac. For $195, the Sony Clié PEG-S360 offers 16-MB of RAM but has a sealed battery that requires professional replacement. The Kyocera and Samsung units combine a PDA and cell phone. Pocket PCs are designed to work with Microsoft software. They also tend to cost and weigh more than Palm OS models. The HP Jornada 565, $550, tops the Pocket PC Ratings with its clear color screen, ease of use, and good battery life. A few PDAs such as the Casio BE-300, $200, use a proprietary operating system, which limits connectivity and available software. Key features for these models are listed in the table on page 172. See product report for explanation of features.

Overall Ratings — In performance order

Ratings key: Excellent ● | Very good ◉ | Good ○ | Fair ◐ | Poor ●

Key No.	Brand & Model	Price	Overall Score (P F G VG E)	Ease of Use	Battery Life	Display	In Sync	Convenience
	PALM-OS MODELS							
1	Sony Clié PEG-S360	$195		○	◉	◉	◉	◉
2	Palm m500	330		◉	◉	○	◉	◉
3	Sony Clié PEG-T415	250		○	◉	◉	◉	◉
4	HandEra 330	300		○	◉	◉	○	◉
5	Kyocera Smartphone QCP6035	450 [1]		○	◉	○	◉	◉
6	Palm m105	150		○	◉	○	◉	◉
7	Handspring Visor Edge	250		○	◉	○	◉	○
8	Handspring Visor Platinum	170		○	◉	○	◉	◉
9	Palm i705	450		○	◉	◉	◉	◉
10	Palm m505	400		○	◉	◉	◉	◉
11	Palm m125	200		○	◉	○	◉	◉
12	Handspring Visor Pro	230		○	◉	◉	◉	◉
13	Handspring Visor Prism	300		○	○	○	◉	○
14	Sony Clié PEG-T615C	400		○	◐	◉	◉	◉
15	Samsung SPH-I300	500 [1]		○	○	◐	○	○
	POCKET PC MODELS							
16	HP Jornada 565	550		◉	○	○	○	◉
17	Compaq iPaq H3835	600		○	○	○	○	◉
18	Casio Cassiopeia E-200	600		○	◐	○	○	◉
19	Compaq iPaq H3765	500		○	◐	○	○	○
	PROPRIETARY SYSTEM							
20	Casio BE-300	200		◐	◐	◐	◐	○

[1] Price varies depending on cellular phone plan or special offers.

See report, page 111. Based on tests published in Consumer Reports in June 2002, with updated prices and availability.

The tests behind the Ratings

Overall score is based on ease of use, battery life, display quality, synchronization with a computer, and convenience. Models with the same score are listed in alphabetical order. **Ease of use** considers ergonomic factors; navigation among tasks; and usability of phone lists, calendar, to-do list, and memo pad. **Battery life** indicates how long fully charged batteries lasted in continuous use (with the backlight mostly turned off for monochrome models): ● 20 hours or more; ◐ 10 to 20 hours; ○ 5 to 10 hours; ◌ fewer than 5 hours. **Display** reflects screen readability in low and normal room light and in sunlight. Monochrome and color displays were scored on a different scale. **In sync** gauges how easy it is to synchronize data (including word-processing and spreadsheet files for models that come with such software) with a computer. **Convenience** considers battery type, expansion capability, bundled software, and fit for shirt pocket. **Price** is approximate retail.

Recommendations and notes

Models listed as similar should offer performance comparable to the tested model's, although features may differ.

Except as noted, all models have: Basic personal-information-management functions (phone lists, calendar, to-do list, memo pad). Ability to transfer e-mail to and from a desktop computer. Docking station to synchronize with a computer; the station usually doubles as a charger for models with a rechargeable battery. Ability to synchronize via universal serial bus port or serial port. User manual on CD only.

PALM-OS MODELS

1 > **SONY** Clié PEG-S360 **Very good and reasonably priced, with an excellent monochrome display.** Overall design better than most. Handy jog dial. Easily readable in sunlight. Includes picture viewer and some multimedia software. Fits easily in shirt pocket. Printed manual. But battery can't be replaced by user. Doesn't include backup program or docking station (comes with cables only). 4¼ oz.

2 > **PALM** m500 **Very good; small, light case.** Overall design better than most. Easily readable in sunlight. Includes eBook reader, picture viewer, expense-tracker, and mobile connectivity software. LED and vibrating alarm. Fits easily in shirt pocket. But battery can't be replaced by user. Word-processing and spreadsheet programs can't use expansion cards, and you can't enter formulas in spreadsheets. Doesn't include backup program. 4 oz.

3 > **SONY** Clié PEG-T415 **Very good; smallest case of any Palm-based unit.** Easily readable in sunlight. Handy jog dial. Includes picture viewer, some multimedia software. Can function as remote control. LED and vibrating alarm. Fits easily in shirt pocket. Printed manual. But battery can't be replaced by user. Default display font hard to read. Thin case not as comfortable to hold as most. 4¼ oz.

4 > **HANDERA** 330 **Very good for peripherals and has many features, though some aren't well integrated.** Two expansion slots. Viewable screen area larger than that of most Palm-based units. Easily readable in sunlight. Includes expense-tracker and voice-recording software. LED alarm. Uses AAA batteries. But word-processing and spreadsheet programs can't use expansion cards. 6 oz.

5 > **KYOCERA** Smartphone QCP6035 **Very good, and one of the better choices for wireless access.** Basic organizer functions easy to use and well integrated with cell-phone functions. Easily readable in sunlight. Includes expense-tracker and voice-recording software. Printed manual. But display is small. Doesn't include backup program. 7¼ oz.

Features at a glance — PDAs

Key no.	Tested products (keyed to the Ratings) Brand	Memory (MB)	Replaceable battery	Color display	Display size (in.)	Expansion slot	Office software
PALM-OS MODELS							
1 >	Sony	16			2.9	MS	•
2 >	Palm	8			3.0	M	•
3 >	Sony	7			2.8	MS	•
4 >	HandEra	8	•		3.7	M, C	
5 >	Kyocera	8	•		2.5		
6 >	Palm	8	•		2.6		
7 >	Handspring	8			3.1	SB	
8 >	Handspring	8	•		3.1	SB	
9 >	Palm	8			3.0	M	•
10 >	Palm	8		•	3.0	M	•
11 >	Palm	8	•		2.7	M	•
12 >	Handspring	16		•	3.3	SB	
13 >	Handspring	8		•	3.2	SB	
14 >	Sony	15		•	3.0	MS	•
15 >	Samsung	8	•	•	2.9		
POCKET PC MODELS							
16 >	HP	32		•	3.5	C	•
17 >	Compaq	64		•	3.8	M	•
18 >	Casio	64	•	•	3.5	M, C	•
19 >	Compaq	64		•	3.8		•
PROPRIETARY SYSTEM							
20 >	Casio	16		•	3.2	C	

6 > **PALM** m105 **A very good, low-cost model.** Basic organizer functions easy to use. Easily readable in bright sunlight. Includes mobile connectivity software. Uses AAA batteries. Fits easily in shirt pocket. But doesn't include backup program. 5 oz.

7 > **HANDSPRING** Visor Edge **A very good, basic model in a slim case.** Basic organizer functions easy to use. Easily readable in sunlight. Includes expense-tracker software. Fits easily in shirt pocket. But battery can't be replaced by user. Doesn't include backup program. Expansion sleeve makes unit bulky. 4¾ oz.

8 > **HANDSPRING** Visor Platinum **A very good, basic model.** Basic organizer functions easy to use. Includes expense-tracker software. Uses AAA batteries. But doesn't include backup program. 6 oz. Discontinued, but the similar Visor Neo is available.

9 > **PALM** i705 **Very good overall, with many features in a small package.** Has built-in wireless modem and the most versatile e-mail capability of any tested PDA. Easily readable in bright sunlight. Includes picture viewer and eBook reader. LED and vibrating alarm. Fits easily in shirt pocket. Printed manual. But battery can't be replaced by user. Doesn't include backup program. 5¼ oz.

10 > **PALM** m505 **Very good; like the m500, with a color display.** Overall design better than most. Basic organizer functions easy to use. Includes eBook reader, picture viewer, expense-tracker, and mobile connectivity software. Fits easily in shirt pocket. But batteries can't be replaced by user. Word-processing and spreadsheet programs can't use expansion cards, and you can't enter formulas in spreadsheets. Doesn't include backup program. 5 oz. Discontinued, but the similar m515 is available; has 16 MB of RAM and allows you to enter formulas in spreadsheets.

11 > **PALM** m125 **A very good, low-cost model with expansion capability.** Easily readable in bright sunlight. Includes eBook reader. Uses AAA batteries. Fits easily in shirt pocket. But doesn't include backup program. Word-processing and spreadsheet programs can't use expansion cards, and you can't enter formulas in spreadsheets. 4¾ oz.

12 > **HANDSPRING** Visor Pro **Very good overall, especially for Palm users looking to upgrade.** Easily readable in bright sunlight. Includes expense-tracker software. But battery can't be replaced by user. Doesn't include backup program. 5¾ oz.

13 > **HANDSPRING** Visor Prism **Good overall.** Basic organizer functions easy to use. Includes expense-tracker software. But battery can't be replaced by user. Doesn't include backup program. 7 oz.

14 > **SONY** Clié PEG-T615C **A good choice for Palm users looking to upgrade.** Handy jog dial. Includes picture viewer, some multimedia software. Can function as remote control. LED and vibrating alarm. Fits easily in shirt pocket. Printed manual. But battery can't be replaced by user. Thin case not as comfortable to hold as most. 5 oz.

15 > **SAMSUNG** SPH-I300 **Good overall, but not the best PDA/cellphone combo we've seen.** Includes expense-tracker and voice-recording software. Vibrating alarm. Fits easily in shirt pocket. Printed manual. But screen washes out in sunlight. Doesn't include backup program. E-mail program cumbersome. Not tested as a cell phone. 6 oz.

POCKET PC MODELS

16 > **HP** Jornada 565 **Good overall, with the best design among the Pocket PCs.** User interface better than most. Basic organizer functions easy to use. Buttons more useful than most. Includes picture viewer, eBook reader, and voice-recording software. Bundled HP applications well integrated with OS. Has handy task-switcher software. LED alarm. Printed manual. 6¼ oz. Similar: HP Jornada 568.

17 > **COMPAQ** iPaq H3835 **Good overall.** User interface better than most. The only iPaq with an integrated expansion card. Includes picture viewer, eBook reader, and voice-recording software. LED alarm. But battery can't be replaced by user. 6½ oz. Similar iPaq H3850.

18 > **CASIO** Cassiopeia E-200 **A good choice if you want to add peripherals.** Two expansion slots. User interface better than most. Includes picture viewer, eBook reader, voice-recording software. LED alarm. Supports USB 2.0. 6¾ oz.

19 > **COMPAQ** iPaq H3765 **Good, but there are better choices.** Includes picture viewer, eBook reader, voice-recording software. LED alarm. But battery can't be replaced by user and can permanently lose charge if unit is not left on charger when idle for long periods. 6¾ oz. Similar iPaq H3760.

PROPRIETARY SYSTEM

20 > **CASIO** BE-300 **Fair.** Includes picture viewer, Word and Excel file viewer. But user interface worse than most. Basic organizer functions hard to use. Battery can't be replaced by user. Requires purchase of MS Outlook to synchronize with a PC. Screen washes out in sunlight. 5½ oz.

Printers

You can purchase an inkjet printer with excellent text and color-photo quality for as little as $100. The two CR Best Buys—the Epson Stylus C60 and Canon Color Bubble Jet S300—each sell for $100. The Epson is faster for photo printing, while the Canon is very economical for printing a page of text. Consider a multifunction machine if you don't have room for a separate fax machine, scanner, copier, and printer. The $300 Canon Multipass F30, though expensive, was superior across the board. For printing lots of text, laser printers are still far less costly to use.

Overall Ratings — In performance order

Ratings key: Excellent ●, Very good ◐, Good ○, Fair ◑, Poor ⬤

Key No.	Brand & Model	Price	Overall Score	Text Quality	Text Speed	Text Cost	Color Photo Quality	Color Photo Time	Color Photo Cost	Graphics Quality
INKJET MODELS										
1	Canon Color Bubble Jet S520	$150		●	4.9 ppm	3.6¢	●	2 min.	$1.00	●
2	Epson Stylus C80	150		●	5.5	6.2	◑	3	0.90	◑
3	Epson Stylus C60 **A CR Best Buy**	100		●	4.5	4.8	●	3	0.90	●
4	Lexmark Z65 Color JetPrinter	200		◑	6.2	10.7	◑	8	1.90	◑
5	Canon Color Bubble Jet S300 **A CR Best Buy**	100		●	4.6	1.9	●	11	0.80	◑
6	Lexmark Z45 Color JetPrinter	90		●	4.4	5.7	◑	12	1.40	◑
7	HP DeskJet 995c	400		●	2.7	4.1	●	9	1.00	●
8	Epson Stylus Photo 785EPX	200		●	1.9	3.4	●	3	0.70	●
9	Epson Stylus Photo 890	300		◑	1.8	3.4	●	3	0.70	●
10	Canon Photo Printer S820D	400		◑	2.1	4.2	●	4	1.10	◑
11	Epson Stylus Photo 820	100		◑	1.8	6.5	●	18	1.10	●
MULTIFUNCTION MODELS										
12	Canon Multipass F30	300		●	5.0	3.6	●	4	1.00	●
13	HP OfficeJet v40xi	200		○	3.4	4.6	◑	9	0.90	○
14	Lexmark X73	150		○	4.0	5.4	●	10	1.40	◑

See report, page 131. Based on tests published in Consumer Reports in September 2002.

The tests behind the Ratings

Brand & model includes printers tested for previous reports. **Overall score** is based primarily on text, color-photo, and graphics quality and on text speed (for multifunction printers, we tested only the print function). **Text quality** indicates how crisply and clearly a printer produced black text in a variety of typefaces, sizes, and styles. **Text speed** is our calculation of the typical output in pages per minute (ppm) for a three-page document at the default setting. **Color-photo quality** is our assessment of a photo's appearance. **Color-photo time** is our measurement, to the nearest minute, of how long it took to produce an 8x10-inch color print at the printer's best-quality setting. **Cost** is for a single text page (including ink and paper, sold by the 5,000-sheet, 10-ream box) or for a single photo (ink and glossy photo paper, plus the amortized cost of the printhead based on the manufacturer's stated life). **Graphics quality** assesses color graphics–illustrations, charts, and drawings. **Price** is approximate retail.

Recommendations and notes

Models listed as similar should offer performance comparable to the tested model, although features may differ.
All models: Work with most versions of Windows and Mac OS. Have a 1-year parts-and-labor warranty. **Most models:** Have parallel and universal serial bus ports (but require a USB for Macs). Can hold 100 sheets or at least 10 envelopes in their input tray. Indicate when ink supply is low. Use water-resistant black ink. Can print banners at least 44 inches long. Have no separate envelope input. Do not include a cable. **All multifunction printers:** Can hold 150 sheets or 10 to 20 envelopes in their input tray.

REGULAR MODELS

1. **CANON** Color Bubble Jet S520 **Among the fastest for color photos and text.**

2. **EPSON** Stylus C80 **Among the fastest for text and photos.** Holds 150 sheets and 15 envelopes. But noisier than most.

3. **EPSON** Stylus C60 **A CR Best Buy Low-priced and fast.** But noisier than most.

4. **LEXMARK** Z65 Color JetPrinter **The fastest for text.** But per-page cost for text and photos the highest. Similar: Z65n

5. **CANON** Color Bubble Jet S300 **A CR Best Buy Low cost for text and photos.** Fast for text, but slow for photos.

6. **LEXMARK** Z45 Color JetPrinter **Low-priced, but relatively slow and expensive for photos (uses a special cartridge).**

7. **HP** DeskJet 995c **Very good but expensive.** Holds 150 sheets or 15 envelopes. Quiet.

8. **EPSON** Stylus Photo 785EPX **Among the slowest for text and fastest for photos.** Can print directly from PC-card adapter. But noisier than most.

9. **EPSON** Stylus Photo 890 **Low printing costs may offset high price.**

10. **CANON** Photo Printer S820D **Expensive, but among the fastest for photos.** Among the slowest for text. Can print directly from PC-card adapter. Similar:S820.

11. **EPSON** Stylus Photo 820 **Good overall, but noisier than most.** Slowest for photos and text.

MULTIFUNCTION MODELS

12. **CANON** Multipass F30 **An excellent choice on all counts.** Produces top-quality text and photos at high speed and relatively low cost. Flatbed design. But noisier than most. Similar: F50.

13. **HP** OfficeJet v40xi **Quieter than most, but text quality is so-so.** Photo quality very good, but speed on the slow side. Has fax function.

14. **LEXMARK** X73 **Inexpensive and delivers excellent photos, but text quality falls short of others in group and per-page cost is a bit higher.** Flatbed design. Similar: X83, X63.

Workstations

Determine how much room you have and how much work space you need, then decide on the type of workstation you want. There are many fine models. Among desks with a hutch, the Sauder Bayshore is a relative bargain at $170. A corner or L-shaped unit requires more floor space. The Intelligent Designs 10342, $400, offered the best combination of functionality, fit, and finish. Another fine choice is the Ridgewood/Charleswood 14032, $150, **A CR Best Buy.** If space or money is a constraint, consider a cart. There are several in the $100 range. An armoire is useful for hiding a computer when it's not in use, but may require considerable floor space.

Overall Ratings — In performance order

KEY NO.	BRAND & MODEL	PRICE	OVERALL SCORE	WORK SPACE	ERGONOMICS	FIT	FINISH	EASE OF ASSEMBLY
	DESKS WITH HUTCH							
1	Sauder Bayshore 4163-267	$170		Large	○	◓	◓	◉
2	O'Sullivan 10443	190		Large	○	◓	○	◉
3	Bush Ashland HM22424	300		Large	○	◓	○	◓
4	Sauder Mission 8437	200		Large	○	○	◓	○
5	Sauder Cornerstone 7337-105	300		Large	○	◓	○	○
6	Bush Ashland HM22418	200		Very large	○	◓	○	◓
7	Ikea Anton 47" Desk	340		Medium	○	◓	◉	◐
8	O'Sullivan 10437	200		Very large	○	◓	◓	◓
9	Sauder 2738	270		Large	○	◓	○	○
10	Ridgewood/Charleswood 74672	140		Medium	◐	○	○	◓
11	Dorel 41152	140		Medium	◐	○	◐	◉
	CORNER DESKS AND L-SHAPED UNITS							
12	Intelligent Designs 10342	400		Very large	○	◓	◓	◉
13	Ridgewood/Charleswood 14032 **A CR Best Buy**	150		Very large	○	◓	○	○
14	Bush Ashland HM22310	180		Large	◐	◓	◓	◉
15	Dorel 46552	150		Large	●	◉	○	○
	CARTS							
16	Sauder Cornerstone 7399-105	110		Small	◐	◓	○	◉
17	Sauder 2799	110		Small	◐	○	○	◉
18	O'Sullivan 61925	100		Small	◐	◓	○	◉
19	Bush Visions MM97401	90		Small	●	◉	○	◓
20	Dorel 41252	65		Small	●	◉	○	◓
21	Sauder 468-110	100		Small	●	◓	○	◉
	ARMOIRE							
22	Sauder Monarch 2749	400		Medium	○	○	○	◓

Ratings key: Excellent ●, Very good ◓, Good ○, Fair ◐, Poor ●

Overall score scale: 0–100 (P, F, G, VG, E)

See report, page 148. Based on tests published in Consumer Reports in September 2001, with updated prices and availability.

CONSUMER REPORTS DIGITAL BUYING GUIDE ◆ 177

The tests behind the Ratings

Overall score is based mainly on ergonomics; fit, finish, and ease of assembly were factored in. **Work space** is our assessment of the usable space a workstation offers. **Ergonomics** reflects how well the furniture fits users of various sizes and considers keyboard-shelf height and design, monitor location, leg and foot room, and copy-shelf compatibility. **Fit** is how well pieces align. **Finish** indicates quality, including edges. **Ease of assembly** reflects ease of setup and quality of instructions. **Price** is approximate retail; it includes a hutch, if sold separately (desks have a hutch unless otherwise noted).

Recommendations and notes

Style and finish are for unit tested; similar models may have different finish. Dimensions are HxWxD. **All models:** Allow monitor to be placed in line with user. Carts have casters. **Except as noted, all models:** Are made of particleboard/laminate. Have a fixed-height keyboard shelf that slides in and out, with room for a mouse.

DESKS WITH HUTCH

1> SAUDER Bayshore 4163-267 **Well made and easy to assemble.** Contemporary, oak laminate, 57x54x23 in. Very good finish. No compartment for tower CPU. Keyboard shelf too low for taller users. Similar: 4163-468.

2> O'SULLIVAN 10443 **A fine choice that's easy to assemble.** Contemporary, oak laminate, 56x59x24 in. Shortest assembly time for desks. But keyboard shelf too low for taller users.

3> BUSH Ashland HM22424 **A good desk, but pricier than some.** Contemporary, maple laminate, 66x59x28 in. Hutch sold separately (HM22425, $70, included in price shown).

4> SAUDER Mission 8437 **Good overall, with very good finish, but some assembly quirks.** Mission, fruitwood laminate, 57x60x24 in. Tricky to install underdesk brace.

5> SAUDER Cornerstone 7337-105 **Good, but many features add to assembly time; pricier than some.** Contemporary, cherry laminate, 54x60x24 in. Adjustable floor glides, easy to level. Tricky to install underdesk brace. Similar: 7337-110, 7337-290.

6> BUSH Ashland HM22418 **A good desk with very large work space.** Contemporary, maple laminate, 59x53x30 in. No compartment for tower CPU.

7> IKEA Anton 47" Desk **Excellent wood-veneer finish, but poor instructions complicate assembly; pricier than some.** Contemporary, beech veneer, 60x47x30 in. Components not labeled. No compartment for tower CPU. Hutch (called shelving unit) sold separately (16-in., $70; 31-in., $90; we used both shelving units together, which are included in price shown).

8> O'SULLIVAN 10437 **Very large work space and very good finish.** Traditional, pine laminate, 56x59x32 in. But overhanging desktop may block access to top row of keyboard. Hard to tell some screw sizes apart. Similar: 10537.

9> SAUDER 2738 **A good choice.** Traditional, cherry laminate, 60x60x24 in. Includes touch-up pen. Similar: 2538, 2638.

10> RIDGEWOOD/CHARLESWOOD 74672 **There are better desks.** Contemporary, oak laminate, 52x54x23 in.

11> DOREL 41152 **Ergonomics only fair; there are better desks.** Contemporary, oak laminate, 55x42x24 in. Similar: 41127.

CORNER DESKS AND L-SHAPED UNITS

12> INTELLIGENT DESIGNS 10342 **A large, easy-to-assemble unit with very good fit and finish.** Contemporary, cherry/granite laminate, 35x67x67 in. Can adjust height of keyboard shelf with tools. Monitor too high for shorter users and too far away for some users. Similar: 10012, 10642.

13> RIDGEWOOD/CHARLESWOOD 14032 **A CR Best Buy Offers plenty of work space and very good value.** Contemporary, oak/black laminate, 52x59x59 in. Can be easily disassembled.

14> BUSH Ashland HM22310 **A compact workstation with very good fit and finish, but ergonomics only fair.** Contemporary, maple/granite laminate, 37x59x40 in. Mouse doesn't fit on keyboard shelf. Similar: HM22510.

15> DOREL 46552 **Ergonomics poor; there are better choices.** Contemporary, oak/black, 55x49x49 in. Similar: 46583.

CARTS

16> SAUDER Cornerstone 7399-105 **A good, basic cart.** Contemporary, cherry laminate, 30x35x20 in. Easy assembly. Sliding printer shelf, touch-up pen. Similar: 7399-290, 7399-110.

17> SAUDER 2799 **A decent choice for a basic cart.** Traditional, cherry laminate, 30x35x20 in. Easy to assemble. Sliding printer shelf. Includes touch-up pen. Similar: 2689, 2799-110.

18> O'SULLIVAN 61925 **A good, basic cart with hutch.** Contemporary, oak laminate, 60x31x24 in. Easy to assemble. Monitor too far away for some users.

19> BUSH Visions MM97401 **Poor ergonomics make this one to avoid.** Contemporary, maple and black laminate, 33x35x29 in.

20> DOREL 41252 **Poor ergonomics make this one to avoid.** Contemporary, oak, 35x25x24 in.

21> SAUDER 468-110 **Poor ergonomics make this one to avoid.** Mission, fruitwood laminate, 48x36x19 in. (with drop leaf open).

ARMOIRE

22> SAUDER Monarch 2749 **A good choice, but time-consuming to assemble.** Traditional, cherry laminate, 72x41x23 in. Monitor too close for some users. Requires considerable floor space when doors open. Similar: 2549, 2649, 8449.

Guide to the Brands

A few large, well-known players dominate the home-computer market, but over the past few years, smaller companies have forged comfortable niches with innovative technology and competitive prices. Some of the giants, such as Hewlett-Packard, market not only desktops and laptop computers but also peripherals such as printers and scanners. Other companies, such as WinBook, have successfully concentrated on a single market—in this case, laptops.

Here's a rundown of the leading companies that sell computers, software, and home-office equipment in the U.S. See the list of brands on page 183 for manufacturers' phone numbers and web addresses.

HARDWARE MANUFACTURERS

AMD *(www.amd.com)*. Advanced Micro Devices is the second-largest microprocessor manufacturer. Despite rival Intel's strength, AMD has managed to grab a share of the market for its Athlon and Duron chips, mostly in budget and midpriced desktops. It was AMD that first broke the psychologically important 1-GHz barrier, in 2000.

APPLE COMPUTER *(www.apple.com)*. The user-friendly Macintosh personal computer revolutionized the market in the early '80s. By the mid '90s, beset by management problems and the dominance of Microsoft's Windows operating system, Apple was forced to regroup under the guidance of its returning founder, Steve Jobs. The company made headlines in mid-1998 with the introduction of its futuristic-looking iMac computer, designed to appeal to users on a budget (it retails for around $1,000) who are interested in ease of use. Apple's strengths have always been in the areas of education, design, and publishing. And Apple owners are very loyal and consistently rate the brand high in performance.

Apple's current offerings include the iMac, the iBook, the Power Macintosh desktop series, and the Macintosh PowerBook laptops. The latest operating system from Apple is version 10 of Mac OS X. Macs are available through Apple, computer and home-electronics retailers, and Apple retail outlets.

CTX INTERNATIONAL (*www.ctxintl.com*). The U.S. division of Chuntex Electronics, one of Taiwan's largest monitor manufacturers, CTX International markets cathode-ray tube (CRT) and liquid-crystal display (LCD) monitors. The brand is available through computer and home-electronics retailers.

DELL COMPUTER CORP. (*www.dell.com*). The world's leading direct marketer of computer systems, Dell was founded by Michael Dell in 1984 to design and customize computer systems to end-user requirements. Much of the company's revenue is from businesses, government, and educational institutions. But Dell has been increasing its home-PC business in recent years. Dell's extensive line includes Dell Dimension desktops and Dell Latitude and Inspiron notebooks. Available exclusively from Dell via its toll-free number or the Internet.

FUJITSU PC CORP. (*www.fujitsupc.com*). Fujitsu PC Corp. was formed in 1996 by the Japanese electronics conglomerate Fujitsu Ltd. to expand its business to the U.S. home-computer market. Its LifeBook series of multimedia laptops ranges from value-based models to pricey, high-performance models designed for corporate and technical power users. Available through computer and home-electronics retailers.

GATEWAY (*www.gateway.com*). The Ben & Jerry's of the personal computer market, Gateway is known for the black-and-white cowhide design on its computer boxes. Gateway was founded in 1985 by two Midwesterners whose goal was to offer home-computer consumers a direct-mail alternative. In doing so, they generated $100,000 during their first four months in business and helped pioneer direct-mail sales of home-PC products. By 1987, Gateway was selling fully configured PCs to consumers sight unseen. The lure was a good price. The company's offerings include the Essential and Performance lines of desktop PCs, and the Solo multimedia laptop line. Their products are available direct and through Gateway Country Stores.

HANDSPRING (*www.handspring.com*). Founded in 1998 by the cofounders of Palm, Handspring manufactures the Visor line of personal digital assistants (PDAs). The Visors are "clones" of Palm PDAs, which means they use the Palm operating system.

HEWLETT-PACKARD (*www.hp.com*). HP was founded in 1939 and its first product, an electronic test instrument known as an audio oscillator, was built in a Palo Alto, Calif., garage. HP's home-computer line is centered around the Pavilion series of desktop and laptop PCs. After acquiring Compaq in 2002, HP also now markets the Compaq Presario line of desktops and laptops, as well as iPaq handheld devices (PDAs).

HP is the market leader in printers, offering several best-selling models in both the laser and inkjet formats under its HP LaserJet and HP DeskJet series. HP also makes multifunction office machines (for faxing, copying, scanning, and printing). The company offers a series of scanners, its ScanJet series, along with the PhotoSmart digital camera and photo printer products. Available through computer and home-electronics stores nationwide. Computers can be configured to order via retail kiosks of on the HP web site.

IBM (*www.ibm.com*). Founded in 1911 as the Computing-Tabulating-Recording

Company and renamed International Business Machines Corp. in 1924, IBM pioneered industrial computing in the 1940s and 1950s, presenting its first large-scale computer to Harvard in 1945. By 1952, the IBM 701, designed for scientific calculations, was in production and keypunch technology was in its heyday. IBM became a billion-dollar company in 1957 and spent the 1960s and 1970s introducing a series of corporate computers known as mainframes, one more powerful than the next.

The company entered the home-PC market in 1981, when it introduced the first IBM personal computer (the origin of the term PC). Then, faced with stiff competition from makers of so-called "IBM-compatible" PCs (computers that ran on MS-DOS), IBM found itself losing market share to industry entrepreneurs. Today, IBM's offerings center around its Net Vista desktops and ThinkPad laptops. Available through IBM by telephone or the Internet.

INTEL *(www.intel.com).* This microprocessor company is the world's largest maker of microchips (the "brains" that control the central processing data). Intel introduced the Pentium processor for both desktop and laptop PCs in 1993, followed by the Pentium with MMX technology for improved multimedia performance in 1996. Then, in 1997, Intel introduced the Pentium II microprocessor, eventually available in speeds of 233 to 450 MHz. Intel also makes a lower-priced line of chips called Celeron, used in budget and moderate-priced desktops. A new generation of enhanced Pentium III chips with speeds starting at 500 MHz and later breaking the 1-GHz barrier debuted in early 1999. Intel's current line is made up of Pentium 4s and Celerons for desktops, and Pentium IIIs, 4s, and Celerons for laptops. Intel also supplies the motherboards used in many PCs.

IOMEGA *(www.iomega.com).* You might be familiar with the brand name Zip—the leading removable-cartridge drive for backup and archival purposes. These drives are manufactured by Iomega. The company also makes portable hard disk drives and CD-RW drives.

PALM *(www.palm.com).* Palm is largely responsible for making personal digital assistants popular. It has retained its lead over the PDA market, but clone makers such as Handspring (formed by Palm cofounders) and Sony are posing formidable challenges. In 2000, 3Com, which acquired Palm when it bought U.S. Robotics in 1997, spun off Palm.

SONY *(www.sony.com).* This Japanese home-electronics giant now has its name on everything from movie theaters to music CDs to microwaves. An innovator—Sony marketed the first all-transistor TV and the first videotape recorder for home use and helped develop the compact disc—the company made a foray into the home-PC market in the '90s with Sony Vaio desktop and notebook computers, plus digital cameras (on top of its already successful line of Trinitron monitors). In 1998, Sony emerged as a leading player in the "ultraportable" laptop business with its Vaio SuperSlim series of subnotebooks weighing under 3 pounds. Sony PC products are available through computer and home-electronics retailers nationwide, and online stores.

TOSHIBA *(www.toshiba.com).* Its laptops include the midpriced Satellite and ultralight Portégé series, along with the more advanced Tecra series for business users. Available through computer and home-electronics retailers nationwide.

WINBOOK *(www.winbook.com).* WinBook, a direct-sales subsidiary of Micro Electronics Inc., has made a name for itself with its line of value-priced laptops. Available direct through the company's toll-free number and its web site.

SOFTWARE MANUFACTURERS

Over the past decade, literally hundreds of software companies have sprung up, offering programs that will help you do everything from creating greeting cards to redesigning your kitchen to saving for retirement to troubleshooting your PC—not to mention just having fun. Here are some of the leading brand names you'll find in the software aisles.

ADOBE *(www.adobe.com)*. The company is a leader in the graphic-arts and photo-imaging software areas. Its products include Adobe Photoshop, Adobe PhotoDeluxe, Adobe PageMaker, and Adobe Illustrator.

COREL *(www.corel.com)*. WordPerfect, the No. 2 word-processing program after Microsoft Word, is one of this company's major offerings. Another is CorelDraw, a paint and creativity program.

DISNEY INTERACTIVE *(disney.go.com/disneyinteractive)*. With new movies and characters in theaters every year, Disney saw software as a natural tie-in. The company now markets more than 20 titles aimed at children from toddlers to teens.

EDMARK *(www.riverdeep.net/edmark)*. This software line, acquired by Riverdeep Interactive Learning in 2000, is a leader in educational and edutainment titles for preschool and school-aged children. Its best-selling series include Let's Go Read!, Thinkin' Things, Mighty Math, and Imagination Express.

HUMONGOUS ENTERTAINMENT *(www.humongous.com)*. Owned by Infogames, this company creates imaginative and entertaining software for kids. Best-selling titles include Blue's Clues, Freddi Fish, and Putt-Putt.

INTUIT *(www.intuit.com)*. This company's leading software, Quicken, receives the bulk of retail dollars spent on personal-finance software. The latest version is Quicken 2000. Intuit also makes TurboTax.

LEARNINGCO.COM *(www.broderbund.com)*. Acquired by Riverdeep Interactive Learning in 2001, The Learning Company has among it offerings the Reader Rabbit series, American Girls Premiere, and Berlitz "Learn to Speak" language programs. LearningCo.com sold its entertainment titles, including the Myst series, to the French company Ubi-Soft in 2001.

LOTUS DEVELOPMENT *(www.lotus.com)*. Office workers have been familiar with this company's spreadsheet software, Lotus 1-2-3, for years. The company, based in Cambridge, Mass., and owned by IBM since 1995, also makes the productivity program Lotus Organizer, the groupware product Lotus Notes, and the program family Lotus SmartSuite.

MICROSOFT *(www.microsoft.com)*. This leading software developer owns the market in PC operating systems. Its Windows operating system (the newest version is Windows XP) is installed in almost every home PC built. Its software titles (which include Microsoft Word and Excel, Encarta Reference Library 2003, and Microsoft Money 2003) are among the best-selling titles on the market.

Founded in 1975, Microsoft got its first serious boost in 1981, when IBM introduced its personal computer featuring Microsoft's MS-DOS 1.0 operating system. The company went public in 1986. In 1990 it introduced its Windows 3.0 operating system in response to demand for a more user-friendly interface. Windows mimics the Apple Macintosh's graphical user interface, which allows the user to run the computer by pointing and clicking with a mouse. In August 1995, Microsoft Windows 95 debuted. Later that year, founder Bill

Gates announced that Microsoft intended to be a serious player in the burgeoning domain of cyberspace with its Internet Explorer browser and its Microsoft Network (MSN) online service. Internet Explorer, preinstalled with Windows 95 and integrated into Windows 98, has wrestled the lion's share of the market away from Netscape Navigator, but MSN has thus far failed to pose a significant threat to the online leader, America Online. In 2000, a federal judge ruled that Microsoft was an illegal monopoly and ordered that it be broken into two. But in 2001, a federal appeals court disqualified the judge and ordered that the breakup be reconsidered. As of the summer of 2002, the case was being heard by a different judge and the parties were working toward a settlement.

SEGA *(www.sega.com)*. A leader in the game arena, this company has sold more than $2 billion in software in the past two years. Many of its products are action-based shoot-'em-ups.

SIERRA *(www.sierra.com)*. With a half-dozen divisions, Sierra makes everything from games to products for do-it-yourselfers. Best-selling titles include HeadRush, NASCAR Racing 3, the MasterCook series, and Sierra Complete Home.

SYMANTEC *(www.symantec.com)*. This company specializes in PC utilities. Its major products include Norton Utilities, Norton AntiVirus, and dozens of other titles designed to keep your PC in top working condition.

HOME-OFFICE EQUIPMENT MANUFACTURERS

AT&T *(www.att.com)*. This telecommunications giant focuses more on services than products since its spinoff from NCR. The At&T Consumer Products division, which sells corded and cordless phones, is owned by VTech, who licenses the At&T brand to use on the phones. AT&T Wireless, a separate company, may put the At&T brand on some cell phones.

BROTHER *(www.brother.com)*. Brother International Corp. is a leader in the value-priced home-office field, manufacturing an array of printers, fax machines, and multifunction devices. The latter combine products such as a phone, an answering machine, a fax, a scanner, a printer, and a copier into single units. The company also has a line of self-contained word processors and low-end notebook PCs. Available through home-electronics and home-office retailers nationwide.

CANON *(www.usa.canon.com/consumer)*. The emergence of color inkjet printers as versatile, value-oriented additions to the home office proved to be a boon to the Japanese photo and optical giant Canon, which staked its claim in the market in 1992, when it formed its Canon Computer Systems Inc. division. The subsidiary introduced its first color Bubble Jet 600 printer in 1993 and now offers an entire line of Bubble Jet and MultiPass printers and scanners and PowerShot digital cameras. Canon also has a well-established business in home copiers. Available through computer and home-electronics/home-office retailers nationwide.

EPSON *(www.epson.com)*. This manufacturer of moderate- to high-priced printers, scanners, and digital cameras, is a division of Seiko Epson Corp. Epson's product lines include its Stylus series of color inkjet printers, its Expression and Perfection scanners, and its PhotoPC digital cameras. Available through computer and home-office retailers nationwide.

LEXMARK *(www.lexmark.com)*. Lexmark was formed in March 1991 as a spin-off of the Information Products division of IBM and became a public company in November 1995. Lexmark sells moderate-priced printers, including its series of Optra laser and Color Jetprinter inkjet printers designed for home and office use. Available through computer and home-office retailers nationwide.

MICROTEK *(www.microtek.com)*. Microtek entered the scanner market in 1983, before scanning became an important element in desktop publishing. Microtek pioneered the technology, and the company's lineup now consists of a variety of color ScanMaker scanners for professional and home use. Available through computer and home-office retailers nationwide, and from a number of mail-order companies.

PANASONIC *(www.panasonic.com)*. The Panasonic brand name, part of the Matsushita electronics conglomerate, has found its way into the home-PC and home-office markets. Panasonic markets laser printers, CD-ROM drives, DVD-ROM drives, copiers, fax machines, multifunction machines, and digital cameras, plus telephones and answerers. Available

---

COMPANY CONTACT INFORMATION

Computers
AMD	800-222-9323	*www.amd.com*
Apple	800-538-9696	*www.apple.com*
Compaq	800-345-1518	*www.compaq.com*
CTX	800-888-2012	*www.ctxintl.com*
Dell	800-879-3355	*www.dell.com*
Fujitsu	800-838-5487	*www.fujitsupc.com*
Gateway	800-846-2000	*www.gateway.com*
Handspring	888-565-9393	*www.handspring.com*
Hewlett-Packard	800-724-6631	*www.hp.com*
IBM	800-426-7235	*www.ibm.com*
Intel	800-628-8686	*www.intel.com*
Iomega	800-697-8833	*www.iomega.com*
Palm	800-881-7256	*www.palm.com*
Sony	800-476-6972	*www.sony.com*
Toshiba	800-457-7777	*www.toshiba.com*
WinBook	800-254-7806	*www.winbook.com*

Home office
AT&T	800-222-3111	*www.att.com*
Brother	800-284-4329	*www.brother.com*
(fax machines, fax modems)		
Brother	800-276-7746	*www.brother.com*
(printers)		
Canon	800-OK-CANON	*www.usa.canon.com*
(copiers)		
Epson	800-463-7766	*www.epson.com*
Lexmark	888-539-6275	*www.lexmark.com*
Microtek	800-654-4160	*www.microtek.com*
Panasonic	800-742-8086	*www.panasonic.com*
Samsung	800-767-4675	*ww.samsungusa.com*
Sharp	800-726-7864	*www.sharpusa.com*

Software
Adobe	800-833-6687	*www.adobe.com*
Corel	800-772-6735	*www.corel.com*
Disney Interactive	800-900-9234	*disney.go.com/disneyinteractive*
Edmark	800-691-2986	*www.edmark.com*
Humongous Entertainment	800-499-8386	*www.humongous.com*
Intuit	800-446-8848	*www.intuit.com*
LearningCo.com	800-395-0277	*www.broderbund.com*
Lotus	800-343-5414	*www.lotus.com*
Microsoft	800-426-9400	*www.microsoft.com*
Sega		*www.sega.com*
Sierra	425-649-9800	*www.sierra.com*
Symantec	800-441-7234	*www.symantec.com*

Online services
America Online	800-827-6364	*www.aol.com*
CompuServ	800-336-6823	*www.compuserv.com*
Lucent	888-4Lucent	*www.lucent.com*
Microsoft Network	800-373-3676	*www.msn.com*
Prodigy	800-776-3449	*www.prodigy.com*

through computer and home-office retailers nationwide.

SAMSUNG *(www.samsungusa.com)*. Known for its value-priced home electronics, this Korean-based manufacturer offers printers, fax machines, multifunction devices, color monitors, and CD-ROM drives for the home office. In recent years, the company has focused on distribution through mass-market outlets. The company is a major force in the memory-chip business.

SHARP *(www.sharpusa.com)*. The company's name dates back to 1915, when its founder, Tokuji Hayakawa, invented the Ever-Sharp mechanical pencil. Today, the Japanese electronics manufacturer sells midpriced home-office copiers, fax machines, multifunction machines, and color monitors. Available through computer and home-office retailers nationwide.

Glossary

ACCELERATED GRAPHICS PORT. See AGP.

ACCESS. Ability to connect to the Internet. To store or retrieve data from a storage device such as a disk or a database. Sometimes access is restricted by an authentication scheme, such as a password.

ACCESSIBILITY. The degree to which hardware or software is designed to allow disabled persons to use a computer. Windowed operating systems have many accessibility features, such as the ability to enlarge fonts, icons, and menus, and to use alternate Human Interface Devices (HIDs).

ACRONYM. A word formed from the initial letters of a phrase, used as an abbreviation. Examples are ASCII, BIOS, and RAM.

ACTIVE MATRIX DISPLAY. A high-quality, flat panel LCD display in which a separate transistor switch is used for each pixel, allowing viewing from wider angles. See also passive matrix display.

ADAPTER CARD. A peripheral, such as a modem, built on a printed circuit board that plugs into an empty expansion slot on the motherboard.

ADD-ON OR ADD-IN. A component that can be attached to a computer by a simple process such as plugging it into a socket.

ADMINISTRATOR. System administrator, the person responsible for managing security, access authorization, and shared resources in a computer network.

AD-WARE. Software that displays advertising when it is being used. See also shovelware, spyware, and trashware.

AGP. Accelerated Graphics Port, an Intel design that, when connected to a compatible graphics adapter, speeds high-resolution images such as those found in "3-D" games. AGP allows main RAM to augment video RAM.

ALL-IN-ONE CASE. A compact desktop computer design with a built-in monitor. Apple's iMac is an example. See also portable computer and tower case.

ALL-IN-ONE LAPTOP. A laptop PC that contains one or more removable-disk drives in addition to the internal hard drive. See also modular laptop and slim-and-light laptop.

ALPHANUMERIC, ALPHAMERIC. Containing only the letters of the alphabet and the 10 digits 0 to 9.

ALT KEY. Short for alternate key, a key found on IBM-compatible keyboards that alters the function of a key pressed simultaneously. See also control key, command key.

ANALOG. A representation of a continuous measurement of some function. A common example is the telephone, where sound is converted to a varying voltage that is transmitted via wires and converted from voltage to sound on the other end. See also digital.

ANSI (AN-SEE). American National Standards Institute, an independent organization that researches and establishes standards in many areas, including computers.

ANTIVIRUS PROGRAM. A program designed to detect, remove, and protect against computer viruses, worms, and Trojan Horses. Antivirus programs must be updated regularly to maintain protection against new threats. See also Trojan Horse, virus, and worm.

APP. Short for application.

APPLE KEY. See command key.

APPLET. A "miniature" application with a specific purpose, usually adjunct to a larger application or the operating system.

APPLICATIONS, APPLICATION SOFTWARE. Programs with a particular function. Typical examples are word processors, spreadsheets, and games. See also OS and system software.

APPLICATION SUITE. A package of programs designed to work together in the operating system environment and share certain common features.

ARCHITECTURE. Internal structure and design of a CPU or computer system.

ARCHIVAL STORAGE. Offline storage of information needed for future reference.

ASCII (ASK-EE). American Standard Code for Information Interchange. This 7-bit code originally developed by ANSI is the standard for text in most computers. Standard ASCII text—a set of 128 common characters—can be used with any word processor. The Extended Set of ASCII—which requires an 8th bit—contains pseudo-graphical symbols for drawing lines and boxes, selected foreign alphabet characters, and a few mathematical symbols.

ASCII FILE. A file that contains only characters from the Standard ASCII character set. Such files have the advantage of being readable on any computer but contain no formatting or layout information.

ATHLON. A series of microprocessors from AMD that competes directly with Intel's Pentium series, and has similar performance. The latest version, called Athlon XP, has clock speeds up to 1.8 GHz, which AMD says is as fast as the more expensive 2.2 GHz Pentium 4. See also Celeron, Duron, 486, and Pentium.

A TO D CONVERSION. The conversion of data or signals from analog to digital format, needed to record, e.g., a wave sound file. See also modem.

AUTHENTICATION. A method by which a system, such as a computer operating system or a network, prevents access or usage by unauthorized persons or other systems. Personal authentication may involve a user ID and password, or a more sophisticated method such as a "smart card" or biometrics. System authentication may use an encrypted software key, a digital certificate, or a list of globally unique system identifiers. See also biometric, certificate, encryption, secure system and smart card.

b. Bit, the smallest unit of data measurement. See also byte.

B. Byte, 8 bits. See also bit.

BACKDOOR. A secret, or unintended, unsecured entry method into a secure system, such as a network, online service, or BBS. See also hacker.

BACKGROUND PROCESS. A relatively low-priority process that is performed when the CPU is free from other processing duties. On a PC, this is most often printing or file transfers. See also foreground process.

BACK UP. To copy data onto a floppy disk, a tape cassette, a second hard drive, or other storage medium such as a disk cartridge or optical disk drive, to store the data safely offline.

BACKUP FILE. A copy of a file saved in case the original is lost or damaged.

BACKUP SYSTEM. A procedure used to maintain a current copy or prevent the loss of data in case it is damaged or destroyed. See also archival storage.

BACKWARD COMPATIBILITY. The ability of a new product to properly work with other products that use older technology. See also upgrade path.

BANDWIDTH. The maximum speed of a data link in bits per second. Ethernet has a bandwidth of 10 to 1000 Mbps, T-1 has a bandwidth of 1.544 Mbps, typical consumer-grade DSL has a download bandwidth of 384 to 768 kbps, and a V.90 modem connection has a bandwidth of 53.3 kbps or less.

BAR CODE. A numerical labeling and recognition method that uses a series of parallel bars of varying widths read by an optical scanner.

BASIC. A simple, high-level programming language that is usually interpreted, rather than compiled, so Basic programs run slower than programs written in, say, C. Later versions of Basic, such as Visual Basic, can be compiled into efficient machine code.

BAUD. A measure of the symbol transfer rate in a modem communications channel. In lower-speed modems, each symbol equals 1 bit, but in higher-speed modems, each symbol represents several bits. "Baud rate" is a common but redundant term, since baud is already defined as a rate. See also bandwidth.

BAY. A position in a computer case to mount a device, such as a drive.

BETA TESTING. The test phase of a new product that takes place under actual use conditions and is conducted by a group of representative users. Many bugs are found and removed in beta testing. (Alpha testing takes place under controlled conditions within the company.)

BIDIRECTIONAL. Capable of transferring information in both directions.

BIOMETRIC. Relating to the measurement of one or more properties of the human body. Used for personal authentication in secure systems, a biometric reader may electronically scan the user's fingerprint or ocular iris pattern. It may also measure facial features or voice characteristics. See also authentication and secure system.

BIOS (BYE-OSE). Basic Input/Output System, the fundamental instructions by which a computer communicates with various peripheral devices. The BIOS usually resides in a firmware chip on the motherboard, allowing the computer to boot. A "flash" BIOS can be updated by overwriting its contents with new data from a file. See also firmware.

BIT. Short for binary digit, it's the smallest piece of data recognized by a computer. See also byte.

BITMAP. A graphics image composed of dots or pixels in a rectangular matrix. A visual object represented in a bitmap cannot be manipulated as an object, only as a group of pixels.

BLUE SCREEN OF DEATH. See BSOD.

BLUETOOTH. A short-range (35 feet) wireless data protocol to link compatible devices in a secure connection, using the 2.5 GHz radio-frequency band, with transfer speeds of up to 720 kbps. Examples are computer-to-printer, PDA-to-computer, and headset-to-telephone. See also WiFi.

BOARD. A thin, usually rectangular unit on which various electronic components are mounted. See also card, IC, and motherboard.

BOOKMARK. An easy way to access frequently visited websites; the user saves web-page URLs to a list (called either Bookmarks or Favorites) through a drop-down menu in the browser.

BOOLEAN. Operations used to combine different sets of objects for retrieval in database searching. During a search, for example, the Boolean operator AND retrieves objects that have information in common between data sets, while OR retrieves objects that have the information in at least one of several sets.

BOOT. To bring a system into operation. This normally includes loading part or all of the operating system into main memory from a storage device. See also cold boot and warm boot.

BOOTABLE DISK. A disk containing the loader program used to boot the system.

BOOT DEVICE. The storage device (usually a disk) from which the operating system was loaded. See also system disk.

BPS. Bits per second, a measure of data transfer rate. Higher rates are usually expressed with the prefixes k- for kilo-, M- for mega-, or G- for giga-. See also bandwidth.

BROADBAND. As commonly used, a connection to the Internet that has a receiving bandwidth greater than that of dial-up modem or ISDN service, about 128 kbps. (The FCC says "256 kb/s in at least one direction".) Common broadband connections are cable modem, DSL, and satellite. Broadband makes streaming audio and video practical.

BSOD. "Blue Screen of Death," a euphemism for the blue-background explanatory text screen that the Windows OS displays when an unrecoverable system error occurs. Usually, the only remedy for a BSOD is a cold boot.

BUFFER. A memory area used to hold data temporarily while it is being transferred from one location or device to another or waiting to be processed. Buffers are essential for the efficient operation of the CPU and are often used in graphics processors, CD-ROM drives, printer drivers and other input/output devices to compensate for differences in processing speed. See also FIFO.

BUG. An error in a computer program that prevents proper operation. See also debug and beta testing.

BUNDLE. 1) The software that comes preloaded with many personal computers. This typically includes a word processor, financial program, encyclopedia, productivity suite, and assorted games. See also preloaded. 2) The combination of a PC and peripheral devices such as a monitor, printer, scanner, or accessories, usually as a sales incentive.

BURNER. See CD-writer.

BUS. A pathway that connects devices inside the computer, usually the CPU and memory, or a peripheral such as an adapter card. Common bus designs include the ISA and PCI. See also local bus, network, and USB.

BUS SPEED. The bandwidth, in megahertz (MHz), of the main data pathway through which a microprocessor reads from main memory and communicates with the chipset on the motherboard. Currently, bus speeds up to 533 MHz (533 million 32-bit data words per second, or about 2.1 GB/s) can be achieved with very fast DDR RAM and 2.266 GHz and faster Pentium 4 processors.

BYTE. The basic storage unit needed to store a single character, nominally 8 bits. See also bit.

C. A family of high-level computer languages that compile to produce relatively efficient machine code. Newer versions include C++, Visual C, and C# (C-sharp). See also Java.

CABLE MODEM. A means of providing high-speed Internet service through a TV cable. See also DSL and ISDN.

CACHE. Memory that is dedicated specifically to improve the performance of a computer. This is accomplished by either setting aside part of main memory using a driver or through special high-speed memory. See also disk cache and memory cache.

CARD. An electronic circuit board that serves a particular function, such as memory or graphics; in a PC, cards are usually plugged into a bus connector on the motherboard. See also chip and PCMCIA card.

CARPAL TUNNEL SYNDROME (CTS). A painful, potentially debilitating injury that can arise from very heavy keyboard use. Symptoms may include weakness, numbness, tingling, and burning in the hands and fingers. See also RSI.

CATHODE RAY TUBE. See CRT.

CD. Compact disc, a 5-inch, aluminum-coated polycarbonate plastic disc with embedded digital data, read by focusing a laser beam on the data tracks and sensing its reflection. CDs can carry about 650 megabytes (MB) of digital information, which can be entertainment like music and motion video or computer data of many sorts. See also CD-ROM and DVD.

CD-R. CD-Recordable, a disc that can be recorded, once only, in a CD-writer.

CD-ROM. Compact Disc-Read Only Memory, referring to the 5-inch disc holding various software programs or the drive that retrieves digital data from the disc.

CD-R/W. CD-Read/Write, a disk that can be used like a large, somewhat slow, removable hard disk, in a CD-writer.

CD-WRITER. A drive that lets you create or copy CD-ROM disks. With the right software, you can also create or copy audio and video CDs. CD writers and blank media have dropped in price significantly over the past few years, and are now virtually standard in PCs.

CELERON. A processor series from Intel that is generally slower than its Pentium counterpart and used in lower-priced PCs. See also Athlon, Duron, 486, and Pentium.

CERTIFICATE (DIGITAL). Also called a "digital signature," a block of data appended to a file with an encrypted section uniquely identifying the sender of the document using technology that makes it virtually impossible to "forge." The encrypted section depends on the file content, so changing even one character in the file invalidates the certificate. A certificate assures the recipient that the file indeed comes from its stated sender, and indeed contains what the sender intended.

CHARACTER SET. The letters and symbols supported by a particular system or software package. The set may consist of only the letters of the alphabet (upper- and lowercase), 10 digits (0-9), and special symbols, such as punctuation marks (the Standard ASCII Character Set), or it may include graphics characters as well. Foreign-language character sets, supported in modern operating systems, have special characters for specific languages.

CHAT. Internet term for any site or service that allows real-time communication between two or more users, using text, graphics, voice, or a combination. Participants often refer to the interface as a "chat room." See also instant messaging and IRC.

CHECK BOX. A box, next to a selection in a dialog window, that is checked to indicate if that particular selection is activated. See also dialog box and radio buttons.

CHIP. An integrated circuit such as those commonly used for a PC's microprocessor and memory systems. Composed of a small, rectangular "chip" of semiconductor material, encased in a larger rectangular carrier with electrical connections.

CHIPSET. The support chips that manage data flow into and between the microprocessor and other parts of a computer.

CLIENT. A single-user terminal or personal computer (workstation) used in a networked environment. See also server.

CLIENT/SERVER. A network architecture in which the client (your computer) issues data processing requests to the server (another designated computer), which returns the information.

CLIP ART. Prepared graphics images that can be incorporated into a document using a program such as a word processor or desktop publisher.

CLIPBOARD. A reserved block of memory to temporarily hold data (either text or graphics) that has been taken from one application to be placed in another, printed, or saved to a file.

CLOCK. A circuit in the PC that regulates all processes by synchronizing them to a defined frequency. See also clock speed and bus speed.

CLOCK/CALENDAR. Part of a computer system that automatically keeps track of the current date and time for reference by application programs.

CLOCK SPEED. The rate at which the CPU clock operates, measured in megahertz (MHz) or gigahertz (GHz). In theory, the faster the clock speed, the faster the CPU will perform its operations. Most new PCs now work at clock speeds ranging from 800 MHz to over 2.5 GHz.

CLONE. Originally used to describe systems based on the architecture of the original IBM PCs. Now applies to PCs sold by smaller "integrators" via mail order or independent stores, assembled from standard, off-the-shelf subassemblies.

CMOS RAM. A small memory chip with battery backup that holds the hardware configuration settings for a personal computer, read by the BIOS at boot time.

COAXIAL CABLE. A type of telecommunications link that carries more data than conventional phone lines. Also used for cable TV. See also optical cable.

CODE. 1) A set of instructions, written by a programmer, that tells the computer what to do. 2) To write a program. 3) One or more characters that perform a specific function such as a control code.

COLD BOOT. To start or restart a computer from the power-off condition, or via a reset button.

COMDEX. Computer Dealers Exposition, an annual trade show (usually in Las Vegas) displaying new personal and business computers, components, and software.

COMMAND. An instruction, usually entered directly from the keyboard or pointing device, designed to cause an action to occur.

COMMAND KEY. A key on many Apple computer keyboards, designated by the symbol of an apple, that functions like a control key.

COMPACT DISK. See CD.

COMPILER. A program that interprets high-level (human-readable) source code written by a programmer and converts it into lower-level (machine-readable) instructions that can be directly executed by a microprocessor. See also interpreter.

COMPRESSED FORMAT. A method of data storage that eliminates all unnecessary and redundant bits, and often encodes the remaining bits to further conserve space. Compression that allows perfect recovery of original data is called "lossless"; if something, such as the sharpness of a graphic image, is degraded, the compression is "lossy." See also file compression.

COMPUTER. A programmable electronic device that can store, retrieve, and process information. All computers consist of the same basic components: the CPU, memory, storage, and input/output devices. See also personal computer.

COMPUTER PROGRAM. See program.

COMMAND. Any immediate instruction given to a computer. Some OSs, such as DOS, provide a "command line" interface that commands may be typed into. See also DOS.

CONFIGURATION. The way various components of a computer system are linked. This normally refers not only to the way the hardware is physically connected but also to how the software is set up to govern the computer and its peripherals; the setup and operating parameters of a software program. See also platform.

CONNECT TIME. The period during which a modem is connected to a remote computer.

CONTEXT-SENSITIVE. Responsive to a specific item or situation. For example, many software programs and operating systems have context-sensitive help windows, which automatically give the correct help for the process or feature you are using.

CONTROL KEY. A key found on IBM-compatible and other computer keyboards, usually designated by Ctl or Ctrl, used to enter codes or issue commands.

CONTROLLER. A chip or board that governs the transmission of data between a peripheral device, such as a disk drive or graphics display, and the CPU and main memory.

CPI. Characters per inch, a measure of print pitch.

CPU. Central Processing Unit, the part of the computer that controls and performs all processing activities. It consists of the ALU (arithmetic logic unit), control unit, and main memory. See also microprocessor.

CRASH. An uncontrolled shutdown of one task or the entire computer. See also BSOD and head crash.

CRIPPLE-WARE. Trial software that has some needed functions deactivated, sometimes only until the user enters an activation code that proves the purchase of a license to use the program fully. See also trial-ware.

CRT. Cathode Ray Tube, the display screen of a computer monitor or a TV. See also LCD.

CTL KEY OR CTRL KEY. See control key.

CURSOR. A symbol that marks the current position on the screen and moves as the position changes. It is most often a single underline, a vertical line, or a block the size of one character. It may be either steady or blinking. See also mouse pointer.

CURSOR CONTROL KEYS. A special group of keys on a keyboard (designated by arrows pointing up, down, left, and right) that perform cursor movement functions. See also numeric keypad.

CYBER-. Relating to the rapidly growing interactive world between humans and computers.

CYBERSPACE. First used by William Gibson in the novel "Neuromancer" to refer to a futuristic computer network into which people plugged their brains and interacted with it. It has come to refer to the interconnection of computers known as the Internet. See also Internet and virtual reality.

CYLINDER. On a hard disk, the collection of all the tracks that are in the same location on each disk surface.

DAISY CHAIN. A group of computers or

peripheral devices connected by a bus in a string, one to the next.

DATA. An item or collection of items of information to be processed, displayed, or stored. Data can be text, numbers, binary code, images, sounds, or any combination.

DATABASE. A collection of data, organized for retrieval, on a specific topic or for a designated purpose.

DATA CARTRIDGE. A removable, high-quality tape cassette designed for the storage of data on a computer. Data cartridges are most often used for backup or archival data.

DATA DENSITY. A measure of the amount of items or values stored in a unit length. On a tape this is usually in bits per inch (bpi), and on a disk it is usually in bits per unit of surface area.

DATA FILE. A collection of information to be used as input to a program for processing, display, or any other useful purpose. See also program file.

DDR. Double Data Rate, memory that delivers twice as much data on each memory clock cycle as single data rate memory. Rapidly becoming standard.

DEBUG. To locate and remove the errors (bugs) from a computer program. See also beta testing.

DEDICATED LINE. Telephone line used solely for data services. See also DSL.

DEFAULT. A value that is automatically assigned to a setting when no other value is entered. A default password, such as "secret," should be changed to ensure security.

DEGRADATION. Slowing down of a system under the load of processing. This is usually noticeable only on multiuser systems or PCs running multiple tasks. Other qualities of a system that can suffer degradation are stability and security.

DESKTOP. In a window-based user interface, the bottom-level window you see when no program window is open. The desktop can be set up as a user prefers, with icons allowing easy launching of often-used programs and documents.

DESKTOP COMPUTER. A PC featuring the traditional full-size case, monitor, and keyboard designed to be used in a stationary, "desk-centered" environment. See also laptop computer and portable computer.

DESKTOP PUBLISHING. Using software designed to create and publish professional-looking page layouts.

DEVICE BAY. A plug-and-play standard for easily installing new disk drives or other devices into a PC.

DHCP. Dynamic Host Control Protocol, a network protocol in which one computer assigns internal IP addresses to all the other computers as they request them.

DIALOG BOX. A window that appears onscreen to convey a message (such as a warning or error) or to request input (such as a choice of alternatives or a confirmation of some action). See also check box and radio buttons.

DIAL-UP LINE. A communications line that connects through the telephone system, usually by dialing touch-tones. See also DSL, ISDN, and POTS.

DIGITAL. Characterized by the representation of data as numbers. Computers are digital. See also analog.

DIGITAL CAMERA OR DIGICAM. A photographic still-image recording device that uses an electronic sensor and memory system instead of film to record images. The images can be subsequently transferred to a computer for long-term storage, editing, inclusion in documents, and transfer to others over the Internet. Some digicams can take short, low-resolution motion-video clips as well.

DIGITAL COMPUTER. An electronic device designed to process data in digital format. Personal computers (PCs) are general-purpose digital computers, suitable for most applications. See also computer.

DIGITAL SIGNATURE. See certificate.

DIGITIZE. To convert an analog signal to digital format.

DIGITIZER. A device that converts an analog signal (such as video or sound) into a series of digital values.

DIMM. Dual Inline Memory Module, a circuit board that can hold up to 256 MB of RAM and plugs into a DIMM socket on the motherboard. See also SIMM.

DIRECTCD. A method of saving data to a CD-R or CD-RW immediately through drag-and-drop file operations. DirectCD writes data in the "Universal Disk Format" (UDF).

DIRECTORY. A listing of the files available on a disk or part of a disk. Typically, files that pertain to a specific application (such as word processing, home finance, database, and games) are grouped together in their own directory, such as *C:\Quicken*. Windows and Mac OS use the term "folder" to refer to a disk directory. See also pathname and subdirectory.

DISK CACHE. A portion of memory set aside to keep recently accessed hard drive data for a period of time, shortening access time if the data is needed again. See also memory cache.

DISK CARTRIDGE. A removable storage unit of 100 MB or more that offers the capacity of a hard disk and the portability of a diskette. See also Zip drive and Jaz drive.

DISKETTE. A small, portable plastic-encased flexible ("floppy") disk used as a magnetic data storage medium. Data is recorded as magnetic signals that are arranged in a series of circular tracks. Most diskettes hold 1.4 megabytes of data, a small capacity by today's standards. See also hard disk.

DISPLAY. Any electronic device that visually conveys information or images, usually graphically. See also CRT and LCD.

DISPLAY ADAPTER. See graphics board.

DLL. Dynamic Link Library, a Windows file associated with one or more applications containing reusable subroutines that are read into memory as needed by the application.

DMA. Direct Memory Access, refers to the direct transfer of data between a peripheral or other device and main memory without going through the microprocessor.

DNS. Domain-Name Service, the translation of domain names into IP addresses performed by a designated computer on the network or the Internet.

DOCK. On Apple's Mac OS X desktop, an icon-filled bar for launching and switching between applications. See also taskbar.

DOCKING STATION. A rectangular platform with a connector and a power supply for a laptop or handheld computer, to connect it with a CRT monitor, printer, and other peripherals. Essentially, it turns a laptop computer into a desktop computer. See also dongle and port expander.

DOCUMENT. Any human-readable file containing information entered by the user. Examples are word-processing, spreadsheets, and databases.

DOCUMENTATION. Material that comes with a software package or a computer system and offers directions for setup and operation, features, capabilities, and troubleshooting advice. More and more, paper documentation is being replaced by "online" help, files installed on the PC's hard disk, a CD-ROM, or the Internet.

DOMAIN. A network or part of a larger network that is managed by a computer called a domain controller, which handles user logins, security, and shared resources.

DOMAIN NAME. A structured, alphabetic name, such as consumerreports.org, for a location on the Internet. These names are aliases for numeric IP addresses, and are leased from an Internet naming authority by the domain-name owner.

DONGLE. Any small peripheral device connected to a computer by a short cord and plug. See also port expander.

DOS. Disk Operating System, a set of programs that activates the computer and allows the user or other programs to perform simple functions; used synonymously with MS- or PC-DOS. A simple command-line DOS was built into Windows 95 and 98, and can be invoked in later versions of Windows if needed.

DOT-MATRIX. An outdated impact printer in which characters are formed by a series of dots. See also impact printer.

DOT PITCH. Indicates the spacing of color phosphor-dot triads on a CRT monitor screen; it should be 0.28 mm or less to avoid eyestrain with text. See also triad and pixel.

DOUBLE-CLICK. A quick double-press of the left button on a mouse to activate a file or icon.

DOWNLOAD. To transfer a copy of a file from a host (server) computer to a client computer. Term frequently used to describe process of transferring a file or data from the Internet to a computer's hard drive. See also upload.

DPI. Dots per inch, a common measure of the resolution of a printer or scanner. The higher the dpi, the better the image quality.

DRAFT MODE. A faster, ink-saving printing mode for ink-jet printers, and a toner-saving mode for laser printers.

DRAG AND DROP. Using a mouse, this is the way to move objects onscreen. Click on the item, representing a folder or file, and drag it while holding the mouse button, then release it wherever you want to place it.

DRAM (DEE-RAM). Dynamic Random Access Memory, chips designed as a matrix of "memory cells" in rows and columns. Each memory cell is used to store bits of data that can be retrieved by indicating the row and column location (or address) of the data. The data in each cell must be electronically "refreshed" several times a second, hence the term dynamic. See also DDR, RDRAM, SDRAM, and SRAM.

DRIVE. A unit that writes data to or reads it from a storage medium such as a tape or disk.

DRIVER. A program that controls some component of the system such as a monitor, disk drive, or printer.

DROP-DOWN MENU. A menu system in which the options are brought down from a menu bar at the top of the screen. The menu bar may be initially hidden or dormant until brought to life using either the mouse or keyboard. See also menu-driven.

DSL. Digital Subscriber Line, provides high-speed Internet access through existing phone lines without affecting normal phone operation. See also cable modem, dial-up line, and ISDN.

D TO A CONVERSION. The change of data or signals from digital to analog format. See also A to D conversion and modem.

DUAL-SCAN LCD. An improved passive matrix display that employs simultaneous scanning of two halves of the display area, thereby doubling the refresh rate and improving brightness. See also active matrix display.

DUPLEX. The ability to transfer data in two directions. If the signals can go both ways at the same time, it is called full duplex; if simultaneous transmission is not permitted, it is known as half-duplex. See also simplex.

DURON. A processor series from AMD that is generally slower than its Athlon counterpart and used in lower-priced PCs. See also Athlon, Celeron, 486, and Pentium.

DVD. Digital Versatile Disk, an optical storage medium the same size as a CD, but with at least 4 times the capacity. DVDs began as Digital Video Discs used for consumer distribution of movies, and were adopted for computer use. There are now drives with write-once (DVD-R) and re-write (DVD-RAM, DVD-RW, and DVD+RW) capabilities.

DVI. Digital Visual Interface, a display-device connection standard for digital displays. A DVI-D port is for digital monitors only, while a DVI-I port can also connect to analog monitors.

DVORAK KEYBOARD. An alternative keyboard layout, that must be learned in order to touch type, offering improved speed and accuracy over the standard "QWERTY" keyboard.

E-ANYTHING. Refers to an electronic or online version of anything traditionally done nonelectronically, such as e-mail or e-commerce. See also i-anything.

EASTER EGG. An undocumented animation, usually featuring the programmers' names, hidden in a program and activated by a "secret" sequence of actions.

ECP. Enhanced Capabilities Port, a type of parallel port on a computer, providing higher speed and bidirectional communication with multiple devices. The parallel port is being supplanted by the USB port on personal computers.

EDIT. To make changes in a document, data, or other file.

EDITOR. A program that permits you to create or make changes in a document. A word processor is an advanced type of editor, with special features such as word wrap, headers and footers, and print attributes (boldface, underline, italics).

EFT. Electronic funds transfer, a system commonly used by banks and other money handlers that involves secure, computer-controlled money transfers between accounts.

EIDE. Enhanced IDE, an advanced version of the IDE disk drive interface standard that runs faster and supports larger drives. See also Ultra DMA.

EISA (EE-SA) BUS. Extended ISA bus, introduced as a 32-bit alternative to IBM's Micro Channel bus, it preserved physical and electrical compatibility with the older ISA bus systems. Now supplanted by PCI, AGP, and USB.

ELECTRONIC COMMERCE. Shopping through electronic catalogs and making purchases using the Internet.

ELECTRONIC FUNDS TRANSFER. See EFT.

E-MAIL. Electronic mail lets you send and receive personal messages, including those with attached files such as text or graphics, through the Internet, an online service, a BBS, a network, or other system.

EMOTICONS. Short for "emotional icons", the use of strings of ASCII characters to represent the user's emotions. Examples are :-) for "that's funny," ;-) for "just kidding," and :-(for "I'm unhappy." Some users call these "smileys."

ENCRYPTION. A process applied to a data file to render its contents unreadable to a nonauthorized user or computer system. Reading an encrypted file requires a software "key" that is available only to an authenticated user. Encryption is a mathematical science whose goal is to create algorithms whose resulting encryption is impossible to "crack" with currently available computing power and hacker tools. See also authentication, certificate, and secure system.

END USER. The final person or business to make use of a product or service. This is generally you, the consumer. See also EULA.

ENERGY STAR. A label that designates compliance with energy efficiency goals developed by the United States Environmental Protection Agency. In order to qualify for the Energy Star standard, a typical computer or monitor must power down to no more than about 10% of normal power consumption after a period of inactivity.

ERGONOMIC. Designed with the needs and comfort of the human user in mind.

ESD. Electrostatic discharge, the great destroyer of digital electronics. Static build-up on your body in the winter can produce enough ESD to damage a keyboard, mouse, or laptop PC. ESD can be reduced through humidifying the air.

ETHERNET. The most common type of local area network (see LAN) used to connect personal computers to each other, and to file, printer, and communications servers.

EULA. End-User License Agreement. A legal instrument accompanying most software that states the terms under which the company is providing its material to the consumer. An EULA is typically written in virtually incomprehensible legal jargon, but must often be agreed with by clicking an on-screen "I Agree" button before one can use the software.

EXPANSION BOARD OR CARD. A unit with electronic components, plugged into a computer's expansion slot. This may be a new feature such as a TV tuner or an interface to an external device. See also PC card.

EXPANSION SLOT. A position in a computer for adding an expansion board or card. Desktop PCs usually have at least two free PCI expansion slots. Laptops use PC cards for expansion.

EXPERT SYSTEM. An AI (Artificial Intelligence) system that employs a database and set of rules for solving some specific problem. Expert systems are commonly used in applications such as medical diagnostics, trip routing, financial forecasting, and behavioral analysis.

EXPORT. To transfer from the file format currently in use to another one. See also import.

EXTERNAL BAY. A front-mounted drive bay that allows physical access. Floppy disks, tapes, and CD-ROMs are normally housed in external bays. See also internal bay and device bay.

EXTERNAL DRIVE. A drive that is physically separate from the computer. Such drives normally have their own power supply and attach to the computer through a FireWire port, SCSI port, or a PC card on a laptop. See also internal drive.

FAQ. A list of Frequently Asked Questions and answers, meant to help users of a product or service understand its features and operation, and perform simple troubleshooting.

FAT. File Allocation Table, a system for organizing files on a disk that keeps track of the locations of all the files in the directories and allocates the remaining disk space to new files. An update to the original FAT scheme for IBM-compatible PCs, called FAT32, was developed to handle disks larger than 2 GB and to store small files more efficiently. See also NTFS.

FATAL ERROR. The cause of premature termination of processing, often as a crash. Fatal errors can occur as a result of read/write errors, program bugs, system conflicts, and hardware defects. Some errors crash only one application, others require the PC to be restarted.

FAXMODEM. A modem that can pass either data or fax protocols, enabling a computer to send and receive fax documents from either another faxmodem or a standard fax machine. See also modem and voice modem.

F CONNECTOR. A type of coaxial connector, most frequently used to connect cable or satellite television signals to components such as TVs, VCRs, and PC tuner cards.

FIBER OPTICS. See optical cable.

FIFO. First-in, first-out. Describes the most common type of data buffer, in which the first data to come in is the first to go out. See also buffer.

FIELD. An individual item in a database record. See also record.

56K. A modem speed, nominally 56 kilobits per second (kbps), used in the fastest modems that will work with normal dial-up telephone lines (see POTS). A connection between 34k and 53k (the U.S. limit) can be established only if both the local telephone line and the ISP (Internet Service Provider) are properly equipped. See also V.90.

FILE. A collection of related records. Computer data and documents are normally stored as files. See also data file and program file.

FILE COMPRESSION. A procedure, such as "zipping," that reduces a file's size, without loss of data, usually for the purpose of storage or transmission. Compressed files must then be decompressed before use. Special utility programs handle file compression and can combine one or more files into a single compressed file for later retrieval. See also archival storage and self-extracting file.

FILE EXTENSION. An identifier of the type or purpose of a file, usually written as one to three letters following the filename and separated from it by a period. For example, the file *My Letter.doc* might be a text document while *Numbers.dat* could be a data file. File extensions are used by Windows to determine what program to use to open a file, and are hidden by default if Windows has registered a program for the extension.

FILENAME. The unique identification given to a program or data file for storage. Filenames were traditionally limited to eight characters (plus a three-character extension) in older operating systems like DOS. Newer operating systems such as Windows and Mac OS allow much longer filenames. See also filespec and pathname.

FILE SERVER. A high-speed computer in a network that provides common storage and retrieval of program and data files shared by the users. See also server.

FILE-SHARING. One of the common uses for a local area network. Files can be designated as shared by their owners on one PC, and accessed by other authorized users in the same network workgroup. See also file-swapping.

FILE SPECIFICATION OR FILESPEC. The complete description of a file, giving the path, filename, extension, and drive indicator, if needed. For example, the file d:\games\bigdice.exe might be an executable program file named Bigdice located in a folder called Games on drive D.

FILE-SWAPPING. An Internet activity popularized by free, peer-to-peer services such as Kazaa and Morpheus, with which users can search designated shared folders on each others PCs for files they are interested in and download them. File-swapping has been criticized because users often trade files containing copyrighted material.

FIREWALL. A network gateway (software or hardware) that "filters" data requests, rejecting those that lack the necessary security clearance; originally used to protect corporate, government, or institutional networks from unauthorized access, but now in use by individuals to keep their computers safe from intruders on the Internet. See also Intranet and proxy server.

FIREWIRE. A common name for the high-speed wired interface standardized by IEEE-1394, that provides synchronous multimedia data exchange between devices, such as a digital camcorder and a PC. Also called iLink.

FIRMWARE. Programs permanently stored on a ROM chip, or on an EPROM chip to allow for occasional updates. Firmware programs usually control the basic processes within a hardware device, such as a modem. See also BIOS and flash memory.

FIXED DISK. An IBM term for hard disk.

FLASH ANIMATION. A programming platform commonly used for embedding animation in Web pages. Flash "movies" are relatively small, allowing them to download quickly on slow dial-up connections. Playing a Flash movie requires a plug-in for the browser.

FLASH MEMORY. A lower-cost, higher-density, erasable RAM memory chip, derived from the EPROM, that is non-volatile but requires that memory be erased in blocks of fixed size rather than individual bytes. Used on motherboards to allow easy BIOS updating, and packaged in PCMCIA cards to act as auxiliary data storage in small portable devices.

FLAT-PANEL DISPLAY. A thin display screen employing one of several technologies, usually LCD. Flat panel displays are commonly used on portables to reduce size and weight, and are beginning to be sold as desktop monitor replacements. See active matrix display, dual-scan LCD, and LCD.

FLAT-SCREEN MONITOR. Refers to a monitor with a screen nearly or completely free of curvature. Flat screens allow square corners and reduce glare and image distortion.

FLOPPY DISK. See diskette.

FLOPS. Floating-point instructions per second, a measure of computer processor performance doing math instructions. See also MIPS.

FOLDER. The Windows 95/98 and Mac OS name for a disk directory.

FONT. A typeface enhancement such as bold or script. Although it is not precisely correct, the term is often used to refer to a typeface style such as Bookman, Times, Courier, or sans serif.

FOOTER. A special message or identification placed at the bottom of a page. See also header and tagline.

FOOTPRINT. The space on a floor or table occupied by a piece of hardware.

FOREGROUND PROCESS. A high-priority process that is performed while any others that are running are assigned to wait until CPU resources are available. See also background process.

FORMAT. 1) To initialize a data-storage disk. 2) To lay out in a specific pattern, such as a screen or report format. 3) The layout or pattern itself.

FORUM. An information exchange, usually found on online services and confined to a single topic or area of interest.

486. Also known as the 80486 or i486, an improved version of Intel's multitasking 386 processor. Some consumers may still own computers with 486 processors, but new Windows-based PCs usually use Intel's Pentium or AMD's Athlon. See also Athlon, Celeron, Duron, Pentium, and PowerPC.

FRAME RATE. Expressed in FPS (frames per second), the rate at which a display of moving graphical images is updated. Motion picture film runs at 24 FPS, the minimum considered to be essentially jitter-free. Computer-generated graphics, such as from games, can run at much higher rates, limited by the graphics processor. Avid gamers look for rates of 50 FPS or higher, producing more realistic motion. See also refresh rate.

FREEWARE. Software that is distributed, mostly via the Internet, without charge (other than a small service fee) to all interested users. See also public domain software and shareware.

FPS. See frame rate.

FTP. File Transfer Protocol, an Internet protocol that allows you to transfer files between your computer and an FTP site. "Anonymous" FTP allows a user to retrieve files without having to establish a user ID and password.

FULL-STROKE KEY. The type found on most keyboards, characterized by a marked give or depression when pressed, often with an associated key click. These keys feel like those on an electric typewriter and are preferred by most users. See also limited-stroke key.

FUNCTION KEY. A key that can be programmed to perform a specific operation. This may be a permanent programming by the operating system or temporary programming by the user or the application software in use.

G4. The newest microprocessor from Apple, available in Macintosh systems ranging in speed from 450 MHz to 1000 MHz.

GAME CONTROLLER. Originally limited to knobs and joysticks, now includes driving simulators, cockpit simulators, movement sensors, and the entire class of human interface devices (HIDs).

GAME PORT. A 15-pin serial port used for attaching joysticks or other game controllers, as well as MIDI music devices. Game ports can handle a pair of controllers and may come as part of the original system or be supplied on sound boards. They are becoming less common on new PCs, supplanted by newer interfaces like USB.

GB. See Gigabyte.

GIF (JIFF). Graphics Interchange Format, a lossless, compressed file format for image bitmaps invented by the CompuServe online service to reduce download time.

GIGABYTE. 1,024 megabytes, which is 1,073,741,824 bytes. Sometimes manufacturers will "inflate" hard drive sizes by defining a GB as a "billion bytes," but that is not strictly accurate.

GIGO (GIG-GO). Garbage-In, Garbage-Out, a colorful way of saying that the output cannot be reliable if the input is not.

GLITCH. A nonreproducible problem in a system. Glitches often result from voltage fluctuations, static discharges, and data transmission errors. See also soft error.

GRAPHICAL USER INTERFACE. See GUI.

GRAPHICS. Special characters or drawings such as graphs, charts, and picture-like representations of various objects. See also bitmap.

GRAPHICS ACCELERATOR. A display adapter that has built-in firmware, processing capabilities, and adequate memory (usually 32 to 128 MB) to relieve the CPU of much of the burden of processing graphics.

GRAPHICS BOARD OR ADAPTER. An expansion card (or circuitry built into the motherboard) that provides the memory and graphics coprocessor necessary to produce text and graphics displays; along with the monitor, determines the resolution and colors that can be displayed.

GUI (GOOEY). Graphical User Interface, a graphics-based user interface that allows you to operate by pointing and clicking with a mouse rather than entering typed text commands. The two main GUIs are Windows and the Macintosh OS.

H. At the end of a number (such as 384H), it indicates the hexadecimal format has been used in expressing that number. See also hexadecimal number system.

HACKER. A nonprofessional computer whiz; usually, one who tries to gain unlawful access to a computer system, or alters programs to allow unlicensed usage.

HALF-HEIGHT DRIVE OR BAY. A disk drive or its bay in a computer case about 1-1/2 inches high (half the physical height of older models).

HANDHELD. Short for any device that is operated while held in the hand. See also PDA.

HANDSHAKE. Control codes exchanged between computers or between a computer and its peripherals to govern the transfer of data. See also protocol.

HARD COPY. Printed text.

HARD DISK OR HARD DRIVE. A magnetic data storage system using one or more rigid platters sealed in a dustproof housing. Data is recorded as magnetic signals arranged in a pattern of concentric circles on the surfaces. Typical storage capacities range from about 20 to 120 gigabytes. See also diskette.

HARD ERROR. A permanent problem that is not removed by rereading the data or any other action. This usually means that there is a flaw, such as a bad memory chip or spot on a disk, that must be avoided in the future. See also glitch and soft error.

HARDWARE. The electronic equipment that makes up a computer system, such as the CPU, monitor, printer, circuit boards, drives, cables, etc. It does not include data or computer programs, which are software.

HARDWARE INTERFACE. A direct connection between two hardware components, such as the processor and video board or modem, usually established by means of cables. See also interface and user interface.

HARD-WIRED. Connected to the PC with a cable; permanently wired.

HEAD. The part of a drive that writes data to the storage medium (disk or tape) or reads data from it.

HEAD CRASH. A condition that results when the read/write head of a hard disk drive comes into contact with the disk surface, causing data loss along with permanent damage to the drive head and disk surface at the point of contact, requiring replacement of the drive. Data can sometimes be recovered from such a drive through an expensive data-recovery service.

HEADER. A special message or identification that is placed at the top of a page; an identifying marker or value in a record, file, or data transfer string. See also footer.

HERTZ OR HZ. A measure of frequency or the number of cycles per second.

HEXADECIMAL NUMBER SYSTEM. A number system that is based on the number 16 and uses the 16 characters 0-9 and A-F. Since a group of four binary digits can be expressed as one hexadecimal digit, this system is often used to express binary values in a more compact format.

HIBERNATION. A shutdown mode in many PCs and most laptops that saves the current state of the machine and all its running processes on the hard drive for quick restoration on demand. Also called suspend-to-disk. See also standby.

HIGH-LEVEL LANGUAGE. A programming language such as BASIC or C that is structured primarily from the logic of the problem rather than the machine design. A high-level program must be compiled or interpreted into machine code to run on a computer.

HIGH-RESOLUTION. Showing great detail; the higher the resolution of a graphics monitor or printer, the greater the detail of a drawing or image it is able to reproduce.

HOME PAGE. The page in a web site usually visited first, that contains links to other pages in the site or other sites. The home page is automatically selected when you type a web address ending in ".com," ".org," or another common domain suffix.

HOST COMPUTER. A computer that serves as a source for data and information retrieval for client computers, usually networked PCs. See also network.

HOTKEY. A key or combination of keys that when pressed take priority in causing some action to take place. Typical uses for hotkeys include initiating menu options or interrupting an ongoing process.

HTML. HyperText Markup Language, the standard language for creating pages on the World Wide Web. Even if you do not understand HTML, you can create it with Web-page authoring programs, popular word-processors, or basic step-by-step instructions at certain Web sites to build pages. See also hypertext and XML.

HTTP. HyperText Transfer Protocol, a protocol developed for exchange of hypertext documents across the Internet. All web addresses begin with http://, which a browser will automatically insert for you. See also hypertext.

HUB. A multiport device that connects several computers together into a wired network, without performing any data management functions. A "switched" hub adds the ability to prevent data "collisions," increasing overall speed. See also router.

HUMAN INTERFACE DEVICE (HID). Refers to any type of hardware device that accepts input from a user to control a computer program. Includes keyboards, mice, trackballs, biometric sensors, joysticks, and various game controllers.

HYPERLINK. A clickable object within a hypertext document that retrieves another location within the document or anywhere else on the Web. These can be either graphics or text; text links are usually blue and underlined.

HYPERTEXT. A method of linking information within and between text or other files. The linked data may be almost anything from text to graphics to programs. The Internet's WorldWide Web is an ad-hoc collection of linked hypertext documents.

I-ANYTHING. Refers to anything done using the Internet that was or is also done in non-Internet ways. See also e-anything.

IBM-COMPATIBLE. Generally, hardware or software that is designed for PCs based on the Intel x86 microprocessor architecture, first popularized by IBM. Most IBM-compatible PCs now run Microsoft Windows.

IC. Integrated Circuit, an assembly of electrical components deposited and connected on an encapsulated silicon wafer.

ICON. A small graphical image that appears on the computer's desktop in a Windows or Mac system. These normally represent a specific file or program or cause a desired action to occur when clicked with a mouse.

IDE. Integrated Drive Electronics, a hard disk interface technology. See also EIDE, SCSI, and Ultra DMA.

IEEE. A standards organization that publishes computer-industry-defined standards for hardware, software, and data communications. IEEE 1394 is the standard for the FireWire interface, and IEEE 802.11b is the standard for WiFi wireless networking.

iMAC. The latest value-line Macintosh computer from Apple, a compact, Internet-ready desktop series with an all-in-one case.

IMPACT PRINTER. One that produces characters on the paper by actually striking the paper through an inked ribbon, much like a typewriter. See also dot-matrix.

IMPORT. To transfer data from another file into the one currently in use. See also export.

INCOMPATIBLE. Unable to work with, usually referring to a program that can't be run under a different operating system than it was created for, or a device not supported by a computer's hardware or BIOS. See also standard.

INITIALIZE. To set up, prepare, or start from the beginning. To initialize a disk is to make it ready for use by a system. See also boot and format.

INK-JET PRINTER. A printer that uses tiny jets or droplets of charged ink particles, projected from a set of nozzles, to create images, usually of high quality. Ink-jet printers are currently the most popular printers for home use and are the most economical means of producing high-quality full-color printouts.

INSTANT MESSAGING. An online system, usually proprietary, that lets you hold a private, real-time text-based conversation between two users. Messaging among more than two users is usually referred to as chat, though it may use the same system. See also chat and IRC.

INSTRUCTION. A command to the CPU to carry out an operation.

INTEGRATED CIRCUIT. See IC.

INTEGRATED SOFTWARE. A software package that offers two or more types of applications, such as a word processor, spreadsheet, and database manager. See also application suite.

INTELLIGENT SYSTEM. An automated system designed to process information and make decisions using written rules that mimic the way a human would work. Intelligent systems can be used to monitor physical processes in real time and make critical decisions in the absence of human interaction. They are also used to help humans decide on a course of action based on a number of existing conditions, such as in medical diagnoses. Some systems are programmed to learn from errors.

INTERACTIVE. Able to respond to a user's wishes. Interactive software usually refers to a multimedia presentation that the user controls, moving at a speed and in a direction the user wishes.

INTERFACE. The connection between two components such as the PC and a printer; to connect two components together. See also hardware interface and user interface.

INTERLACED. Video display in which odd and even scan lines are displayed on alternate cycles. Interlaced signals require less processing and tend to be faster but can produce flicker. Standard televisions use an interlaced display. See also noninterlaced.

INTERNAL BAY. A drive bay that holds a drive not requiring physical access to the outside. Hard disks are normally housed in internal bays. See also external bay.

INTERNAL DRIVE. A drive housed within the computer. Such drives normally derive power from the computer's power supply. See also external drive.

INTERNET. A "super" network consisting of a collection of many commercial, academic, and governmental networks throughout the world. Public access to the Internet, now used by millions of people, is obtained through a contract with an Internet Service Provider (ISP). See also FTP and World Wide Web.

INTERNET GATEWAY. A device or computer that provides the connection and protocols to link a single computer or a network to the Internet.

INTERPRETER. A program that translates source code written in a high-level language to object code in machine language, executing each line as it is converted. BASIC is an interpreted programming language.

INTERRUPT. A pause in the normal execution of a computer program during which the operating system transfers control to another process. See also IRQ.

INTRANET. An "Internet-like" hyperlinked information-exchange system established within an organization or institution, for its own purposes, protected from unauthorized public access. See also firewall and proxy server.

I/O. Input/output, referring to data transfer.

IP OR IP ADDRESS. Internet Protocol address, a means of referring to locations on the Internet. Composed of four numbers from 0 through 255, separated by decimal points. All machines on the Internet have one, often assigned by the ISP at connection time.

IP TELEPHONY. Use of IP protocols to establish two-way voice communications between two or more users.

IRC. Internet Relay Chat, Internet communication where anyone can carry on real-time conversation by typing back and forth. See also instant messaging and chat.

IRQ. Interrupt Request, one of several control lines into a computer's CPU to provide a means for hardware components such as disk controllers, printers, and modems to gain the attention of the CPU. See also interrupt.

ISA (EYE-SA). Industry Standard Architecture, a bus standard developed for IBM-PC expansion cards. Originally it was 8-bit and eventually expanded to 16-bit architecture. Now supplanted by 32-bit interfaces. See also PCI and AGP.

ISDN. Integrated Services Digital Network, a high-speed telephone line that is a faster but expensive alternative to traditional dial-up modems, and available farther from the telephone office than DSL. See also DSL and POTS.

ITERATIVE. A software process using repetition to arrive at a precise result.

JAVA. A programming language that brings animation and interactivity to web pages by embedding program code that gets run on the client PC.

JAZ DRIVE. A drive, installed either internally or externally, that allows users to store data on relatively expensive 1- or 2-GB removable cartridges for backup, transferal, or archival purposes. See also Zip drive.

JOYSTICK. A device used with games and other interactive programs to manually control the cursor, an object, or the action by moving a stick back and forth, right and left, or by the push of a "fire" button.

JPEG. Joint Photographic Experts Group, an image file format allowing several levels of file compression from lossless (high quality, large file) to quite lossy (lower quality, small file), to suit different needs. Commonly used on web pages. See also compressed format.

JUMPER. A small, plastic-covered metal clip used to close a connection (circuit) between two pins such as for configuring settings on a board.

JUSTIFICATION. The alignment of text or images in a document, usually to the left and/or right margins, or centered.

K OR KB. Kilobyte, which is exactly 1,024 bytes but is usually thought of as 1,000 bytes. Sometimes incorrectly represented by a small k, which is just the prefix kilo.

Kb. Kilobit.

KERNEL. The most rudimentary part of a program, most typically of an operating system, that remains in memory at all times. Making the kernel "crash-proof" is a primary goal of operating system designers. See also interface.

KEY. In a database, an item, usually a field within a record, used to identify the record uniquely; a button on a keyboard.

KEYBOARD. The typewriter-like panel used to enter and manipulate text or data and enter instructions to direct the computer's operations. See also multifunction keyboard.

KEYPAD. A set of keys grouped together and performing a particular function. The most common keypads are the numeric and cursor control.

KILO-. A prefix meaning 1,000. Because of the binary nature of computers, kilo is also used to refer to 1,024. See also K.

KILOBIT. 1,024 bits (2 to the 8th power), usually thought of as 1,000 bits.

KILOBYTE. 1,024 bytes (2 to the 8th power), usually thought of as 1,000 bytes.

LAN. Local Area Network, a system of two or more computers within an area (typically a building) that share some of the same facilities, such as disks, printers, and software. See also Ethernet and token-ring.

LANDSCAPE. The page or screen orientation in which information is printed across the longer dimension. See also portrait.

LANGUAGE. In programming, a command syntax comprising the lexicon a programmer uses when writing source code. Languages include Basic, C, Pascal, Cobol, Lisp, Java, HTML, XML, Forth and Perl, among many others.

LAPTOP COMPUTER. A class of portable, battery-equipped computers with flat screens, small enough to be used on the lap or small table. Some are complete systems offering advanced features nearly the equal of desktop PCs. See also portable computer.

LASER PRINTER. A fast, economical page printer that produces very high-quality print and graphics. Only black-and-white laser printers are currently affordable for consumers.

LAUNCH. Load and run a program.

LCD. Liquid Crystal Display, a technology allowing thin, flat, high-resolution color displays, used for laptop computers and some desktop monitors. See also active matrix display and passive matrix display.

LED. Light-emitting diode, a small electrical component that produces light when a current is passed through it.

LED's can now produce virtually any color of light.

LIMITED-STROKE KEY. The type of key found on some keyboards and laptop computers that depresses only slightly when pressed. See also full-stroke key.

LINK. See hyperlink.

LINUX. A freely downloadable, user-supported open-source OS, based on UNIX. Linux is touted as an alternative to Windows, but is more suited to certain business applications such as web-servers. See also open source and UNIX.

LIST. An ordered sequence of information. See also queue.

LOAD. To read a program or data into a PC's memory. See also launch, retrieve, and save.

LOCAL AREA NETWORK. See LAN.

LOCAL BUS. A parallel bus that attaches a peripheral device within the PC directly to the CPU, permitting much faster data transfer rates. See also PCI.

LOGICAL DRIVE. A section of a physical drive that has been designated as an independent storage device. For example, a single hard drive could contain logical drives C: and D:. See also partition.

LOST CLUSTER. Units of disk storage that have lost the information that links them to the proper file name. Lost clusters can occur if a computer is shut down with files left open, such as when power is suddenly lost or the system is turned off with applications still running. Running a utility, such as Windows' ScanDisk, can locate and repair lost clusters and other defects.

MAC ADDRESS. Media Access Control address, a globally unique hexadecimal string, such as 00-10-3C-B6-45-DG, embedded into every hardware device that can connect to a network. MAC addresses are used by routers to direct Internet packets to the right user.

MAC. Short for Apple's Macintosh computer.

MAC OS. The windowed operating system of the Apple Macintosh computer family. Mac OS X (version ten) departed radically from earlier versions in being UNIX-based, and having its user-interface modernized with an equivalent to the Windows taskbar called the "dock."

MACHINE LANGUAGE OR CODE. Programming instructions in binary format, the basic coding of a particular microprocessor family.

MACHINE-SPECIFIC. Software or hardware that can be used on only one type or model of computer.

MACINTOSH. A computer from Apple that was the first to use a mouse and icon-based operating system to make it user friendly.

MACRO. A series of commands that can be initiated easily, often by a solitary keystroke or simple combination of keys; a sequence of instructions embedded in a spreadsheet or other document that can be easily executed at will.

MAGNETIC TAPE. See tape.

MAILING LIST. A list of subscribers to a topical information exchange that operates through e-mail. Most mailing list users refer to the group of postings as "the list." The list-server is the host software, residing on a server computer that manages the traffic for the list. Mailing list programs include listserv, majordomo, and listproc. A directory of over 50,000 public lists is at *www.lsoft.com/catalist.html*.

MAINFRAME. A large, expensive, multi-processor computer system capable of handling many users and running many programs simultaneously. Such systems are extremely fast and support a wide range of peripherals. They are normally found in large businesses, universities, and government agencies. See supercomputer.

MAIN MEMORY. The data storage locations inside a computer and directly accessible by the CPU; memory can range from as little as 1 MB to more than 8 GB.

MATRIX. An array or an ordered arrangement. For example, 63 dots might be arranged into a rectangular matrix or array of nine rows and seven columns.

Mb. Megabit.

MB. Megabyte.

MEDIA. The physical object, usually a disk or tape, upon which digital data is stored.

MEDIA PLAYER. Generically, a program that decodes file- or Internet-based multimedia material into an audible and/or visual presentation. Examples are Windows Media Player, RealOne Player, and MusicMatch Jukebox.

MEG. Short for megabyte or megahertz.

MEGA-. A prefix usually meaning one million, but because of the binary nature of computers, used to refer to 1,048,576 (or 2 to the twentieth power).

MEGABIT. 1,024 kilobits, yielding 1,048,576 bits, usually considered a million.

MEGABYTE. 1,024 kilobytes, yielding 1,048,576 bytes, usually considered a million.

MEGAHERTZ. 1 million hertz.

MEMORY. See main memory, RAM, and VRAM.

MEMORY CACHE. A high-speed block of memory that acts between the main memory and processor to speed the execution of instructions and processing of data. See also disk cache.

MEMORY-RESIDENT. See resident.

MENU. A list of available options, often in a "drop-down" list activated via a mouse-click. See also drop-down menu and shell.

MENU BAR. A bar across the top of the screen that presents the first level of options for a drop-down menu system.

MENU-DRIVEN. A program or system that uses a series of menus to make it easier to use. The user selects the desired option by clicking on an entry with the mouse, typing the corresponding letter or number, or moving the cursor to the proper selection and hitting the Enter key, and the program will then perform the chosen function. See also drop-down menu.

MERGE. Typically, to merge a name and address file with a form letter using functions built into a word-processing program.

MHz. Megahertz.

MICRO. A shorthand term for microcomputer.

MICROCHIP. A small semiconductor chip.

MICROCOMPUTER. See personal computer.

MICRON. One-millionth of a meter or

one-thousandth of a millimeter.

MICROPROCESSOR. The CPU of a personal computer, such as the Pentium 4 or Athlon XP. Microprocessors have an ALU and control unit with limited memory such as an instruction cache. The main memory is added externally.

MICROSECOND. One-millionth of a second.

MIDI. Musical Instrument Digital Interface, standard for the exchange of information between various musical devices, including instruments, synthesizers, and computers that are MIDI capable. See also sound board.

MINICOMPUTER. A medium-size computer capable of handling several users and multiple tasks, and acting as a database host. Normally found in small businesses and schools.

MINITOWER CASE AND MICROTOWER CASE. Smaller versions of the tower case.

MIPS. Million Instructions Per Second, a very rough measure of the performance of a processor in terms of the number of instructions carried out in one second. 1 MIPS = 1,000,000 instructions per second. But MIPS values alone are not good indicators of relative system performance. See also FLOPS.

MM. See multimedia.

MODE. A condition or set of conditions for operation. A printer may have modes for different print qualities, or a serial port for different transmission speeds or protocols.

MODEM. Modulator/Demodulator, used to connect a digital device (computer) to a data communications channel (telephone line, cable or radio link). Modems perform the necessary D-to-A (modulation) and A-to-D (demodulation) conversions. A modem is needed to send a fax, to access e-mail, and to get online to the Internet.

MODULAR LAPTOP. A laptop PC that contains one or more bays allowing various drives or a battery to be inserted as desired, or removed to save travel weight. See also all-in-one and slim-and-light.

MONITOR. The "face" of the computer, most often a CRT screen. Monitors are similar to TVs but usually do not have a tuner and so cannot directly receive television broadcast signals. See also CRT and LCD.

MONOCHROME. One color, usually referring to a monitor or printer.

MOTHERBOARD. The main board inside a PC into which the memory, microprocessor, and other components are plugged.

MOUSE. A palm-size device that controls the cursor, an object on the screen, or other screen action by moving around on a flat surface. A small ball or optical sensor on the bottom of the mouse senses direction of the motion, transferring this action to the screen. One or more buttons are also used for additional control, such as clicking and dragging. See also trackball.

MOUSE POINTER. A type of cursor used by a mouse or other pointing device to indicate a specific screen location. The pointer may be any number of different shapes, but the most common types are the arrow and crosshair.

MPEG. Motion Picture Experts Group, modern standard format for compression and storage of video files. MPEG-1 allows a full-length movie to be stored on a standard CD-ROM disc with a moderate amount of visual artifacts; MPEG-2 allows a full-length movie to be stored on a DVD-ROM with few visual artifacts.

MP3. Nickname for "MPEG-1 Layer-3", an encoding format for compressed digital music files that offers high quality with less than one-tenth the data rate of an uncompressed CD-music bitstream. The small files required for typical songs allow for fairly fast transfer over consumer-grade Internet connections, and have spawned a hobby of sharing music over the Internet, both legally as well as in violation of copyright laws.

MS-DOS. Microsoft DOS, the version of the IBM PC-DOS disk operating system used by IBM-compatible computers. It has been replaced by Windows.

MSN TV. Formerly called WebTV, a Microsoft-owned service that uses a TV setup box to access the Internet.

MULTIFREQUENCY. See multiscan.

MULTIFUNCTION KEYBOARD. A computer keyboard that has additional keys to launch e-mail, the Internet, and selected applications, and control computer functions like the CD or DVD drive, sound volume, and sleep mode.

MULTIFUNCTION PRINTER. An ink-jet, laser, or thermal printer that, in addition to printing, may serve as a phone, fax machine, scanner, copier, or other device.

MULTIMEDIA. Generally, any system or application that incorporates two or more of graphics, text, audio, and video into an integrated presentation.

MULTIMEDIA PC. A PC equipped for multimedia use. Common multimedia systems for home use are equipped with high-resolution graphics, CD-ROM drives, and sound boards in addition to the traditional disk drives.

MULTISCAN. A type of monitor that accepts various combinations of screen resolution and refresh rate.

MULTIPROCESSOR. A computer that has more than one processor, which can improve performance when combined with an OS that supports multiprocessing.

MULTITASKING. The ability to run more than one program or process at the same time. For example, printing a document while surfing the web. The increasing power of 32-bit and 64-bit processors has made multitasking more efficient and popular. See also time-sharing.

MULTIUSER. Designed to support more than one user at a time. Although most microcomputers are single-user PCs, a few upper-end systems have multiuser capability.

NAGWARE. Software, normally shareware, that displays messages to remind (nag) the user to register and, usually, to pay a fee.

NETWORK. Any system of two or more connected computers along with their peripherals, organized to share files and resources. See also bus and LAN.

NEWSGROUP. One of the informal information-sharing message boards on Usenet.

NIC. Network Interface Card, an expansion card used to connect a computer to a LAN.

NODE. A computer (client or server) or peripheral device in a network.

NOISE. Unwanted electrical or communication signals; interference.

NOISE FILTER. An electric device

designed to reduce electrical noise on a data line or AC line.

NONINTERLACED. Video display mode in which every scan line is displayed progressively. Noninterlaced images are more stable to view, but place more demands on the monitor. See also interlaced.

NONVOLATILE. A memory design in which the stored data is not lost when the power is removed from the system. See also flash memory and volatile.

NOTEBOOK COMPUTER. See laptop computer.

NTFS. New Technology File System, an advanced hard drive file-allocation scheme developed by Microsoft for Windows NT and used in newer versions of Windows, including 2000 and XP. NTFS is much more robust and reliable than the earlier FAT, and it has several fail-safe and recovery features that help prevent data loss in the event of an unexpected shutdown. But NTFS is more complex than FAT and is not visible to earlier operating systems, except across a network.

NUMERIC. Containing only numbers, which may include only the 10 digits 0-9, a plus or minus sign, and a decimal point.

NUMERIC KEYPAD. A group of keys set aside for the entry of numeric data and performing simple arithmatic operations. See also cursor control keys.

OCR. Optical Character Recognition, a text-recognition program that can convert scanned paper documents into a word-processing file format for storage, editing, and incorporation into other documents. See also scanner.

OEM. Original Equipment Manufacturer; technically, the original maker of a piece of equipment who usually markets to a reseller, but may also market direct to the end-user. See also VAR.

OFFICE SUITE. An application suite of office-oriented programs. Examples are Microsoft Office, Corel WordPerfect office, Lotus SmartSuite, and Sun StarOffice.

OFFLINE. Not currently accessible by the PC; a PC that is not networked.

OFFLINE STORAGE. See archival storage.
ONLINE. Connected to the Internet or to another computer via modem, cable, or satellite. Going online refers to using the Internet.

ONLINE HELP. A feature of many programs that provides assistance with how to operate the program. It is normally accessed by hitting a key such as F1 or selecting a menu option. Online help is often all that is needed to become proficient in using an application. See also context-sensitive.

ONLINE SERVICE. A collection of information databases and other offerings that can be accessed via a modem. The various features range from reference material (encyclopedias and atlases) to current updates (weather and stocks) to interactive features with other users (bulletin boards and games). Popular services include America Online, CompuServe, and Microsoft Network.

OPEN SOURCE. Describing a program or system whose code is freely available and publicly-supported. Anyone can modify open source programs for their own needs, and make those modifications available to other users through web sites established for the purpose.

OPERATING SYSTEM. See OS.

OPTICAL CABLE. Cable that contains very thin, flexible glass or plastic fibers through which data is carried using a light beam. Used in cable TV and in high-speed data communication links.

OPTICAL DISK. Generally refers to any disk read or written to by a laser or other light-emitting/sensing device.

OS. Operating System, the software that is necessary to control the basic operation of the computer. Examples are DOS, Windows, Mac OS, and Linux. A computer's OS determines to a large extent the "look-and-feel" of the machine.

PACKET. A "chunk" of digital information carried on a data channel from a specific source addressed to a specific destination. Packets meant for many different users can be sent in any order, and will be sorted out by a router according to their addresses. See also MAC address and router.

PAGE. 1) A section of a program or data file of fixed length. 2)The amount of a document that will fit on one printed page.
PAGING. The division of main memory to speed up access.

PAINT PROGRAM. An application that lets a user draw a graphical "bitmap" image directly by moving the pointing device.

PALETTE. The range of colors and shades that are available within a graphics program, that are displayable on a certain monitor, or that are printable with a certain printer.

PALMTOP COMPUTER. A PDA.

PARALLEL PORT. A type of connection that transmits data one byte or data word at a time. Parallel ports were most frequently used for printers on IBM-compatible systems, but are being supplanted by the faster USB port. See also serial port.

PARALLEL PROCESSING. A computer design in which more than one operation can be performed simultaneously.

PARTITION. The division of a physical drive into two or more logical disks. For example, a 6-GB hard disk drive might be partitioned into three 2-GB disks.

PASSIVE MATRIX DISPLAY. A flat panel LCD display in which all transistors are outside the display area. Passive matrix displays lose brightness when not viewed from straight on, and blur moving images. See also active matrix display.

PASSWORD. A series of characters used as a code to access a system, program, or file. A password should be chosen that is hard to guess, and not a common word.

PATHNAME. The sequence of subdirectory (or folder) names needed to specify the location of a file on a disk. The string *C:\windows\system\shell.dll* is a pathname.

PC. Personal Computer; sometimes used to denote any IBM-compatible personal computer; printed circuit. See also personal computer.

PC CARD. A credit card-size, plug-and-play module commonly used to attach expansion devices (such as memory, modems, and drives) to portable computers.

PC-COMPATIBLE. Loosely used to mean IBM PC-compatible.

PC-DOS. The original, command-driven, text-based disk operating system for IBM

PCs, based on Microsoft's MS-DOS which IBM licensed from Microsoft.

PCI. Peripheral Component Interconnect, a local bus design, popular on Pentium-based systems, that provides high-speed communications between various components and the processor. See also local bus.

PCMCIA CARD. See PC card.

PDA. Personal Digital Assistant, a small handheld computer that functions as a personal organizer, with a calendar/reminder, to-do list, notepad, and address/phone directory. Usually uses a stylus for input, though some have small keyboards. Some PDAs offer optional wireless access to such services as e-mail, Internet, or cellular phone service. See also PIM.

PEER-TO-PEER. A network architecture in which data can flow directly between any of the nodes without a server being necessary.

PEN COMPUTER. A portable computer, larger than a PDA, with wireless communications capabilities and a stylus-sensitive screen that the user writes on to enter information and commands. See also portable computer.

PENTIUM. An Intel microprocessor employing a fast, 32-bit architecture (with a 64-bit internal bus) that makes extensive use of RISC technology, employs internal memory caches, and can execute multiple independent instructions in the same clock cycle, giving it higher performance than its predecessors. The most recent series is the Pentium 4, which is available in clock speeds up to 2.5 GHz. See also 486, Athlon, and PowerPC.

PERIPHERAL. Any hardware attachment to a computer such as a keyboard, monitor, disk, or printer.

PERIPHERAL COMPONENT INTERCONNECT. See PCI.

PERSONAL COMPUTER. A small, single-user computer that uses a microprocessor as its CPU and is designed to be both user-friendly and available at relatively low cost.

PERSONAL DIGITAL ASSISTANT. See PDA.

PHYSICAL DRIVE. The entire disk consisting of all logical drives into which that drive has been partitioned. For example, if a 6-GB disk drive is partitioned into three 2-GB logical disks, then 6 GB is the size of the physical drive.

PICOSECOND. One-trillionth (10 to the minus 12th power) of a second.

PIM. Personal Information Manager, an application that organizes information on a day-to-day basis. PIMs routinely include features such as a reminder calendar, notepad, address book, phone dialer, calculator, alarm clock, and other utilities. See also PDA.

PINCUSHION EFFECT. A bowing-in on each side of the image on a CRT monitor screen, usually correctable with the monitor's controls. LCD monitors do not have this effect.

PITCH. A print size, such as pica (10 characters per inch) and elite (12 per inch). See also point.

PIXEL. Short for picture element, the smallest individually controllable unit of a visible image on a display monitor. Often erroneously used to refer to the triad of dots on a CRT screen. On flat-panel (LCD) displays, there is always one pixel per triad of stripes, but there is no such mapping on a CRT monitor. See also dot pitch and triad.

PLATFORM. The hardware architecture on which software applications are intended to run; the operating system or user interface under which the software application is intended to be used. See also configuration.

PLUG AND PLAY. A standard for managing the installation of expansion cards and peripherals in modern PCs and OSs. If both a PC and a device are plug-and-play compatible, the computer should handle the installation automatically.

PLUG-IN. A small add-on program that when downloaded expands the capability of a web browser. Examples are Acrobat for text, Flash for graphical animation, and RealPlayer for audio.

PnP. See plug and play.

POCKETZIP. A removable magnetic disk and drive, formerly called a "Clik" disk, from Iomega. The PocketZip disk holds 40 MB, costs about $10, and is small enough to fit into a Type II PC-card-size drive. See also Zip and Jaz.

POINT. A measure of the vertical height of a print character, equal to 1/72 of an inch. See also pitch. Also, to select a screen location with a pointing device such as a mouse.

POINTER. See mouse pointer; a marker as to a place in memory or in a file.

POINTING DEVICE. A hand-operated device used to move a pointer on the screen of a graphical user interface, selecting program objects, activating controls, or manipulating objects. See also mouse, tablet, and trackball.

POP. Post Office Protocol, an e-mail system that communicates between your primary mailbox in your own computer and the one at your access provider's site. POP mail is the usual protocol for incoming mail, while SMTP is used for outgoing.

POP-UP. A message or window that appears on a computer screen, often in response to a user or program action. Pop-ups are also a favorite way to present advertising associated with web sites. Pop-up ads that appear when you close a browser window are called "pop-under" ads.

PORT. A socket on a computer to connect a peripheral such as a printer or modem. See FireWire, parallel port, SCSI, serial port, and USB port.

PORT EXPANDER. A small plastic box or bracket with connectors for attaching peripheral devices to laptop computers. See also dongle.

PORTABLE COMPUTER. A computer that is easily moved from place to place and that normally contains battery power for use on the go. Types include PDAs, laptops, and pen computers.

PORTRAIT. The page or screen orientation in which information is printed across the shorter dimension. See also landscape.

POSTSCRIPT. A standard for formatting output files for printing that is device-independent. A file formatted for one PostScript printer should be able to be printed correctly by any other PostScript printer.

POTS. Plain Old Telephone Service, the low-bandwidth, twisted-pair wiring and associated equipment at the local telephone central office that provides for voice telephone calls and up to 53-kbps modem connections. See also DSL, 56k, and ISDN.

POWER CONDITIONER. An electrical device designed to eliminate both voltage spikes and noise from input power sources.

POWERMAC. A newer version of the Apple Macintosh that employs the PowerPC microprocessor.

POWERPC. A fast, 32-bit chip that employs advanced RISC technology. See also Athlon and Pentium.

POWER STRIP. An AC electrical device that provides multiple outlets, usually having an on/off switch, a circuit breaker, and surge protection.

PPM. Pages per minute, a measure of the speed of a printer.

PPP. Point-to-Point Protocol, a convention for transmitting packet-switched data over long-distance networks such as the Internet.

PRELOAD. The operating system and usually a selection of applications loaded onto the hard disk of a computer prior to purchase. See also bundle, shovelware, and turnkey system.

PRESENTATION GRAPHICS. A software program designed to create charts and graphs suitable for business or educational presentations.

PRINTER. A device designed to produce hard copy of either text or graphics. There are several types of printers, both monochrome and color-capable.

PRINTER CABLE. A cable that connects the printer to the computer.

PRINTHEAD. The part of a character printer that produces the characters.

PRINT SERVER. A small device that connects a printer directly to a network for shared use.

PRINT SPOOLER. A background applet that keeps a list of files to be printed and sends these to the printer as soon as it is available, thus freeing the system for other uses.

PRIVILEGES OR RIGHTS. Granted to a user by a system administrator, the set of operations that the user may perform on a system, such as ability to access, change or delete files in certain directories, or change the configuration of the system. Usually tied to a user's login ID.

PROCESSOR. The "brain" of a computer. See CPU and microprocessor.

PRODUCTIVITY SOFTWARE. Applications for the office, such as word-processor, spreadsheet, and database software.

PROGRAM. A logical sequence of instructions designed to accomplish a specific task, written in such a way that it can be read and executed by a computer. Also to construct a program. See also application and language.

PROGRAM FILE. A file that contains a program. Program files may also be data files if they serve as the input or output for other programs. See also data file.

PROGRAMMABLE KEY. See function key.

PROGRAMMING LANGUAGE. A language used to create a program that can be loaded into and executed by a computer. See also language.

PROGRAMMER. One who writes programs.

PROMPT. A character, symbol, sound, or message sent to the screen to signal the user that the computer is ready for input; to issue a prompt.

PROPORTIONAL SPACING. The characteristic of some print fonts (such as this text) in which narrow characters such as I and J use less space than wider ones such as M and W.

PROPRIETARY. Incompatible with others of the same type; patented or copyrighted; exclusively owned by a company or individual. See also standard.

PROTOCOL. A standardized sequence of bits, characters, and control codes used to transfer data among computers, peripherals, and networks. See also handshake.

PROXY SERVER. A network service intended to link multiple users on a protected LAN with specified resources on the Internet, while maintaining security. See also firewall.

PS/2. Short for Personal System/2, an IBM designation for a line of PCs popular in the late 1980s and early 1990s, after which the mouse and keyboard interfaces still used today were named.

PUBLIC DOMAIN SOFTWARE. Programs that are neither owned nor copyrighted by anyone and are available to all who want them without restriction. These programs can usually be obtained for a small service fee. See also freeware and shareware.

PULL-DOWN MENU. See drop-down menu.

QUERY. A request for information from a database; to issue a query.

QUEUE. An ordered list of data in temporary storage. Data in a queue are usually handled as a FIFO (First-In, First-Out) list, in which the first to be added to the list is the first to be processed.

QUICKTIME. A multimedia extension to the Macintosh operating system. A version is also available for Windows-based multimedia applications.

QWERTY KEYBOARD. The traditional keyboard layout familiar to most typists and keyboard users. Named for the first six letters from the left on the top alphabet row. The keyboard has compromises in layout (due to limitations of early typewriters) that lead to errors in fast typing. See also Dvorak keyboard.

RADIO BUTTONS. A set of onscreen options, only one of which is available at any one time. Once a selection is made (usually indicated by a dot or similar symbol), any previous choice is turned off (the dot is removed). See also check box and dialog box.

RAM. Random Access Memory, a read/write type of memory that permits the user to both read the information that is there and write data to it. This is the type of memory available to the user in most systems. See also DDR, DRAM, ROM, SDRAM, SRAM, and RDRAM.

RDRAM. Rambus DRAM, a type of DRAM that is faster, but more expensive than SDRAM. See also DDR and RAM.

REALAUDIO OR REALMEDIA. Popular streaming audio and video formats for the web. Downloading the free RealOne Player plug-in applet turns your web browser into an Internet radio/television.

RECORD. A group of related fields or data items. A collection of records is a database. See also file.

REFRESH. To continuously renew or update, as contents of DRAM; to redraw information after alteration, such as a graphics image that is being edited.

REFRESH RATE. The number of times each second that a CRT monitor redraws the image on the screen. A refresh rate below about 72 Hz can appear to "blink" as the image fades between refreshes. See also frame rate.

REMOTE ACCESS. Access to a computer through a data communications channel.

RESIDENT. Permanently present; a program that is resident in memory stays there between uses.

RESOLUTION. Indicates the degree of detail that can be perceived. The higher the resolution, the finer the detail.

RETRIEVE. To obtain data from main memory or disk storage. See also load and save.

RGB VIDEO. Short for red/green/blue, a color description method for video that provides for individual control of the intensity of the three primary colors (red, green, and blue).

RIBBON CABLE. A flat, multiwire cable design that is commonly used to connect devices within the computer.

RIGHTS. See privileges.

R/O. Read-Only, indicates a file, disk, or device that data may be read from but not written to. CD-ROMs and ROM chips are examples of R/O devices. See also R/W and write-protected.

ROM. Read-Only Memory, storage that permits reading and use of data but no changes. ROMs are preprogrammed at the factory for a specific purpose and are found on many boards such as graphics and in many systems that automatically boot when they are turned on. See also RAM.

ROM BIOS. A BIOS routine contained in a ROM chip, enabling a computer device to boot. The system BIOS on a PC's motherboard is one example; however, some components have their own ROM BIOS chips.

ROUTER. A device in a network that manages the flow of data packets between the network and the computers connected to the router's ports. See also packet.

RSI. Repetitive Stress Injury, a disorder of the hands, arms, back, neck, and even eyes that can arise from very heavy computer use. See also carpal tunnel syndrome.

RS-232C INTERFACE. A standard serial data transmission protocol using a 9- or 25-pin connector, found in most PCs. It is frequently used for a mouse, modem, or similar device.

RTFM. "Read The Flaming Manual," the PG-rated version of a somewhat stronger expression that states the solution for the all-too-true tendency of computer users to read the manual only as a last resort in resolving problems.

RUN. To execute a program. See also launch and load.

R/W. Read/Write, indicates a file, disk, or device for which data may be both read and written. Although individual files may be set to R/O status, hard disks, diskettes, tapes, and main memory are examples of components that are normally R/W. See also R/O and write-protected.

SAVE. To store a file on a disk storage device. See also load and retrieve.

SCALABLE. 1) Capable of being sized up or down, as with a font. 2) A computer system whose speed or data throughput can be increased in stages by adding modules.

SCALABLE FONT. A font for which each character can be set to the desired size from a stored pattern. The most common scalable fonts are TrueType fonts.

SCANNER. A peripheral device that digitally translates and then transfers photos, graphics, or text onto a computer's hard drive. See also OCR.

SCREEN SAVER. An applet that produces a moving image on the monitor screen to prevent permanent after-images from being burned into the phosphors by lingering, unattended displays. Does not really save the screen on modern monitors, which are better served by using the power-saving standby mode.

SCROLL. To move onscreen graphics or text up, down, right, or left in a smooth, usually continuous and reversible action.

SCROLL BAR. A screen element consisting of a horizontal or vertical bar with a slider that moves within the bar both to control scrolling and to indicate position in the document.

SCSI (SCUZZY). Small Computer System Interface, a parallel interface that can handle several daisy-chained peripheral devices such as disk, tape, and CD-ROM, with high data transfer rates. See also IDE.

SDRAM (S-D-RAM). Synchronous Dynamic RAM, a faster type of main memory chip, used in fast Pentium-class PCs. See also DDR, DRAM, and RDRAM.

SECTOR. A unit of data on a disk. Each track is divided into the same number of sequentially numbered sectors, which are further divided into clusters.

SECURE SITE. A web site that uses encrypted pages that cannot be read by unauthorized persons such as hackers. Many commercial and financial web sites have secure sections for exchange of personal information with customers. See also encryption and certificate.

SECURE SYSTEM. A computer or network to which access is restricted to authorized users or other systems, and whose critical data communications is encrypted.

SEEK TIME. The time required for disk drive to move the read/write heads to the proper track, usually a few milliseconds.

SELF-EXTRACTING FILE. A compressed file that is executable. When run, the self-extracting file will release and decompress all the files that have been stored within it. See also file compression.

SERIAL PORT. A type of connection that transfers data one bit at a time. Serial ports are commonly used by most input/output devices. See also parallel port, RS-232C interface, and USB port.

SERVER. A computer in a network, the resources of which are shared by part or all of the other users. See also file server.

SHAREWARE. User-supported software that is copyrighted and usually available on the Internet; the author usually requests a ($10 to $50) fee from those who use the program. See also public domain software.

SHEET FEEDER. A device that attaches to some scanners that automatically feeds a stack of sheets through it for scanning, thus eliminating the need to hand-feed the pages. Useful for OCR of large printed documents.

SHELL. An onscreen menu- or icon-driven user interface that attempts to make operation easier. They tend to shield the user from the underlying operating system, which may not be desirable.

SHELL ACCOUNT. A nongraphical interface to the Internet, using UNIX commands.

SHIFT KEY. A key that changes the function of a character printed by another key when pressed along with that key. See also alt key and control key.

SHORTCUT. An icon on the OS desktop or program list that launches a program or document when activated. There can be many shortcuts to one program.

SHOVELWARE. Limited-function or promotional software of questionable value that comes preloaded onto a new PC. Often, the PC manufacturer pays little or nothing for shovelware. See also ad-ware, bundle, preloaded, spyware, and trashware.

SHUTDOWN. To power off a PC or other computing device. See also standby and hibernation.

SIMM. Single Inline Memory Module, a circuit card that can hold from 1 to 64 MB of RAM and plugs into a SIMM socket on the motherboard. See also DIMM.

SIMPLEX. The ability to transfer data in only one direction at a time, sometimes called half-duplex. See also duplex.

SLEEP MODE. See standby.

SLIM-AND-LIGHT LAPTOP. A laptop PC that contains only the components needed to run installed applications, operate on stored documents and files, and communicate with external devices. Removable-disk drives are connected externally when needed, and the focus of the design is on reducing travel size and weight. See also all-in-one and modular.

SLOT. Similar to a port but usually used for internal expansions such as memory, graphics, and so forth, by the addition of boards. See also PCMCIA card.

SMART CARD. A plastic card containing memory and a processor that communicates with a computer through a reader into which it is inserted. The data on the card may authenticate a user, and/or may provide personal or financial information enabling a transaction. The memory on smart cards can be updated by the system as part of the transaction.

SMTP. Simple Mail Transfer Protocol, the usual protocol for outgoing Internet e-mail. See also POP.

SNAIL MAIL. The U.S. Postal Service's product.

SNEAKERNET. A humorous reference to carrying files between computers on a floppy disk in absence of a "real" network or Internet connection.

SOFT BOOT. Restarting a computer under program control, rather than shutting off the power.

SOFT ERROR. A temporary problem that can be removed by rereading the data or some other action. See also glitch and hard error.

SOFTWARE. The programs that are run on a computer. See also application software and system software.

SOFTWARE LICENSE AGREEMENT. See EULA.

SOFTWARE-CONFIGURED OR -SELECTED. The ability to select certain features of a hardware component in a computer system directly from software.

SORT. To arrange information in a specified order, such as alphabetical, numerical, or chronological.

SOUND BOARD/CARD/SYSTEM. A component of multimedia PCs that can realistically reproduce (through attached speakers or headphones) almost any sound from music to speech to sound effects. Sound boards often interface with various devices such as joysticks, MIDI devices, CD-ROM drives, and input/output from other sound equipment.

SOURCE CODE. High-level (human-readable) program instructions that must be converted to machine-readable object code before a microprocessor can execute them.

SPAM. Slang term for unsolicited commercial e-mail, thought to come from a skit by the Monty Python comedy troupe in which the word spam was repeated over and over until it became annoying. Spam is the Internet's equivalent of junk mail, and proliferates despite many efforts to reduce it.

SPAM FILTER. A feature built into e-mail programs that attempts to identify spam messages and remove them from your main Inbox. Spam filters on individual PCs have mixed success. Some ISPs offer a spam filter option that can work quite well.

SPEECH SYNTHESIZER. An output device that simulates human speech using phonetic rules. When used with the appropriate software, a speech synthesizer can "speak" the words that are displayed on the monitor screen. See also voice recognition.

SPREADSHEET. A software package, such as Lotus 1-2-3 or Microsoft Excel, which allows the user to enter into "cells" numbers and equations that the program automatically calculates. Eases the development of financial applications.

SPYWARE. Software that often rides in on a useful program, but runs in the background and transmits statistics about your Internet activities to a marketing database for their use and resale. See also ad-ware, shovelware, and trashware.

SRAM (ES-RAM). Static Random Access Memory, a form of memory chip that does not need to be refreshed but still needs to have power applied to maintain the data. See also DRAM and SDRAM.

STANDARD. Industry-agreed design guidelines for a hardware or software product intended to make it interoperable between different manufacturers. Given the choice, it's usually wise to choose a standards-based product rather than a proprietary one.

STANDBY. A power-saving state in a PC, in which some subsystems are shut off but can resume full-speed operation almost immediately when a key or the pointing device is touched. PCs in standby can also respond to modem ringing signals or timed events by resuming. Also called suspend mode or sleep mode. See also hibernation.

START MENU. A feature of the Microsoft Windows desktop that provides a single pop-up menu to launch any installed program and access other features of the operating system. See also taskbar.

STATEMENT. See instruction.

STATUS BAR. An area usually at the top or

bottom of a window that provides information on the current operation of the software in use.

STORAGE. Any disk (fixed or removable), tape, CD, or online service that stores data.

STORE. See save.

STREAMING. Playing an audio or video presentation directly from an Internet web site without having to download it first. Requires cooperation between the web server and a "media player" applet on the user's PC.

STRING. A set of characters treated as a unit.

SUBDIRECTORY. A directory that is contained by another directory, such as C:\windows\system.

SUBPROGRAM OR SUBROUTINE. A sequence of instructions that perform a specific task that is repeated several times within a program or by different programs.

SUPERCOMPUTER. An extremely fast and costly computer that is capable of handling very complex problems and vast amounts of data, for tasks such as weather prediction. See mainframe.

SUPERVGA. See SVGA.

SURGE SUPPRESSOR OR PROTECTOR. An electrical device, often built into a power strip, designed to prevent damage to the computer by voltage spikes from the power source. See also power conditioner.

SUSPEND MODE. See standby.

SVGA. SuperVGA, a high-resolution (800 x 600 pixels) graphics display mode. See also VGA and XGA.

SWITCH BOX. A unit that lets more than one device share a single connection but not simultaneously. Used to share a printer between two computers.

SYNCHRONOUS TRANSMISSION. Characterized by operations guided by regularly timed signals.

SYNTAX. Comparable to the grammar of a language, syntax is a set of rules used for forming commands in an operating system or programming language.

SYSOP. System Operator, person responsible for physical operations of a computer system, network, or network service.

SYSTEM. A single computer, or any group of interconnected computers and the network itself.

SYSTEM ADMINISTRATOR OR SYSADMIN. See administrator.

SYSTEM DISK, DRIVE, OR VOLUME. The currently active data-storage device that contains the critical operating-system files for a running computer. See also boot disk.

SYSTEM SOFTWARE. Programs required for the basic operation of the computer and its components. For PCs, this normally consists of the operating system and any associated utilities. See also application software.

SYSTEM UTILITIES. Programs usually supplied as part of the system software that permit and assist in basic control and maintenance of the computer and its components.

T-1 LINE, T-3 LINE. Leased telecommunications line connections capable of carrying data at 1,544,000 and 44,736,000 bits per second, respectively.

TABLE. An ordered arrangement of data, often presented in rows and columns.

TABLET. An input device often used by designers. Tablets consist of a touch-sensitive membrane, pressure on which (using a stylus or even a finger) is transferred to the corresponding position on the screen.

TABLET PC. Microsoft name for a pen computer.

TAGLINE. A short quip or quote at the end of an e-mail message.

TAPE. A magnetic data storage or backup medium on which files are stored in a predetermined and rigid sequence. Updating a tape usually requires making a new copy of the entire tape. The 1/4-inch data cartridge (QIC or TRAVAN) is most common on home systems.

TASK. Any process currently running on a computer. An application may have several tasks running simultaneously.

TASKBAR. On the Microsoft Windows desktop, a bar with icons and window titles, used to launch programs, switch between running tasks, and view the status of programs running in the background. See also Start menu.

TCP/IP. Transmission Control Protocol/Internet Protocol, a shorthand name for the "language" of Internet communication.

TELECOMMUNICATIONS. Communications between devices that are not located near each other and must make use of a data communications channel. This occurs when PCs link to a host computer for an exchange of data. See also network.

TELECONFERENCING. The simultaneous communication between three or more persons. This may be via the telephone, computer telecommunications link, Internet, or a special network.

TELNET. A standard protocol for text-based terminal remote connection over the Internet.

TEMPLATE. A document guide, similar to a paper form, permitting the user to simply fill in the blanks to create a new document.

TERMINAL. Any device that acts as an input/output unit for a computer. Terminals usually have a keyboard and a CRT screen but vary in design. See also monitor.

TERMINATOR. An electrical circuit, often contained in a connector, that is placed at the end of a data bus to prevent reflections from corrupting the data signals.

TEXT EDITOR. See editor.

TEXT FILE. A file that usually contains only ASCII characters, readable by practically any program that uses text.

TEXT RECOGNITION. See OCR.

TFT LCD. Thin film transistor LCD, an active-matrix LCD display that is commonly used on top-line, color portables.

THERMAL PRINTER. A printer, often used as part of a fax machine, that produces images by using heat interaction with special paper.

THROUGHPUT. The amount of work done in a given amount of time by a computer or a component of a system such as a printer; the amount of data transferred per second in a network link.

THUMBNAIL. A miniature reproduction of an image, usually for display as an example.

TIME-SHARING. A method of processing used in multiprogramming that shares the CPU time between two or more processes. With rapid processing speeds, the CPU can alternate between the processes without any significant loss in speed. See also multitasking.

TLD. Top-level domain, the suffix on a web site URL, such as ".com". See also URL.

TOGGLE. A soft switch or control code that turns a setting on and off by repeated action; to turn something on and off by repeating the same action.

TONER. A very fine, black, powdery ink, supplied in a cartridge, used in copy machines and laser printers. Toner particles become electrically charged and adhere to the pattern of an image defined by charges on a plate or drum.

TOWER CASE. A computer case design that employs an upright (stacked) arrangement of drives. Tower cases can sit on a tabletop, but more frequently they are placed on the floor or a low stand adjacent to the work area. Often prefixed by full-, mid-, mini-, or micro-, indicating the relative size and expansion space of the case.

TRACK. A circular path used for recording data on a floppy or hard disk; a parallel data channel on a magnetic tape; a spiral path on a CD for recording data.

TRACKBALL. A pointing device similar to a mouse, which uses a ball mounted on a fixed base to control onscreen cursor movement. The ball is rolled with the fingers or thumb in the direction the user wants the onscreen pointer to go.

TRANSPARENT. A running program or process that does not interfere with (is transparent to) other operations, even though it may have an effect on them. Also used to indicate a change in hardware or software that causes no apparent change in system performance.

TRASHWARE. Poorly designed or useless software that is good for nothing but the trash can. See also ad-ware, shovelware, and spyware.

TRIAD. A triangular cluster of three colored phosphor dots (red, blue, and green) that form the smallest point viewable on a monitor screen. The distance between triads is called dot pitch, and is commonly considered adequately small if 0.28 mm or less. Some monitors use stripes instead of dots, and need a "stripe-pitch" of 0.25 mm or less. On flat-panel (LCD) displays, there is always one pixel per triad of stripes, but there is no such mapping on a CRT monitor. See also dot pitch and pixel.

TRIAL-WARE. Software that is either "crippled" to remove functionality or set to stop working after a period of days, in order to let the user try it out before buying it.

TRINITRON. A Sony Corp. trademark for its cylindrical- and flat-face CRT monitors, which use a fine grid of taut wires as the color-separating element. Some other brands of computer monitors use Trinitron CRTs, which are touted for their viewing quality.

TROJAN OR TROJAN HORSE. A general class of computer programs that gain system entry by riding in on legitimate-appearing programs or e-mail attachments. The best-known examples are malicious programs that provide hackers remote access to infected systems; however, not all Trojan Horses are necessarily destructive. See also adware, spyware, and virus.

TRUETYPE. A type of scalable font primarily used in Microsoft Windows and Mac OS.

TTL. Transistor to Transistor Logic, a generic designation for digital signals, as a TTL monitor is a digital monitor.

TURNKEY SYSTEM. A ready-to-use system, usually supplied by a single vendor, that includes hardware, software, and training. See also preload.

TYPEFACE. The design or style of a set of print characters such as Helvetica, Orator, or Times-Roman. See also font.

UDF. Universal Disk Format. See DirectCD.

UI. User interface, the means through which a user controls a computing device.

ULTRA DMA OR UDMA. A further enhancement to the EIDE disk drive interface that can transfer data as fast as 133 MB per second in bursts. A compatible drive is required.

UNINTERRUPTIBLE POWER SUPPLY. See UPS.

UNIX. A popular but not user-friendly operating system that runs on many platforms from mainframe to microcomputer. It employs cryptic but powerful commands, shells, and pipes, and has TCP/IP protocols built in, making it popular for use in Internet servers. See also Linux and Mac OS.

UPDATE OR UPGRADE. The process of changing software or hardware to a newer, more powerful, or possibly less-buggy version.

UPGRADABLE. A system whose components are designed to be easily upgraded to newer ones, usually by simply unplugging the old one and inserting the new one.

UPGRADE PATH. Refers to the means for a computer, hardware component, or software application to be changed to a more powerful or newer version without adversely affecting the remainder of the system or any pertinent data files. See also backward compatibility.

UPLOAD. To transfer a copy of a file from one computer, usually a PC, to another computer, called the host. See also download.

UPS. Uninterruptible Power Supply, an electrical device that contains a battery pack and will supply adequate power to a system for a short time in the event of a power failure, permitting it to be shut down in an orderly manner. See also power conditioner.

URL. Uniform Resource Locator, an Internet/intranet address, such as *http://www.consumerreports.org*. Every place on the web has such an address. All web addresses begin with *http://*, and most web sites start with "www." Site URLs end with a "top-level domain" (TLD) suffix: commercial sites end in ".com," organizations in ".org", educational sites in ".edu," and government sites in ".gov." Other TLDs have been established, such as .info and .biz. URLs can also address FTP and other types of sites, as well as resources on a LAN.

USB. Universal Serial Bus, a high-speed external interface on newer PCs, used to connect peripheral devices like printers, scanners, and digital cameras. A recent enhancement, dubbed USB-2, has a much higher speed, providing enough bandwidth for digital video and external hard drives.

USENET. A large but informal collection of Internet servers that host groups of users known as newsgroups to exchange news and information on specific topics.

USER FRIENDLY. Easy to understand and use.

USER INTERFACE. Any device, either hardware or software, that provides a bridge between the computer and the user. Examples include the keyboard, mouse, and menu programs. See also GUI.

USER-PROGRAMMABLE KEY. See function key.

USER-SUPPORTED SOFTWARE. See shareware.

V.90. A standard for 56-kbps modems. A later standard, V.92, alleviates some of the shortcomings of dial-up Internet access, such as lengthy call-setup times, slow upload speed, and tying up a phone line.

VAPORWARE. Hardware or software products that are announced by a company but do not appear on the market for a very long time, if ever.

VAR. Valued Added Reseller, a company that assembles systems, usually for a specific purpose or application, using components from various vendors. See also OEM.

VDT. Video Display Terminal, any device used to give a visual display of computer output, such as on a screen. For personal computers this is most commonly a single CRT unit called a monitor. See also terminal.

VENDOR. A supplier of computer hardware or software.

VERSION NUMBER. A number, such as 3.2, that indicates an application or driver's place in the history of its development. In general, the larger the version number, the longer the program has been around and under development, and the more revisions it has undergone. Also, the larger the difference between two version numbers, the greater the change in the program.

VESA (VEE-SA). Video Electronics Standards Association, a group of manufacturers of video products working toward the establishment of better industrywide video standards.

VGA. IBM's Video Graphics Array, a medium-resolution, 640-by-480-pixel color graphics system. VGA was originally designed for professional applications on top-of-the-line PCs; however, it is now considered to be standard equipment. See also SVGA and XGA.

VIDEOCONFERENCING. Teleconferencing in which video images are exchanged. Although this traditionally involved using video cameras and monitors, routine video conferencing via computer over the Internet is starting to become reality.

VIDEO DISPLAY ADAPTER, VIDEO CARD. See display adapter.

VIDEO DISPLAY TERMINAL. See VDT.

VIDEO RAM. See VRAM.

VIRTUAL MEMORY. Using disk file overlays to make the total amount of available memory appear to be larger and hold more than its actual capacity would permit, though with slower access.

VIRTUAL REALITY. A computerized simulation of three-dimensional space in which the user can interact with and manipulate objects in the virtual world. This may be as simple as the movement through three-dimensional environments that is simulated by many games, or it may be complex, involving special devices such as a glove and helmet through which the user interacts with the projected world. See also cyberspace.

VIRUS. A typically small, malicious computer program embedded in a legitimate-appearing "host" file, often a downloaded program or e-mail attachment. A computer becomes "infected" with the virus when a user runs the host file. Viruses replicate themselves in an attempt to infect other computers, and attach to user files causing annoyance or damage to the infected system. See also Trojan Horse and worm.

VIRUS SIGNATURE. The unique machine code (binary) pattern of a computer virus program. Most antivirus programs include a search for known virus signatures as a means for quick detection of these viruses.

VOICE RECOGNITION. The ability of a computer to accept input commands or data using the spoken word. Voice recognition technology has advanced greatly in recent years, and is likely to become a common alternative to keyboard control and data entry.

VOICE MODEM. A modem that is able to send and receive speech as well as, or instead of, data or faxes. Such a modem, with appropriate software, can act as a voicemail system or a speakerphone.

VOICE SYNTHESIZER. See speech synthesizer.

VOLATILE. A memory design in which the stored data is lost when the power is removed from the system. See also nonvolatile.

VOLTAGE SPIKE. A sudden jump in electrical power. These can be very dangerous to data and, if large enough, to computer hardware as well. See also power conditioner and surge suppressor.

VOLUME. See logical drive.

VRAM (VEE-RAM). Video RAM, memory dedicated to handling video processing and output.

WARM BOOT. To restart a system from the keyboard. This method does not always completely clear and re-initialize the system, and a cold boot may be required.

WAV. Also known as a wave file, this is a file format for storing uncompressed digital audio. See also MP3.

WEB. See World Wide Web.

WEBCAM. Web camera, a small camera connected to a computer, intended to send still or moving pictures to others over the Internet.

WEBMAIL. E-mail account access through a web-page interface, allowing the mail user to send and receive mail anywhere an Internet connection is available.

WEBMASTER. The individual responsible for maintaining a web site's content and links. Usually, the webmaster operates remotely, and does not have (or need) direct control of the computer that serves the web site.

WEB PAGE. The page of text and graphics that fills your screen after you type a URL into a web browser or click on a hyperlink. Each web page is designed using HTML. See also home page.

WEBTV. See MSN TV.

WiFi. Nickname for a medium-range (150 feet) wireless connectivity standard, officially known as IEEE 802.11b. WiFi enables secure networking of PCs in either a peer-to-peer or a workstation-to-base configuration. It operates in the 2.4 GHz radio-frequency band, and provides data transfer at up to 11 Mbps.

WILDCARD. A generic symbol (such as * or ?) that can stand for either a single character or for several characters. Wildcards are frequently used in system commands.

WINDOW. A portion of the screen set aside for a specific display or purpose.

WINDOWS. A multitasking, graphical user interface developed by Microsoft for IBM-compatible systems. The program gets its name from using movable and sizable windows in which applications are displayed. Windows supports multimedia, common printer management, TrueType fonts, and copy and paste between Windows applications. The first release of Windows was Windows 3.1, which has been superseded by Windows 95, 98, 2000, and most recently, XP.

WINDOWS XP (HOME, PROFESSIONAL, SERVER, ETC.). The latest versions of Windows 2000. Windows XP Home replaces prior versions of Windows, bringing many of the features of the Windows 2000 operating system to the consumer.

WIRELESS. Descriptive of any communications link that doesn't use wiring as a transmission medium. Examples are WiFi (802.11b) networking, and Bluetooth.

WIZARD. A program that takes you one step at a time through a complex process, such as setting up a home network, asking simple questions to set up configuration options.

WORD. A group of bits treated as a unit of storage. The larger the word size, the faster the computer can process data. Most microcomputers use 16-, 32-, or 64-bit words.

WORD PROCESSOR. A software application, like Corel WordPerfect or Microsoft Word, designed to accept and process normal text (words) as data. Word processors range from simple programs that are little more than screen typewriters to those with complex screen handling, editing, enhancements, and assistance features. Also refers to a stand-alone machine dedicated to word processing.

WORD WRAP. A feature of most word processors in which the text is automatically continued from one line to the next.

WORKGROUP. A named group of computers connected as a peer-to-peer network. See also domain.

WORKSTATION. A single-user personal computer, often on a LAN, especially a high-performance system designed for a special function such as CAD or CAM.

WORLD WIDE WEB (WWW OR W3). A global, multimedia portion of the Internet featuring text, audio, graphics, and moving image files. The web is the most popular part of the Net and is accessed with a program called a browser.

WORM. Write-Once-Read-Many, an optical disk system in which data may be written to the disk only once but read an unlimited number of times. Updating data on the disk involves physically destroying the old data, rendering that part of the disk unusable, and then writing the new data to an unused part of the disk. A CD-R is a type of a WORM disc.

WORM (AS A NON-ACRONYM). A kind of malicious computer program that, once released into a computer, is designed to repeatedly and rapidly reproduce itself without the user's knowledge or consent.

One effect is that the system may soon have all available disk, memory, and other resources gobbled up, leading to a system crash. Worms can also spread to other connected systems over a network. See also Trojan Horse and virus.

WRITE-PROTECTED. Cannot be written to or changed. See also R/O and R/W.

WRITE-PROTECT WINDOW. 3-1/2-inch diskettes use a small sliding window to indicate write-protect status. The disk is protected when the window is open.

WYSIWYG (WIZ-EE-WIG). "What You See Is What You Get," indicating that the screen display is essentially the same as how the printed output will appear.

X, AS IN 24X. Denotes the rate at which a CD- or DVD-ROM drive reads or writes data, in multiples of the speed of the earliest models of that type of drive. For a CD-ROM, 1X is 150 kilobytes per second. For a DVD-ROM, 1X is about the speed of an 8X CD-ROM.

X86. Refers to Intel's series of microprocessor chips beginning with the 8086/8088 and progressing through the 80286, 386, 486, and Pentium ("586").

XGA. IBM's eXtended Graphics Array, a high-resolution, 1024-by-768-pixel color graphics mode that is very similar to SVGA. See also SVGA and VGA.

XML. Extensible Markup Language, a "superset" of HTML that allows web page designers to incorporate new, interactive objects into their pages.

ZIP DRIVE. A removable-disk drive whose cartridges can hold 100 MB each at a cost of about $10. See also Jaz drive.

ZIP FILE. See file compression.

Index

A
Advertising, online, 75
Airlines
 security measures, 68
 web-site Ratings, 93-94
Anti-virus software, 21-23
AOL (America Online), 14, 18, 26, 31
Apparel, web-site Ratings, 85
Apple computers
 iPhoto, 37
 networking, 26
 processor, 100
Appliances, web-site Ratings, 90
Appraisal services, 79, 82
Armoires, 149
Auctions, online, 77-83
 bidding, 79-82
 proxy bidding, 80
 search engines, 82, 92
 sellers, feedback scores, 78
 variations, 81
 web-site Ratings, 92
Audio-file formats, 50
Authentication services, 82

B
Baby gear, web-site Ratings, 85
Banking, online, 55, 57-60
 fees, 59
 Ratings, 58
Batteries
 cameras and camcorders, 117
 cell phones, 138
 laptops, 105
 MP3 players, 129
 PDAs, 112
Blocking software. See Filtering software
Books, web-site Ratings, 86
Broadband access, 14, 16-17

C
Cable modem, 16, 17
Camcorders, 115-118
 batteries, 117
 features, 116-118
 formats, 115-116
 Ratings, 156
Cameras. See Digital cameras
Car rentals, web-site Ratings, 94
Carts (workstations), 149
CD burners, 52, 54, 125-127
CD player/recorders, 52, 54, 125-127
CDs, do-it-yourself, 50, 52, 54
Cell phones, 136-139
 batteries, 138
 digital phones, 138
 features, 138-139
 Ratings, 159
 service plans, 136-137
Cell phones, alternatives, 143-144
 Ratings, 161
Chairs, ergonomic, 145-146, 148
Children's Online Privacy Protection Act, 29
Chips. See Processors
Computer games. See Games
Computers. See also Desktop computers; Laptops
 recycling, 110
 repair histories, 15
 technical support, 15, 16
 troubleshooting, 112
 web-site Ratings, 87
Cookies (internet), 27-28
Copyright laws, music, 53, 128
Creativity software, 39-40
Cruise lines, web-site Ratings, 95

D
Desks, 148-149
Desktop computers, 99-104
 drives, 100
 keyboards, 101
 monitors, 100, 107-111
 ports, 102
 processors, 99-100, 104
 Ratings, 163
 tower, 100
Dial-up modem, 14, 16
Digital cameras, 34, 118-121
 card reader, 34
 features, 119-120
 memory cards, 34
 Ratings, 165
DirecWay, 17
Discs, music, 54
DoubleCLick, 27
DSL (digital subscriber line), 17, 18

E
Electronic gear, web-site Ratings, 87
E-mail
 attachments, 20, 22
 and doctors, 61-62
 spam, 28-29
Ergonomics, 146
Escrow services, online auctions, 82, 83
Ethernet, 24
Expedia, 65-66

F
File formats, 36, 50, 122
Filtering software, 29-32
Financial planning, online, 56
Financial software, 60
Firewalls, 19-21, 22

G
Games
 accessories, 43
 downloading, 47
 news and reviews, 46, 47-48
 online, 48
 portable, 47
 price comparisons, 45
 rating codes, 44
 shopping tips, 42
 types, 46
 used, 44
 web-site Ratings, 91
Gift shopping, online, 76-77
Greeting-card software, 40

H
Hackers, 18-19, 22
Health & beauty, web-site Ratings, 88

Health information, online, 63-64
Home office, designing, 147
Homeplug, 25
Home PNA, 24
Homework web sites, 69
Hotels, web-site Ratings, 95-96
House & home, web-site Ratings, 88

I
Image-handling software, 34-35, 119-120, 123
Image-handling web sites, 37-38
Internet access, 13-14, 16-18
Internet Content Rating Association (ICRA), 30
Internet Fraud Complaint Center, 80
Internet providers, 14, 18
   switching, 16
Investment research, online, 56

K
Keyboards, 101
   laptops, 105-106
   positioning, 149, 150

L
Laptops, 104-107
   batteries, 105
   configurations, 104-105
   features, 105-107
   uses, 106
Lighting, workstation, 149

M
Mail Abuse Prevention System, 29
Medical information. See Health information, online
Medical records, online, 62
Microprocessors. See Processors
Modems, 14, 16, 17
Monitors, 100, 107-111
   CRTs, 108, 109
   flat-panel LCDs, 108, 109
   laptops, 106
   positioning, 149, 150
   Ratings, 167
   refresh rate, 109
   resolution, 109
Mouse, 100
MP3 players, 49-50, 127-130
   batteries, 129
   features, 129
   Ratings, 169
   software, 129
Multifunction devices, 134-135
   resolution, 135
Music-management software, 50
Music recording, legal issues, 53, 128
Music web sites, 51
   Ratings, 86

N
Networks, home, 23-27
   Ratings, 26

O
Office & mailing supplies, web-site Ratings, 89
Online shopping. See also Auctions, online
   customer service, 73-74
   gifts, 76-77
   privacy, 72, 73
   returns, 72, 77
   search options, 74-75
   security, 72, 73
   web-site design, 74
Orbitz, 66, 67

P
Pagers, 143
Painting software, 39
Paper
   photo, 34, 133
   printer, 133
Passwords, protecting, 22
PDAs (personal digital assistant), 111-114
   batteries, 112
   features, 113-114
Palm OS models, 112-113
Pocket PC, 113
   processors, 114
   Ratings, 171
Pet supplies, web-site Ratings, 89
Phoneline, 24
Photofinishing web sites, 38
Portfolio tracking, online, 56
Powerline, 25
Printers, 131-134
   cartridges, 120, 133
   costs, controlling, 134
   features, 132, 134
   ink and toner, 133
   inkjet, 132-134
   laser, 132
   paper, 133
   photos, 37, 120
   Ratings, 174
   resolution, 132
Privacy, 27
   banking online, 57
   e-mail, 61-62
   shopping online, 72, 73
Processors, 99-100, 104, 114

R
Radios, two-way, 143-144
Railways, web-site Ratings, 96
Research, web sites, 69-70

S
Satellite-based internet service, 17
Scanners, 34, 35-36, 121-124
   commercial services, 36-37
   driver software, 123
   resolution, 35-36
Second opinions, online, 62
Security
   banking online, 57
   credit cards, 77
   shopping online, 72, 73
Security measures, travel, 68
Shopping. See Online shopping
Shopping bots, 73
Software
   anti-virus, 21-23
   creativity, 39-40
   filtering, 29-32
   financial, 60
   firewalls, 19-21
   image-handling, 34-35, 119-120, 123
   web-site Ratings, 90
Spam, 28-29
Sports & camping, web-site Ratings, 91
Surge suppressors, 151-152

T
Tax software, 60
Telephones. See also Cell phones
   corded, 142-143
   cordless, 139-142
   directory assistance, 143
Text-messaging services, 143, 144
Theme parks, web site Ratings, 96
Toys, web-site Ratings, 91
Travel, online, 64-68
   bias of sites, 66
   buying tips, 65
Travelocity, 66, 67

V
Video editing, 38-39
Video games. See Games
Videos, web-site Ratings, 86
Viruses, 20, 21-23

W
Web sites. See also Online shopping
   financial, 56
   health information, 63-64
   homework, 69
   music, 51
   photo, 37-38
   Ratings, 85-96
   research, 69-70
   travel, 65-68
Wi-Fi, 25-26
Workstations, 148-151
   assembling, 151
   Ratings, 176